Alexander Stewart, Thomas Maclauchlan

**Elements of Gaelic Grammar in Four Parts**

Alexander Stewart, Thomas Maclauchlan

**Elements of Gaelic Grammar in Four Parts**

ISBN/EAN: 9783743417861

Manufactured in Europe, USA, Canada, Australia, Japa

Cover: Foto ©Thomas Meinert / pixelio.de

Manufactured and distributed by brebook publishing software (www.brebook.com)

Alexander Stewart, Thomas Maclauchlan

**Elements of Gaelic Grammar in Four Parts**

# ELEMENTS

OF

# GAELIC GRAMMAR

## IN FOUR PARTS

I. OF PRONUNCIATION AND ORTHOGRAPHY
II. OF THE PARTS OF SPEECH

III. OF SYNTAX
IV. OF DERIVATION AND COMPOSITION

BY

## ALEXANDER STEWART

MINISTER OF THE GOSPEL AT DINGWALL
HONORARY MEMBER OF THE HIGHLAND SOCIETY OF SCOTLAND

Royal Celtic Society Edition.

FOURTH EDITION REVISED,

WITH PREFACE BY THE REV. DR M'LAUCHLAN

EDINBURGH
JOHN GRANT, GEORGE IV. BRIDGE
1892

# PREFACE.

For several years the Grammar of the Gaelic language by the Rev. Dr Stewart of Moulin has been out of print. This has been a source of regret to scholars and students of that tongue. Not but that there are other Grammars of real value, which it would be unjust either to ignore or to depreciate, and which have served, and are serving, an excellent purpose in connection with Celtic Literature. But the Grammar of Dr Stewart has peculiar features of its own which give it a permanent value. It is distinguished by its simplicity, conciseness, and philosophical accuracy. No Grammar of any language bears on its pages the marks of real and profound scholarship, in so far as it goes, more than does the Grammar of Dr Stewart. One cannot read a sentence of it without seeing how carefully he had collected his materials, and with what judgment, caution, and sagacity he has compared them and drawn his conclusions. His discussions upon the Article, the Noun, the Verb, and the Preposition, are ample evidence of this. It is no doubt true that a much fuller discussion is, with the more abundant resources of modern scholarship, competent and desirable, but, so far as he goes, Dr Stewart's treatment of the subject is of a masterly character.

That there are defects to be found in the work is very true. On the subject of Syntax his disquisitions are deficient in fulness, and there is a want of grammatical exercises throughout. It was at first thought desirable by the publishers and their advisers to remedy these defects by introducing fuller notices on the subject of Syntax, and a considerable number of grammatical exercises from other sources open to them. But it was finally deemed best in every view of it to give Stewart's work just as he had left it, and that is done here with the exception of a list of subscribers' names in the introduction. Messrs Maclachlan and Stewart are doing the literary community a service in republishing this volume, and thanks are specially due to the Royal Celtic Society of Edinburgh, a society which has done much to foster the interests of education in the Highlands, and which has given substantial aid towards the accomplishment of this undertaking.

THOS. M'LAUCHLAN.

EDINBURGH, 1st August 1876.

# CONTENTS.

# PART III.

### OF SYNTAX.

# PART IV.

### OF DERIVATION AND COMPOSITION.

# INTRODUCTION.

THE utility of a Grammar of the Scottish Gaelic will be variously appreciated. Some will be disposed to deride the vain endeavour to restore vigour to a decaying superannuated language. Those who reckon the extirpation of the Gaelic a necessary step toward that general extension of the English which they deem essential to the political interest of the Highlands, will condemn every project which seems likely to retard its extinction. Those who consider that there are many parts of the Highlands, where the inhabitants can, at present, receive no useful knowledge whatever except through the channel of their native tongue, will probably be of opinion that the Gaelic ought at least to be tolerated. Yet these too may condemn as useless, if not ultimately detrimental, any attempt to cultivate its powers, or to prolong its existence. Others will entertain a different opinion. They will judge from experience, as well as from the nature of the case, that no measure merely of a literary kind will prevail to hinder the progress of the English language over the Highlands; while general convenience and emolument, not to mention private emulation and vanity, conspire to facilitate its intro duction, and prompt the natives to its acquisition. They will perceive at the same time, that while the Gaelic continues to be the common speech of multitudes,—while the knowledge of many important facts, of many necessary arts, of morals, of religion, and of the laws of the land, can be conveyed to them only by means of this language,—it must be of material service to preserve it in such a state of cultivation and purity, as that it may be fully adequate to these valuable ends ; in a word, that while it is a living language, it may answer the purpose of a living language.

To those who wish for an uniformity of speech over the whole kingdom, it may not be impertinent to suggest one remark. The more that the human mind is enlightened, the more desirous it becomes of farther acquisitions in knowledge. The only channel through which the rudiments of knowledge can be conveyed to the mind of a remote Highlander is the Gaelic language. By learning to read and to understand what he reads, in his native tongue, an appetite is generated for those stores of science which are accessible to him only through the medium of the English language. Hence an acquaintance with the English is found to be necessary for enabling him to gratify his desire after further attainments. The study of it becomes, of course, an object of importance ; it is commenced, and prosecuted with increasing diligence. These premises seem to warrant a conclusion which might at first appear paradoxical, that, by cultivating the Gaelic, you effectually, though indirectly, promote the study and diffuse the knowledge of the English.

To public teachers it is of the highest moment that the medium through which their instructions are communicated be properly adapted to that use, and that they be enabled to avail themselves of it in the fittest manner. A language destitute of grammatical regularity can possess neither perspicuity nor precision, and must therefore be very inadequate to the purpose of conveying one's thoughts. The Gaelic is in manifest danger of falling into this discreditable condition, from the disuse of old idioms and distinctions, and the admission of modern corruptions, unless means be applied to prevent its degenerating. It is obvious that a speaker cannot express himself with precision without a correct knowledge of grammar. When he is conscious of his ignorance in this respect, he must deliver himself sometimes ambiguously or erroneously, always with diffidence and hesitation; whereas one who has an accurate knowledge of the structure and phraseology of the language he speaks, will seldom fail to utter his thoughts with superior confidence, energy, and effect.

A competent degree of this knowledge is requisite to the hearer also, to enable him to apprehend the full import and the precise force of the words of the speaker. Among the readers of Gaelic, who are every day becoming more numerous, those only who have studied it grammatically are qualified to understand accurately what they read, and to explain it distinctly to others. Yet it cannot be denied that comparatively few ever arrive at a correct, or even a tolerable knowledge of grammar, without the help of a treatise composed for the purpose. Whoever, therefore, allows that the Gaelic must be employed in communicating to a large body of people the knowledge of revealed Truth and the way of eternal Life, will readily admit the extensive utility of investigating and unfolding its grammatical principles. Impressed with this conviction, I have been induced to offer to the public the following attempt to develop the grammar of the Scottish Gaelic.

While I have endeavoured to render this treatise useful to those who wish to improve the knowledge of Gaelic which they already possess, I have also kept in view the gratification of others, who do not understand the Gaelic, but yet may be desirous to examine the structure and properties of this ancient language. To serve both these purposes, I have occasionally introduced such observations on the analogy between the Gaelic idiom and that of some other tongues, particularly the Hebrew, as a moderate knowledge of these enabled me to collect. The Irish dialect of the Gaelic is the nearest cognate of the Scottish Gaelic. An intimate acquaintance with its vocables and structure, both ancient and modern, would have been of considerable use. This I cannot pretend to have acquired. I have not failed, however, to consult, and to derive some advantage from such Irish philologists as were accessible to me, particularly O'Molloy, O'Brien, Vallancey, and Lhuyd. To these very respectable names I have to add that of the Rev. Dr Neilson, author of "An Introduction to the Irish Language," Dublin, 1808; and E. O'C., author of "A Grammar of the Gaelic Language," Dublin, 1808; to the latter of whom I am indebted for some good-humoured strictures, and some flattering compliments, which, however unmerited, it were unhandsome not to acknowledge. I know but one publication professedly on the subject of Gaelic grammar written by a Scotsman*. I have consulted it also, but in this quarter I have no obligations to acknowledge.

With respect to my literary countrymen who are proficients in the Gaelic, and who may cast an eye on this volume, less with a view to learn than to criticise, while I profess a due deference to their judgment, and declare my anxiety to obtain their favourable suffrage, I must take the liberty to entreat their attention to the following considerations.

* Analysis of the Gaelic Language, by William Shaw, A.M.

The subject of Universal Grammar has been examined in modern times with a truly philosophical spirit, and has been settled on rational and stable principles; yet, in applying these principles to explain the grammar of a particular language, the divisions, the arrangements, and the rules to be given are, in a good measure, mechanical and arbitrary. One set of rules may be equally just with another. For what is it that grammatical rules do? They bring into view the various parts, inflections, or, as they may be termed, the *phenomena* of a language, and class them together in a certain order. If these *phenomena* be all brought forward, and stated according as they actually appear in the language, the rules may be said to be both just and complete. Different sets of rules may exhibit the same things in a different order, and yet may all be equally just. The superiority seems, on a comparison, to belong to that system which follows most nearly the order of nature, or the process of the mind in forming the several inflections; or rather, perhaps, to that system which, from its simplicity, or clear and comprehensive arrangement, is most fitted to assist the memory in acquiring and retaining the parts of speech with their several inflections.

In distributing the various parts of language into their several classes, and imposing names on them, we ought always to be guided by the nature of that language, and to guard against adopting, with inconsiderate servility, the distributions and technical terms of another. This caution is the more necessary because, in our researches into the grammar of any particular tongue, we are apt to follow implicitly the order of the Latin grammar, on which we have been long accustomed to fix our attention, and which we are ever ready to erect into a model for the grammar of all languages. To force the several parts of speech into moulds formed for the idioms of the Latin tongue, and to frame them so as to suit a nomenclature adapted to the peculiarities of Latin grammar, must have the effect of disguising or concealing the peculiarities, and confounding the true distinctions, which belong to the language under discussion.

Although, in treating of Gaelic grammar, the caution here suggested ought never to be forgotten, yet it is needless to reject indiscriminately all the forms and terms introduced into the grammar of other languages. Where the same classifications which have been employed in the grammar of the Latin, or of any other well-known tongue, will suit the Gaelic also, it is but a convenient kind of courtesy to adopt these, and apply to them the same names which are already familiar to us.

In stating the result of my researches into Gaelic grammar, I have endeavoured to conform to these general views. The field of investigation was wide, and almost wholly untrodden. My task was not to fill up or improve the plan of any former writer, but to form a plan for myself. In the several departments of my subject that distribution was adopted which, after various trials, appeared the most eligible. When there were terms already in use in the grammars of other languages that suited tolerably well the divisions which it was found requisite to make, I chose to adopt these, rather than load the treatise with novel or uncommon terms. If their import was not sufficiently obvious already, it was explained, either by particular description, or by reference to the use of these terms in other grammars. In some instances it was found necessary to employ less common terms, but in the choice of these I endeavoured to avoid the affectation of technical nicety. I am far from being persuaded that I am so fortunate as to have hit on the best possible plan. I am certain that it must be far from complete. To such charges a first essay must necessarily be found liable. Still there is room to hope that the work may not prove wholly useless or unacceptable. Imperfect as it is, I may be allowed to think I do a service of its kind to my countrymen by frankly offering the fruits of my labour to such as may choose to make use of them. It has been, if I mistake not, the misfortune of Gaelic grammar that its ablest friends have done nothing directly in its support, because they were apprehensive that they could not do everything.

I confess that my circumscribed knowledge of the varieties of dialect used in different parts of the Highlands, may have left me unacquainted with some genuine Gaelic idioms which ought to be noticed in a work of this kind. The same cause may have led me to assert some things in too general terms, not being sufficiently informed concerning the exceptions which may be found in use in some particular districts. I respectfully invite, and will thankfully receive, the correction of any person whose more accurate and extensive information enables him to supply my omissions, or to rectify my mistakes.

In a few particulars I have differed from some of the highest living authorities,—I mean those gentlemen whose superior abilities are so conspicuous in the masterly translation of the sacred Scriptures with which the Highlands of Scotland are now blessed.* Here I have been careful to

---

* A few examples of what I conceived to be deviations from grammatical propriety are given from the Gaelic version of the Bible. As the translation of the Prophetical Books underwent a revision, the exceptionable passages in those Books have been changed in the second edition from what they were as they came out of the hands of the original translator. The criticism on those passages is, however, allowed to remain in this edition of the Grammar, because the first edition of the Gaelic Prophets is still in the hands of many, and because it often happens that "we can best teach what is right by showing what is wrong."—*Lowth.*

state the grounds on which my judgment was formed. In doing this, I would always be understood to advance my opinion and propose my reasons with the view of suggesting them to the consideration of my countrymen, rather than in the expectation of having my conclusions universally sustained and adopted.

Among my grammatical readers, it is probable that some may have formed to themselves arrangements on the subjects different from mine. Of these I have to request that they do not form a hasty judgment of the work from a partial inspection of it, nor condemn it merely because it may differ from their preconceived schemes. Let them indulge me with a patient perusal of the whole, and a candid comparison of the several parts of the system with each other. To a judicious critic, some faults and many defects may appear, and several improvements will occur. On this supposition, I have one request more to make : that he join his efforts with mine in serving a common cause, interesting to our country, and dear to every patriotic Highlander.

# ADVERTISEMENT

TO THE

# SECOND EDITION.

---

In preparing a Second Edition of the following treatise, the author has endeavoured to avail himself of every assistance in his power, from books, observation, and the communications of some literary friends, to whom he is indebted for several judicious remarks.   In comparing the opinions of different critics, it was not to be expected that all should be found to agree together.   It sometimes happened that one approved what another would have rejected.   If the author has not adopted every hint that was offered him, but used the privilege of exercising his own judgment, the responsibility must rest with himself.   He hopes those gentlemen who most obligingly favoured him with their remarks will forgive him for mentioning their names, for he is unwilling to withhold from the public the satisfaction of knowing that he has had the best assistance which his country could afford him in compiling and modelling his work.   He thankfully acknowledges his obligations to the Rev. Dr Robertson, of Callander; Dr Graham, of Aberfoyle; Dr Stuart, of Luss; Dr Macleod, of Kilmarnock; and Mr Irvine, of Little Dunkeld.

From these sources of emendation, omissions have been

supplied, idiomatic phrases have been collected and inserted, some alterations have been made by simplifying or compressing particular parts, and new examples and illustrations have been introduced throughout, according as the advantages which the author enjoyed enabled him to extend his knowledge of the language, and served to correct, or to confirm, his former judgments. He thought it might be acceptable to Gaelic scholars to have a few lessons subjoined as exercises in translating and analysing. For this purpose he has selected some specimens of original prose composition, extracted from unpublished manuscripts, and from the oldest Gaelic books that are known to be extant. These specimens, short as they are, may suffice to exhibit something of the powers and elegances of the language in its native purity, unmixed with foreign words and idioms, as well as to show the manner in which it was written two or three centuries ago.

The present edition owes its existence to the generous patronage of Sir John Macgregor Murray of Lanrick, Bart., to whom the author is happy in avowing his obligations for the unsolicited and liberal encouragement given him in the execution and publication of his work. To the same gentleman he is indebted for the honour of being permitted here to record the names of those patriotic sons of Caledonia who, in concert with the honourable baronet, and at his suggestion, though residing in the remote provinces of India, yet mindful of their country's fame, contributed a liberal sum of money for promoting Celtic literature, more especially for publishing the poems of Ossian in their original language. It is owing, in a principal degree, to their munificent aid, that the anxious expectation of the public has been at last so richly gratified by Sir John Sinclair's elegant and elaborate edition of the poems of that tender and lofty bard.

# ELEMENTS OF GAELIC GRAMMAR.

## PART I.

### OF PRONUNCIATION AND ORTHOGRAPHY.

THE Gaelic alphabet consists of eighteen letters: a, b, c, d, e, f, g, h, i, l, m, n, o, p, r, s, t, u. Of these, five are vowels, a, e, i, o, u; the rest consonants.

In explaining the powers of the letters, and of their several combinations, such obstacles lie in the way that complete success is not to be expected. In order to explain, in writing, the sounds of a particular language, the only obvious method is to represent them by the letters commonly employed to exhibit similar sounds in some well-known living language. But there are sounds in the Gaelic to which there are none perfectly similar in English, nor perhaps in any modern European tongue. Besides, the same combination of letters does not invariably represent the same sound in one age that it did in a former, or that it may do in the next. And this may be equally true of the letters of the Gaelic alphabet, whose powers are to be taught; and of the letters of any other language, by whose sounds the powers of the former are to be explained. A diversity of pronunciation is very distinguishable also in different districts of the Highlands of Scotland, even in uttering the same words written in the same manner. Though the powers of the letters, then, may be explained to a certain degree of accuracy, yet much will still remain to be learned by the information of the ear alone.

Á

Although tne chief use of the vowels be to represent the *vocal sounds* of speech, and that of the consonants to represent its *articulations*, yet, as in many languages, so in Gaelic, the consonants sometimes serve to modify the sound of the vowels with which they are combined; while, on the other hand, the vowels often qualify the sound of the consonants by which they are preceded or followed.

It may not appear obvious at first sight how a vowel should be employed, not to represent a vocal sound, but to modify an articulation. Yet examples are to be found in modern languages. Thus, in the English words, George, sergeant, the *e* has no other effect than to give *g* its soft sound; and in guest, guide, the *u* only serves to give *g* its hard sound. So in the Italian words giorno, giusto, and many others, the *i* only qualifies the sound of the preceding consonant. The same use of the vowels will be seen to take place frequently in Gaelic orthography.

Besides the common division of the letters into Vowels and Consonants, it is found convenient to adopt some further subdivisions.

The Vowels are divided into *broad* and *small:* a, o, u, are called *broad* vowels; e, i, *small* vowels.

The Consonants are divided into *Mutes* and *Liquids:* *Mutes*, b, c, d, f, g, m, p, t; *Liquids*, l, n, r, s (*a*). They are also divided into *Labials*, *Palatals*, and *Linguals*, so named from the organs employed in pronouncing them : *Labials*, b, f, m, p; *Palatals*, c, g; *Linguals*, d, l, n, r, s, t.

The aspirate *h* is not included in any of these divisions (*b*).

(*a*) It will immediately occur to any grammarian that there is a slight difference between this and the common division into *mutes* and *liquids*, by the letter *m* being removed from the class of liquids to that of mutes. This is not an oversight, but an intentional arrangement ; as the *accidents* of the letter *m* are, in Gaelic, the same with those of the mute, not of the liquid consonants. For a like reason, *s* is included in the class of liquids.

(*b*) Writers, who have touched on this part of Gaelic Grammar, following the Irish grammarians, have divided the consonants further into *mutable* and *immutable*. The former name has been given to consonants which, in writing, have been occasionally combined with the letter *h ;* and the latter name to those consonants which have not, in writing, been

## OF THE SOUNDS OF THE VOWELS (c).

All the vowels are sometimes long, sometimes short. A long vowel is often marked with an accent, especially when the *quantity* of the vowel determines the meaning of the word; as, bàs *death,* sàil *the heel,* càraid *a pair,* rìs *again,* mò *more,* lòn *a marsh;* which are distinguished by the accent alone from bas *the palm* of the hand, sail *a beam,* caraid *a friend,* ris *to,* lon *the elk.*

All the vowels, but especially the broad ones, have somewhat of a nasal sound when preceded or followed by m, mh, n, nn. No vowels are doubled in the same syllable like *ee,* *oo,* in English.

In almost all polysyllables, excepting some words compounded with a preposition, the accent falls on the first syllable (*d*). The other syllables are short and unaccented, and the vowels in that situation have in general the same short obscure sound. Hence it happens that the broad vowels in these syllables are often used indiscriminately

There are no quiescent final vowels.

## A.

*A* has three sounds.

1. The first is both long and short : long, like *a* in the English words *far, star;* as, àr *slaughter,* àth *a ford,* gràdh

combined with *h.* But, in fact, both classes of consonants are alike *mutable* in their pronunciation ; and their *mutation* ought to have been marked in the orthography, though it has not. This defect in Gaelic orthography has been often observed and regretted, though it has never been corrected. Rather than continue a distinction which has no foundation in the structure of the language, I venture to discard the division of *mutable* and *immutable* consonants, as not merely useless, but as tending to mislead the learner.

(*c*) In explaining the sounds of the letters I have availed myself of the very correct and acute remarks on this subject annexed to the Gaelic version of the New Testament, 1767.

(*d*) If it be thought that this renders the language too monotonous, it may be observed, on the other hand, that it prevents ambiguities and obscurities in rapid speaking, as the accent marks the initial syllable of polysyllables. Declaimers, of either sex, have often found their advantage in this circumstance.

*love*, sàruich *oppress;* short, like *a* in *that;* as, cath *a battle*, alt *a joint*, abuich *ripe.*

2. Both long and short, before *dh* and *gh.* This sound has none like it in English. Long, as, adhbhar *a cause*, adhradh *worship;* short, as, lagh *a law*, magh *a field*, adharç *a horn.*

3. Short and obscure, like *e* in *mother;* as, an, a *the*, ar *our*, ma *if*, and in the plural termination a or an.

### E.

*E* has three sounds.

1. Both long and short : long, like *e* in *where, there;* as, è, sè *he*, rè *during.* This *e* is generally marked with a grave accent. Short, like *e* in *met;* as, le *with*, leth *half.*

2. Long, as, ré *the moon*, cé *the earth*, an dé *yesterday.* This *e* is commonly marked with an acute accent.

3. Short, like *e* in *mother;* as, duine *a man*, ceannuichte *bought.*

### I.

*I* has two sounds.

1. Both long and short, like *ee* in *seem :* long, as, mìn *smooth*, righ *a king ;* short, as, min *meal*, crith *trembling.*

2. Short and obscure, like *i* in *this;* as, is *am, art, &c.*

### O.

*O* has three sounds.

1. Both long and short : long, somewhat like *o* in *more;* as, mòr *great*, òr *gold*, dòchas *expectation;* short, like *o* in *hot;* as, mo *my*, do *thy*, dochann *harm.*

2. Both long and short : long, nearly like *o* in *old;* as, lom *bare*, toll *a hole ;* short, as, lomadh *making bare*, tolladh *boring.*

3. Both long and short, like (2) a (*e*): long, as, foghlum *to learn ;* short, as, roghuinn *choice*, logh *to forgive.*

(*e*) That is the second sound assigned to *a.*

## U.

*U* has one sound, both long and short, like *oo* in *fool :* long, as, ùr *fresh,* ùraich *to renew;* short, as, ubh *an egg,* urras *a surety.*

### OF THE DIPHTHONGS.

There are thirteen Diphthongs reckoned in Gaelic : ae, ai, ao, ea, ei, eo, eu ; ia, io, iu ; oi ; ua, ui. Of these, ao, eu, ia, ua, are always long ; the others are sometimes long, sometimes short.

### AE.

The sound of *ae* is made up of (1) *a* long, and (1) *e* short. This diphthong hardly occurs, except in Gael *a Gaul* or *Highlander,* and Gaelic the *Gaelic* language (*f*).

### AI.

The sound of *ai* is either made up of the sounds of both the vowels, or like that of the former.

1. Made up of (1) *a* and (1) *i :* the *a* long, the *i* short ; as, fàidh *a prophet;* the *a* short, the *i* short; as, claidheamh *a sword.*

2. Made up of (2) *a* and (1) *i :* the *a* long, the *i* short ; as, saighde *arrows.*

Before a Lingual or a Palatal, not quiescent, the *i* often loses its sound, and only serves to qualify the sound of the following consonant (*g*); hence,

3. Like (1) *a* alone : long, as, fàisg *squeeze,* fàilte *salutation;* short, as, glaic *a hollow,* tais *soft.*

4. Like (2) *a* alone : short, as, airm *arms,* gairm *a call.*

### AO.

1. The sound of *ao* is like (2) *a,* long : as, caora *a sheep,* faobhar *the edge of a tool,* saothair *labour.*

(*f*) The plural of la or latha *a day,* is sometimes written laeth ; but it is doubtful how far this is a proper mode of writing it.

(*g*) The effect of the vowels in qualifying the sound of the adjoining consonants will be explained in treating of the Palatals and Linguals.

## EA.

The sound of *ea* is either made up of the sounds of both the vowels, or like that of one of them.

1. Made up of (2) *e* and (1) *a:* *e* very short, *a* long, as, beann *a summit, pinnacle*, feall *deceit ;* *a* short, as, meal *to enjoy*, speal *a scythe.*

Before a Lingual or a Palatal, not quiescent, the *a* frequently loses its sound, and only qualifies that of the following consonant ; hence,

2. Like (1) *e*, long : as, dean *do ;* short, us, fear *a man*, bean *a woman.*

3. Like (2) *e*, long : as, easlan *sick ;* short, as, fead *whistle.*

After a Lingual or a Palatal, not quiescent, the *e* loses its sound, and only qualifies that of the preceding consonant ; hence,

4. Like (1) *a*, long : as, cèard *an artificer ;* short, as, geal *white.*

5. Like (3) *a*, short : as, itheadh *eating*, coireach *faulty.*

## EI.

The sound of *ei* is either made up of the sounds of both the vowels, or like that of *e* alone.

1. Made up of (1) *e* and (1) *i :* *e* long, *i* short, as, sgeimh *beauty ;* *e* short, as, meidh *a balance.*

2. Made up of (2) *e* and (1) *i:* *e* long, *i* short, as, feidh *deer ;* *e* short, as, greigh *a herd, stud.*

Before a Lingual or a Palatal, not quiescent, the *i* loses its sound, and only qualifies that of the following consonant ; hence,

3. Like (1) *e* alone : long, as, mèise *of a plate.*

4. Like (2) *e* alone : long, as, éigin *necessity ;* short, as, eich *horses.*

## Eo

The sound of *eo* is either made up of the sounds of both vowels, or like that of *o* alone.

1. Made up of (2) *e* and (1) *o*: *e* very short, *o* long, as, beo *alive*, eolas *knowledge;* *o* short, as, beothail *lively.*

After a Lingual or a Palatal, not quiescent, the *e* loses its sound, and only qualifies that of the preceding consonant; hence,

2. Like (1) *o*: long, as, leomhann a *lion;* short, as, deoch *drink.*

## Eu.

The sound of *eu* is like (2) *e* alone : long, as, teum *to bite,* gleus *trim, entertainment.*

One of the most marked variations of dialect occurs in the pronunciation of the diphthong *eu*, which, instead of being pronounced like long *e*, is over all the North Highlands commonly pronounced like *ia;* as, nial, ian, fiar, for neul, eun, feur.

## Ia.

The sound of *ia* is made up of the sounds of both the vowels.

1. Made up of (1) *i* and (1) *a*: both of equal length, as, fial *liberal*, iar *west.*

2. Made up of (1) *i* and (2) *a*: of equal length, as, fiadh a *deer*, ciall *common sense.*

In cia *which?* iad *they, ia* is often found like (1) *è*.

## Io.

The sound of *io* is either made up of the sounds of both the vowels, or like one of them alone.

1. Made up of (1) *i* and (3) *o*: *i* long, *o* short, as, diol *to pay*, fior *true;* *i* short, as, iolach a *shout*, ionnsuidh *an attack.*

Before a Lingual or Palatal, not quiescent, the *o* sometimes loses its sound, and only qualifies that of the following consonant; hence,

2. Like (1) *i*: long, as, iodhol *an idol;* short, as, crios a *girdle*, biorach *pointed.*

After a Lingual or a Palatal, not quiescent, the *i* sometimes loses its sound, and only qualifies that of the preceding consonant; hence,

3. Like *u* in *fun*, short and obscure: as, cionta *guilt*, tiondadh *to turn*.

## Iu.

The sound of *iu* is either made up of the sound of both the vowels, or like *u* alone.

1. Made up of (1) *i* and (1) *u:* *i* short, *u* long, as, fiù *worthy;* *u* short, as, iuchair *a key*.

After a Lingual or a Palatal, not quiescent, the *i* loses its sound, and only qualifies that of the preceding consonant; hence,

2. Like (1) *u:* long, as, diù *worst part, refuse;* short, as, tiugh *thick*, giuthas *fir*.

## Oi.

The sound of *oi* is either made up of the sounds of both the vowels, or like that of *o* alone.

1. Made up of (1) *o* and (1) *i:* *o* long, *i* short, as, òigh *a virgin;* *o* short, as, troidh a *foot*.

2. Made up of (3) *o* and (1) *i:* *o* long, *i* short, as, oidhche *night*.

Before a Lingual or a Palatal, not quiescent, the *i* loses its sound, and only qualifies that of the following consonant; hence.

(3.) Like (1) *o* long: as, mòid *more;* short, as. toic *wealth*.

4. Like (2) *o* long : as, fòid *a turf;* short, as, fois *rest*.

5. Like (3) *o* short; as, coileach *a cock*, doire *a wood*.

## Ua.

The sound of *ua* is made up of the sounds of both the vowels.

1. Made up of (1) *u* and (1) *a*, equally long; as, cuan *the sea*, fuar *cold*.

2. Made up of (1) *u* and (2) *a;* as, tuadh *a hatchet*, sluagh *people*.

## Uɪ.

The sound of *ui* is either made up of the sounds of both the vowels, or like that of *u* alone.

1. Made up of (1) *u* and (1) *i* : *u* long, *i* short, as, suigh-eag *a rasp-berry;* *u* short, as, buidheann *a company*.

Before a Lingual or a Palatal, not quiescent, the *i* loses its sound, and only qualifies that of the following consonant; hence,

2. Like (1) *u* long: as, dùil *expectation*, cùig *five;* short, as, fuil *blood*, muir *the sea*.

### OF THE TRIPHTHONGS.

There are five Triphthongs, in each of which *i* is the last letter : aoi, eoi, iai, iui, uai. In these the two first vowels have the same sounds and powers as when they form a diphthong. The final *i* is sounded short ; but before a Palatal or a Lingual, not quiescent, it loses its sound, and only qualifies that of the following consonant.

### Aoɪ.

1. Made up of *ao* and (1) *i ;* as, caoidh *lamentation*, aoibhneas *joy*, laoigh *calves*.

2. Like *ao ;* as, caoineadh *wailing*, maoile *baldness*.

### Eoɪ.

1. Made up of (2) *eo* and (1) *i ;* as, geoigh *geese*.
2. Like (1) *eo ;* as, meoir *fingers*.
3. Like (2) *eo ;* as, deoir *tears*, treoir *ability*.

### Iaɪ.

1. Like (1) *ia ;* as, fiaire *more awry*.

### Iuɪ.

1. Like (2) *iu ;* as, ciùil *of music*, fliuiche *more wet*.

## UAI.

1. Made up of (1) *ua* and (1) *i ;* as, luaithe *quicker.*
2. Made up of (2) *ua* and (1) *i ;* as, cruaidh *hard,* fuaim *sound.*
3. Like (1) *ua ;* as, uair *time, an hour,* cluaise *of an ear.*

## OF THE POWERS OF THE CONSONANTS.

The simple powers of the consonants differ not much from their powers in English. Those called *mediae* by the writers on Greek grammar, viz., *b, d, g,* approach nearer in force to the corresponding *tenues p, t, c,* than they do in English.

In accented syllables, where, if the vocal sound be short, the voice necessarily rests on the subsequent articulation, the consonants, though written single, are pronounced with the same degree of force as when written double in English ; as, bradan *a salmon,* cos *a foot ;* pronounced braddan, coss. No consonants are written double except *l, n, r.*

A propensity to aspiration is a conspicuous feature in the Gaelic tongue (*h*). The aspirating of a consonant has been

(*h*) This propensity is seen in the aspirating of consonants in Gaelic words, which have an evident affinity to words in other languages, where the same consonants are not so aspirated. The following list will sufficiently illustrate and confirm the truth of this remark :—

| Greek. | Latin. | Gælic. |
|---|---|---|
| Διαβολος | Diabolus | Diabhol. |
| | Scribo* | Scriobh, *write.* |
| | Febris* | Fiabhrus, *a fever.* |
| | Baculum | Bacholl, *a staff.* |
| Δεκα | Decem | Deich, *ten.* |
| | Lorica | Lùireach, *a coat of mail.* |
| | Clericus | Cleireach, *a clerk.* |
| | Modus | Modh, *manner.* |
| | Gladius | Claidheamh, *a sword.* |
| Καρδια Κραδια } | Cord-is | Cridhe, *the heart.* |
| | Medium | Meadhon, *middle.* |
| | Laudo | Luadh, *mention.* |
| | Lego | Leugh, *read.* |
| | Greg-is | Greigh, *a herd.* |

* So in French, from Aprilis, *Avrilis; habere, avoir; Febris, Fièvre;* επισκοπος, *svéque*

usually marked, in the Irish dialect, by a dot over the letter aspirated ; in the Scottish dialect by writing *h* after it. All the consonants have their sounds changed by being aspirated, and the effect is different on different consonants. In some cases the articulation is changed, but still formed by the same organ. In others the articulation is formed by a different organ. In others the *h* alone retains its power. And sometimes both the *h* and the consonant to which it is subjoined become entirely quiescent.

| *Greek.* | *Latin.* | *Gælic.* |
|---|---|---|
|  | Reg-is | Righ, *a king.* |
|  | Plaga | Plaigh, *a plague.* |
|  | Sagitta | Saighead, *an arrow.* |
|  | Magister | Maighistir, *master.* |
|  | Imago | Iomhaigh, *an image.* |
|  | Primus | Priomh, *chief.* |
|  | Remus | Ràmh, *an oar.* |
|  | Similis | Samhuil, *like.* |
|  | Humilis | Umhal, *humble.* |
|  | Capra | Gabhar, *a goat.* |
| Μητηρ | Mater | Mathair, *mother.* |
|  | Rota | Roth, Rath, *a wheel.* |
|  | Muto | Mùth, *change.* |

It is probable that the consonants, thus aspirated, were pronounced without aspiration in the older dialects of the Celtic tongue ; for we are told that in the Irish manuscripts of the first class for antiquity, the consonants are for the most part written without any mark of aspiration. See "Lhuyd's Archæol. Brit.," p. 301, col. 1.

The tendency to attenuate the articulations shows itself in a progressive state, in a few vocables which are pronounced with an aspiration in some districts, but not universally. Such are deatach or deathach *smoke,* cuntart or cunthart *danger,* ta or tha *am, art,* tu or thu *thou,* troimh or throimh *through,* tar or thar *over,* am beil or am bheil *is there?* dom or domh *to me,* &c. Has not this remission or suppression of the articulations the effect of enfeebling the speech, by mollifying its bones and relaxing its nerves ? Ought not therefore the progress of this corruption to be opposed, by retaining unaspirated articulations in those instances where universal practice has not entirely superseded them, and even by restoring them in some instances, where the loss of them has been attended with manifest inconvenience? It is shameful to see how many monosyllables, once distinguished by their articulations, have in process of time, by dropping these articulations, come to be represented by the solitary vowel *a,* to the no small confusion of the language and embarrassment of the reader. The place of the absent consonant is often supplied, indeed, in writing, by an apostrophe. This, however, is at best but an imperfect and precarious expedient.

In treating of the consonants separately, it will be convenient to depart a little from the alphabetical order of the letters, and to consider first the *Labials,* next the *Palatals,* and lastly the *Linguals.*

### LABIALS.

### P.

1. Plain. Like *p* in English ; as, poll *a pool,* pill *return.*
2. Aspirated. Like *ph* or *f* in English ; as, a' phuill *of the pool,* phill *returned* (*i*).

### B.

1. Plain. Like *b* in English ; as, baile *a town,* beo *alive.*
2. Aspirated. Like *v* in English ; as, bhuail *struck.* In the end of a syllable the articulation is sometimes feeble, and often passes into the vocal sound of *u* (*k*) ; as in marbh (*l*) *dead,* garbh *rough,* dabhach *a vat.*

### M.

1. Plain. Like *m* in English ; as, mac *a son,* cam *crooked.*
2. Aspirated. Somewhat like *v* in English, but more feeble and nasal; as, mhathair *O mother,* lamh *the hand.* The sound *mh* has the same relation to that of *bh,* as the sound of *m* has to that of *b.* Sometimes, like *bh,* it becomes a vocal sound like a nasal *u;* as, in damh *an ox,* samhradh *summer:* and sometimes the articulation becomes so feeble as not to be perceived; as, comhradh *speech,* domhainn *deep.*

(*i*) Ph is found in no Gaelic word which is not inflected, except a few words transplanted from the Greek or the Hebrew, in which *ph* represents the Greek φ, or the Hebrew פ. It might perhaps be more proper to represent פ by *p* rather than *ph ;* and to represent φ by *f,* as the Italians have done in *filosofia, filologia,* &c., by which some ambiguities and anomalies in declension would be avoided.

(*k*) The affinity between the sounds of *v* and *u* is observable in many languages, particularly in the Hebrew, Greek, and Latin.

(*l*) Agreeably to the like pronunciation, the Welsh write this word *marw,* the Manks *marroo.*

## F.

1. Plain.    Like *f* in English ; as, faigh *to get,* fòid *a turf.*
2. Aspirated.    Quiescent ; as, fheara *O men.*    In fhuair *found,* the aspiration is retained, and the word is pronounced as if written *huair.*    It is probable that it was originally written and pronounced fuair (*m*) ; that huair is but a provincial pronunciation (*n*) ; and that to adapt the spelling in some shape to this pronunciation, the word came to be written fhuair.

### PALATALS AND LINGUALS.

In treating of the Diphthongs (ai, ea, ei, &c.) notice has been often taken of the powers of certain vowels in modifying the sound of the adjoining consonants.    This refers to a twofold mode of pronouncing the Palatal and Lingual consonants, whether *plain* or *aspirated.*    The difference between these two modes of pronunciation is, in some consonants, abundantly striking ; in others it is minute, but sufficiently discernible to an ear accustomed to the Gaelic.    The one of these modes of articulation belongs to Palatals and Linguals, chiefly when connected with a *broad vowel;* the other belongs to them when connected with a *small vowel.*    Hence, the former may be called the *broad* sound, the latter the *small* sound of a *Palatal* or a *Lingual.*

These sounds are not distinguished in writing, but may be known, for the most part, by the relative situation of the letters.

## C.

1. Plain.    *Broad:* like *c* in *come, curb;* as, cùl *the back,* cridhe *the heart.*

---

(*m*) It is still pronounced fuair in the Northern Highlands, and it is so written in Irish.    See Irish Bible, Gen. xxxv. 18, 19; John ii. 14, viii. 62, 53.

(*n*) So fathast *yet,* fein *self,* are in some places pronounced as if they began with an *h* instead of an *f.*    The latter word is, by the Manks, written hene.

2. *Small:* like *c* in *care, cure;* as, taic *support,* circe *of a hen* (*o*).

3. Aspirated. *Broad:* like the Greek χ, as pronounced in Scotland, in χωρα; as, croch *to hang,* chaidh *went.*

4. *Small:* like χ in χιων; as, chi *shall see,* eich *horses.*

## G.

1. Plain. *Broad:* like *g* in *go, rogue;* as, gabh *to take,* glor *speech,* bog *soft.*

2. *Small:* like *g* in *give, fatigue;* as, gin *to produce,* thig *shall come,* tilg *to throw.*

3. Aspirated. *Broad:* has no sound like it in English; ghabh *took,* ghleidh *kept.*

4. *Small:* nearly like *y* in *young;* as, ghin *produced.*

5. *Gh* in the end of a syllable is often quiescent; as, righ *a king,* tiugh *thick,* fuigheall *remainder.*

## T.

1. Plain. *Broad:* nearly like *t* in *tone, bottom;* as, tog *to raise,* trom *heavy,* brat *a covering.*

(*o*) Over a considerable part of the Highlands that propensity to aspiration, which has been already remarked, has affixed to *c,* in the end of a word, or of an accented syllable, the sound of *chc;* as, mac *a son,* torc *a boar,* acain *moaning;* pronounced often machc, torchc, achcain.

There is reason to believe that this compound sound of *chc* was not known of old, but is a modern corruption. For,

This pronunciation is not universal over the Highlands. In some parts the *c* retains its proper sound in all situations.

If the articulation in question had, from the first, been compounded, it is highly probable that it would have been represented, in writing, by a combination of letters, such as *chc;* especially as we find that the same sound is represented at other times, not by a single consonant, but by a combination, as in the case of *chd.* Why should it be thought that boc *a buck,* and bochd *poor,* were originally pronounced alike, when they are distinguished both in writing and signification?

The word שׂק *a sack,* has been transplanted from the Hebrew into many languages, among the rest the Gaelic, where it has been always written sac, although now pronounced sachc. In none of the other languages in which the word is used (except the Welsh alone), has the final palatal been aspirated. It would appear therefore that the sound sachc is a departure from the original Gaelic pronunciation. The same change may have happened in the pronunciation of other words; in which the plain *c* is now aspirated, though it may not have been so originally.

2. *Small:* like *ch* in *cheek, choose;* as, tinn *sick,* caillte *lost.*

3. Aspirated. Like *h* in *house;* as, thig *shall come,* throisg *fasted,* maith *good.*

4. *Quiescent:* in the middle of a polysyllable, in the end of a long syllable, and in certain tenses of a few irregular verbs when preceded by *d';* as, snitheach (*p*) *watery,* sìth *peace,* an d' thug e? *did he give?* also in the pronoun thusa *thou.*

## D.

1. Plain. *Broad:* nearly like *d* in *done;* as, dol *going,* dlù *near, close,* ciod *what.*

2. *Small:* like *j* in *June, jewel;* as, diù *refuse,* maide *a stick,* airde *height.*

*D*, after *ch,* is commonly sounded like *c;* as, bochd *poor,* pronounced as if written bochc (*q*).

(*p*) Though *th* be quiescent in the middle of a polysyllable, over the North and Central Highlands, yet it is, with more propriety, pronounced, in the West Highlands, as an aspiration ; as, athair *father,* mathanas *pardon,* pronounced a-hair, mahanas.

(*q*) I am informed that this pronunciation of *chd* is not universal ; but that in some districts, particularly the East Highlands, the *d* has here, as in other places, its proper lingual sounds. In many, if not all the instances in which *chd* occurs, the ancient Irish wrote *ct.* This spelling corresponds to that of some foreign words that have a manifest affinity to Gaelic words of the same signification ; which, it is therefore presumable, were all originally pronounced, as they were written, without an aspiration, such as,

| *Latin.* | *Old French.* | *Gaelic.* |
|---|---|---|
| Noct-u Noct-is, &c. | Nuict | an nochd, *to night.* |
| Oct-o | Huict | Ochd, *eight.* |
| Benedict-um | Benoict | Beannachd, *blessing.* |
| Maledict-um | Maudict | Mallachd, *cursing.* |
| Ruct-us | | Bruchd, *evomition.* |
| Intellect-us | | Intleachd, *contrivance.* |
| Lact-is, -i, &c. | | Lachd, *milk.* |
| Dict-o, -are, &c. | | Deachd, *to dictate.* |
| Rego | | Reachd, *a law, institution.* |
| Rect-um | | |

From the propensity of the Gaelic to aspiration, the original *c* was converted into *ch,* and the words were written with *cht,* as in the Irish acht *but,* &c., or with the slight change of *t* into *d,* as in ochd, &c. This is the

3. Aspirated (*r*).    *Broad:* like broad *gh*, as, dhruid *did shut*, gradh *love.*

4. *Small:* like small *gh;* as, dhearc *looked.*

5. *Quiescent;* as, fàidh *a prophet,* cridhe *a heart,* radh *saying,* bualadh *striking.*

RULE.—*The consonants c, g, t, d, have their* SMALL *sound, when, in the same syllable, they are preceded, or immediately followed, by a* SMALL VOWEL; *in all other situations they have their* BROAD *sound.*

## S.

1. Plain.    *Broad:* like *s* in *sun, this;* as, speal *a scythe,* cas *a foot,* sùil *an eye,* scian *a knife.*

2. *Small:* like *sh* in *show, rash ;* as, bris *to break,* sèimh *quiet,* sniomh *to twine,* stéidh *foundation.*

3. Aspirated : like *h* in *him;* as, shuidh *sat,* shrann *snorted.*    Before *l* and *n,* it is almost, if not altogether, quiescent ; as, shlanuich *healed,* shniomh *twisted.*    *S* followed by a *mute* consonant is never aspirated.

RULE.—*S has its* SMALL *sound, when, in the same syllable, it is preceded or followed by a* SMALL VOWEL, *with or without an intervening Lingual.    In all other situations it has its* BROAD *sound.*    EXCEPT.    *S is broad in* is *am.    It is small in* so *this,* sud *yon.*    It is customary to give *s* its *broad* sound in the beginning of a word, when the former word ends with *r,* in which case the *r* also has its broad sound; as, chuir sinn *we put,* air son *on account.*

opinion of O'Brien, when he says the word lecht is the Celtic root of the Latin *lectio*—the aspirate *h* is but a late invention.—*O'Br. Ir. Dict. voc. lecht.*    In process of time the true sound of *cht* or *chd* was confounded with the kindred sound of *chc,* which was commonly, though corruptly, given to final *c.*

(*r*) It is certain that the natural sound of d aspirated is that of [the Saxon đ] or *th* in *thou;* as the natural sound of *t* aspirated is that of *th* in *think.*    This articulation, from whatever cause, has not been admitted into the Gaelic, either Scottish or Irish, although it is used in the kindred dialects of Cornwall and Wales.

## OF L, N, R.

A distinction between a consonant when *plain*, and the
same consonant when *aspirated*, has been easily traced thus
far. This distinction readily discovers itself, not only in
the pronunciation and orthography, but also (as will be seen
in its proper place) throughout the system of inflection. It
takes place uniformly in those consonants which have been
already considered. With respect to the remaining linguals,
*l, n, r,* a corresponding distinction will be found to take place
in their pronunciation, and likewise in the changes they
suffer by inflection. This close correspondence between the
changes incident to *l, n, r,* and the changes which the other
consonants undergo, seems to be a sufficient reason for still
using the same discriminative terms in treating of their powers,
though these terms may not appear to be so strictly applicable to these three consonants as to the rest. The powers
of *l, n, r,* shall accordingly be explained under the divisions
*plain* and *aspirated, broad* and *small.*

### L.

1. Plain. *Broad:* has no sound like it in English; lom
*bare,* labhair *speak,* mall *slow,* alt *a joint,* ald *a brook,* flat *a
rod,* dlù *near.*
2. *Small:* like *ll* in *million;* as, linn *an age,* lion *fill,*
pill *to return,* slighe *a way.*
3. Aspirated. *Broad:* like *l* in *loom, fool;* as, labhair
*spoke,* lom feminine of lom *bare,* mol *to praise,* dhlù feminine
of dlù *near.*
4. *Small:* nearly like *l* in *limb, fill;* as, a linn *his age,*
lion *filled,* mil *honey,* dligheach *due, lawful.*

### N.

1. Plain. *Broad:* has no sound like it in English; nuadh
*new,* naisg *bind,* lann *a blade,* carn *a heap of stones.*
2. *Small:* like *n* in the second syllable of *opinion;* as,
nigh *wash,* binn *melodious,* cuirn *heaps of stones.*

B

3. Aspirated. *Broad:* like *n* in *no, on;* as, nuadh fem-minine of nuadh *new,* naisg *bound,* shnamh *swam,* sean *old* (*s*), chon *of dogs,* dàn *a poem.*

4. *Small:* like *n* in *keen, near;* as, nigh *washed,* shniomh *twisted,* coin *dogs,* dàin *poems.*

In an when followed by a Palatal, the *n* is pronounced like *ng* in English; as, an gille *the lad,* an comhnuidh *always.*

*N,* after a mute, is in a few instances pronounced like *r* (*t*); as in mnathan *women,* cnatan *a cold,* an t-snàth *of the yarn;* pronounced mrathan, cratan, &c.

## R.

1. Plain. Nearly like *r* in *roar;* as, ruadh *reddish,* righ *a king,* ruith *run,* torr *a heap,* ceartas *justice.*

2. Aspirated. *Broad:* nearly like *r* in *rear;* as, car *a turn,* ruith *ran,* mòr *great.*

3. *Small:* has no sound like it in English; a righ *O king,* seirbhe *satiety,* mòir gen. of mòr *great.*

The *plain, aspirated, broad,* and *small* sounds of these Linguals are not distinguished in writing; but they may, for the most part, be known from the relative position of the letters.

RULE.—L, N, R, *have their* PLAIN *sound when, in the same syllable, they are immediately preceded by a plain Liquid, or immediately followed by a plain Lingual; also in the beginning of certain cases and tenses ; in all other situations, they have their* ASPIRATED *sound. They have their* SMALL *sound when, in the same syllable, they are pre-ceded or followed by a small vowel, with or without an inter-vening Liquid ; in other situations, they have their* BROAD *sound.*

(*s*) In sean *old,* the *n* has its *plain* sound when the following word begins with a Lingual. Accordingly it is often written in that situation seann; as, seann duine *an old man,* an t-seann tiomnaidh *of the old Testament.*

(*t*) So in Latin, *canmen* from *cano* was pronounced, and then written *carmen ; genmen* from the obsolete γενω passed into *germen.*

# H

H is never used as an independent radical letter. When prefixed to a word beginning with a vowel, it is pronounced like h in *how ;* as, na h-òighean *the virgins*, na h-oidhche *of the night.*

The following scheme exhibits a succinct view of the letters, both singly and in their several combinations. The first column contains the letters whose sound is to be exhibited; the prefixed figures marking the number of different sounds denoted by the same letter. The second column explains the sounds by examples or by references. The third column contains Gaelic words, with their translation, in which the several sounds are exemplified.

## VOWELS.

| | | | |
|---|---|---|---|
| 1 a | long | far star | àr *slaughter*, àth *a ford.* |
| | short | that | ar *to plow*, abuich *ripe.* |
| 2 a | long | | adhradh *worship*, adhbhar *reason.* |
| | short | | adharc *a horn*, adhart *a bolster.* |
| 3 a | short | similar | ma *if*, an *the*, a *his, her.* |
| 1 e | long | there | è sè *he*, gnè *sort, kind.* |
| | short | met | le *with*, leth *half.* |
| 2 e | long | | an dé *yesterday*, cé *the earth.* |
| 3 e | short | mother | duine *a man*, briste *broken.* |
| 1 i | see | | mìn *smooth*, righ *a king.* |
| | | | min *meal*, crith *a shaking.* |
| 2 i | short | this | is *am, art, is.* |
| 1 o | long | more | mòr *great*, lòn *food.* |
| | short | hot | mo *my*, do *thy*, lon *the ouzle.* |
| 2 o | long short | old | lom *bare*, toll *a hole.* |
| | | | lomadh *making bare.* |
| 3 o | long short | (2) a | roghnuich *to choose.* |
| | | | roghuinn *choice.* |

1 u  { long / short } fool    { ùr *fresh*, sùgh *juice*. / ubh *an egg*, tur *quite*.

## DIPHTHONGS.

1 ae  (1) a (2) e   laeth *days*.
1 ai  (1) a (1) i   fàidh *a prophet*, claidheamh *a sword*.
2 ai  (2) a (1) i   saidhbhir, *rich*.
3 ai  (1) a         fàisg *squeeze*, tais *soft*.
4 ai  (2) a         airm *arms*, gairm *to call*.
1 ao  (2) a         faobhar *edge* of an instrument.
1 ea  (2) e (1) a   beann *a pinnacle*, meal *enjoy*.
2 ea  (1) e         dean *to do, make*, bean *a woman*.
3 ea  (2) e         easlan *sick*, fead *whistle*.
4 ea  (1) a         ceard *an artificer*, geal *white*.
5 ea  (3) a         coireach *faulty*.
1 ei  (1) e (1) i   sgèimh *beauty*, meidh *a balance*.
2 ei  (2) e (1) i   feidh *deer*, greigh *a herd*.
3 ei  (1) e         mèise *of a plate*.
4 ei  (2) e         éigin *necessity*, eich *horses*.
1 eo  (2) e (1) o   beo *alive*, beothail *lively*.
2 eo  (1) o         leomhann *a lion*, deoch *a drink*.
1 eu  (2) e         teum *to bite*, gleus *trim*.
1 ia  (1) i (1) a   fial *liberal*, fiar *oblique*.
2 ia  (1) i (2) a   fiadh *a deer*, biadh *food*.
1 io  (1) i (3) o   diol *to pay*, iolach *a spout*.
2 io  (1) i         iodhol *an idol*, crios *a girdle*.
3 io  fan          cionta *guilt*.
1 iu  (1) i u       fiù *worth*, iuchair *a key*.
2 iu  u            diù *refuse*, tiugh *thick*.
1 oi  (1) o (1) i   òigh *a virgin*, troidh *a foot*.
2 oi  (3) o (1) i   oidhche *night*.
3 oi  (1) o         mòid *more*, toic *wealth*.
4 oi  (2) o         fòid *a turf*, fois *rest*.
5 oi  (3) o         coileach *a cock*, goirid *short*.
1 ua  u    (1) a    cuan *the sea*, fuath *hatred*.
2 ua  u    (2) a    tuadh *a hatchet*, sluagh *people*.

1 ui　u　(1) i　sùigheah *a raspberry*, buidheann
　　　　　　　　　*a company.*
2 ui　u　　　　dùil *expectation*, fuil *blood.*


## TRIPHTHONGS.

1 aoi (1) ao (1) i　caoidh *lamentation.*
2 aoi (1) ao　　　　caoin *mild*, saoil *to think.*
1 eoi (2) eo (1) i　geoigh *geese.*
2 eoi (1) eo　　　　meoir *fingers.*
3 eoi (2) eo　　　　deoir *tears.*
1 iai (1) ia　　　　fiaire *more oblique.*
1 iui (2) iu　　　　ciùil *of music.*
1 uai (1) ua (1) i　luaithe *quicker.*
2 uai (2) ua (1) i　cruaidh *hard*, fuaim *sound.*
3 uai (1) ua　　　　gluais *to move*, uair *time.*


## CONSONANTS

### *Labials.*

1 p　part　　　　poll *a pool*, streap *to climb.*
2 ph　Philip　　phill *returned.*
1 b　boil　　　　baile *a town*, breab *to kick.*
2 bh　vile　　　bhuail *struck*, gabh *to take.*
1 m　my　　　　mòr *great*, anam *life, soul.*
2 mh　　　　　mhothuich *perceived*, damh *an ox.*
1 f　feel　　　　fill *to fold.*
2 fh　*quiescent*　fheara *O men.*


### *Palatals.*

1 c　cock　　　can *to say, sing*, creid *to believe.*
2 c　kick　　　ceann *end, head*, reic *to sell.*
3 ch　χωρα　　chaidh *went*, rach *go.*
4 ch　χειμων　chi *shall see*, criche *of a boundary.*
1 g　go　　　　gabh *to take*, rag *stiff.*

| | | | |
|---|---|---|---|
| 2 | g | give | geinne *a wedge*, ruig *to reach.* |
| 3 | gh | | ghabh *took*, ghleidh *kept.* |
| 4 | gh | you | gheibh *will get.* |
| 5 | *quiescent* | | righ *a king*, sluagh *people.* |

### Linguals.

| | | | |
|---|---|---|---|
| 1 | t | tone | tog *to raise*, slat *a rod.* |
| 2 | t | chin | tinn *sick*, àite a *place.* |
| 3 | th | have | thainig *came.* |
| 4 | th | *quiescent* | maith *good*, fàth *occasion.* |
| 1 | d | done | dol *going*, dragh *trouble.* |
| 2 | d | join | diom *resentment*, maide *a stick.* |
| 3 | dh | (3) gh | dhall *blind.* |
| 4 | dh | (4) gh | dhearc *looked.* |
| 5 | dh | *quiescent* | radh *saying*, bualadh *threshing.* |
| 1 | s | so | sannt *desire*, sloc *a pit.* |
| 2 | s | show | sèimh *gentle*, so *this.* |
| 3 | sh | how | shuidh *sat*, shaoil *thought.* |
| 1 | l | | lom *bare*, slat *a rod*, moll *chaff.* |
| 2 | l | million | lìnn *an age*, caillte *lost.* |
| 3 | l | look | blàth *blossom*, shlanuich *healed.* |
| 4 | l | believe | leum *leaped*, shleamhnuich *slipped.* |
| 1 | n | | crann *a tree*, naomh *holy*, naisg *bind.* |
| 2 | n | opinion | seinn *to sing*, nigh *wash.* |
| 3 | n | no | fan *to stay*, naisg *bound.* |
| 4 | n | near | coin *dogs*, nigh *washed.* |
| 1 | r | roar | fearr *better*, righ *a king*, ruith *run.* |
| 2 | r | rear | fear *a man*, ruith ran. |
| 3 | r | | fir *men*, a righ *O king*, treoir *strength.* |

There is no doubt that the Gaelic has been for many ages a written language. It is equally certain that its orthography, since it was first committed to writing, has undergone considerable changes.    In this respect it has shared the common fate of all written languages.

In the first exhibition of the sounds of a living language, by alphabetical characters, it is probable that the principle which regulated the system of orthography was, that every elementary sound should be represented by a corresponding character, either simple or compounded, and that the same sound should be represented by the same character. If different sounds were represented by the same letter; if the same sound were represented by different letters; if more letters were employed then were necessary to exhibit the sound; or if any sound were not represented by a corresponding character; then the *written* language would not be an adequate representation of the *spoken*.    It is hardly to be supposed that, in the first rude attempts at alphabetical writing, the principle above laid down could be strictly and uniformly followed.    And though it had, yet, in the course of a few generations, many causes would occur to bring about considerable departures from it.    A gradual refinement of ear, and increasing attention to *euphonia ;* contractions and elisions brought into vogue by the carelessness or the rapidity of colloquial speech, or by the practice of popular speakers ; above all, the mixture of the speech of different nations would introduce numberless varieties into the pronunciation. Still, those who wrote the language might choose to adhere to the original orthography for the sake of retaining the radical parts, and preserving the etymon of vocables undisguised, and for maintaining an uniformity in the mechanism of the inflections.    Hence the pronunciation and the orthography would disagree in many instances, till at length it would be found expedient to alter the orthography, and to adapt it to such changes in the speech or spoken language as long use had established, in order to maintain what was most necessary of all, a due correspondence between the mode of speaking and the mode of writing the same language.

It will probably be found on inquiry that in all languages when the *speech* has undergone material and striking changes,

the *written language* also has varied in a considerable degree
in conformity to these changes, but that it has not scrupu-
lously kept pace with the spoken language in every smaller
variation. The written language of the Greeks suffered
many changes between the time that the old Pelasgic was
spoken and the days of Demosthenes. The various modes
of pronunciation used in the different districts of Greece are
marked by a diversity in the orthography of the written language.
The writing of the Latin underwent considerable alterations
between the era of the *Decemviri* and the Augustan age,
corresponding, no doubt, to the changes which had taken
place during that interval in speaking the Latin. English
and French books printed within the last century exhibit
a mode of orthography very different from what is found in
books printed two or three hundred years ago. These
instances show the tendency which the written language has
to follow the lead of the spoken language, and to maintain a
certain degree of conformity to those modes of pronunciation
which are from time to time adopted by those who speak it.

On the other hand, numberless examples might be adduced
from any living language to prove that the written language
does not adapt itself, on all occasions and with strict
uniformity, to the sounds of speech. Words are written
differently which are pronounced alike. The same combinations of letters, in different situations, represent different
sounds. Letters are retained in writing, serving to point
out the derivations of words, after they have been entirely
dropped in speaking.

From such facts as these, it appears a just conclusion that
*written language* generally follows the *spoken language* through
its various revolutions, but still at a certain distance,—
not dropping so far behind as to lose sight of its precursor,
nor following so close as to be led through all its fantastic
deviations.

Here a question occurs of importance in settling the orthography of any particular tongue : How near ought the
*written language* to correspond to the *spoken*, and where
may a disagreement between them be allowed with pro-

priety? The following observations may serve to throw some light on the subject of this question, though by no means sufficient to furnish a complete answer.

It is obvious that in speech the *articulations* (which are represented by consonants in writing) are the least liable to variation. *Vowel sounds* are continually varying. In this variety chiefly consists that diversity of tone and dialect which is found in the speech of different districts of the same country, where the same words are spoken. The changes, too, which are introduced by time fall with greater effect on the vowel sounds than on the articulations. This circumstance will strike an observer who steps into any deliberative assembly, where the speakers are of different ages. St Jerome makes a remark on the reading of Hebrew, which is applicable, in some measure, to the pronunciation of all languages : " Nec refert utrum *Salem* aut *Salim* nominetur; cum vocalibus in medio literis perraro utantur Hebraei; et pro voluntate lectorum, ac *varietate regionum*, eadem verba *diversis sonis* atque accentibus proferantur." It may be observed that the superior stability of the articulations above the vowel sounds is the natural consequence of the position of the organs of speech in uttering them. The different modifications of the vowel sounds are effected by minute changes in the conformation of the organs ; those of the articulations are made by more distinct and operose inflections of the organs.

It seems, then, a warrantable conclusion that, of the elementary constituents of speech, viz., articulations and vowel sounds, the *articulations* are, in their own nature, ESSEN-TIAL, PERMANENT, and PREDOMINANT; the *vowel sounds*, comparatively considered, are ADJUNCTIVE, FLUCTUATING, and SERVILE.

Further, all the vowel sounds that usually occur in speech seem to be uttered with equal ease, in whatever situation they occur, as the same organs are employed for all. In forming the common articulations of speech, as different organs are employed, a degree of difficulty is sometimes felt in making a transition from one articulation to another.

Thus a difficulty will occasionally occur in pronouncing certain words, where the general analogy of inflection or of collocation has brought together articulations which do not easily coalesce. Hence a necessity arises of departing in such a case from the general analogy, and altering or displacing some of those discrepant articulations, for the sake of ease and convenience in pronunciation, and to relieve the ear from an offensive discordant sound. Departures are made from the general rules of speech in the case of the vowel sounds also, of which the Greek tongue abounds with examples. These departures, however, seem to have been made from a desire to indulge the ear in certain national predilections or aversions which it had conceived with regard to particular sounds. In examining the anomalies of speech, or those peculiarities which have been reckoned anomalous, it will be found that such of them as affect the articulations have, for the most part, been adopted for the purpose of ease and convenience in pronunciation ; while those which affect the vowel sounds have proceeded from the peculiar taste of the speakers. Thus the former spring from a cause urgent and constant in its nature, and uniform in its operation ; the latter, from a cause local and temporary in its nature, and variable in its operation.

If this theory be just, it ought to follow that, in all polished tongues, an agreement will be found among those irregularities which affect the articulations, that is not so observable in those which affect the vowel sounds. There is reason to believe that, if a full comparison were made between different languages, this would accordingly be found to be the case. Let it be observed, then, that in speech a deference has been usually paid to the articulations which has not been paid to the vowel sounds, inasmuch as the latter have been changed from the state in which the structure of each tongue had at first placed them, frequently and from peculiar taste or humour ; the former more rarely, and for the most part from necessity. If this observation be found to be well supported, we shall have the sanction of general practice in favour of the conclusion that was formerly drawn from the nature of articulate sounds, viz., that the articulations are ESSENTIAL, PERMANENT, and PRE-DOMINANT ; the vowel sounds ADJUNCTIVE, FLUC-TUATING, and SERVILE.

If it appear, then, that the vowel sounds in speech are perpetually varying in the mouths of different speakers, from causes which either elude our search, or, when discovered, are seen to be of small importance, may we not judge that it would be equally vain and improper to attempt to make *Writing* follow all these minute variations ; and that, however it may happen that the same vowel sound may be represented in many instances by different letters, and different vowel sounds by the same letters, yet this disagreement between *Speech* and *Writing* must be connived at, for the sake of preserving some degree of uniformity, where alone it can be preserved, in the *written language ?*  If it appear, again, that the variations from the established analogy which are made on the articulations are less frequent, and proceed from causes obvious and cogent, ought not these variations to be exhibited in writing, for preserving that general correspondence between the written and the spoken language which ought to be preserved, as far as the limited powers of letters will permit, and without which the words I speak and those I write do not belong to the same language ?

One exception from this principle seems allowable in the case of quiescent consonants.  It may be inferred, from the practice of all living languages, that consonants whereof the corresponding articulations have been suppressed in speaking may yet be retained with propriety in writing, when they are requisite to point out the derivation of vocables, or the radical part of declinable words.  But this exception ought to be allowed only to a moderate extent, for the reasons already assigned ; to which it may be added, that the far greater part of the suppressed articulations can be easily discovered and retraced to their roots, without any index in the *written* any more than in the *spoken* language to point them out.

These observations being premised, I shall proceed to explain the present state of Gaelic Orthography, and shall endeavour to assist the reader in forming a judgment of its merit, and how far it may admit of improvement.

I. It may be laid down as one settled principle in orthography, that each letter or combination of letters in the written language ought always to denote one and the same sound. From the explanation that has been given of the powers of the letters, it may be seen how far this principle has been regarded in the Gaelic. Though almost every one of the letters represents more than one sound, yet there is an evident affinity between the several sounds of the same letter. And it may be readily allowed that less confusion and inconvenience follow from exhibiting a few kindred sounds by the same letter, than would have taken place had the characters been multiplied to such a degree as that a separate one could have been appropriated to each minute variety of sound.

It is obvious to remark, as a departure from this principle, that in the case of the consonants *l, n, r,* the distinction between their *plain* and their *aspirated* state is not marked in writing, but that in both states the consonant is written in one way. In the middle and end of words, as has been shown, this distinction may be known from the relative situation of the letters. In the beginning of certain cases and tenses of declinable words, it may often be known from their *grammatical* connection, but is not marked by any *graphical* index whatever. The proper reading is to be determined by the sense of the passage, instead of the sense being understood by the proper reading. It is not easy to discover how those who first committed the Gaelic to writing neglected to mark such a material distinction. Inconveniencies and ambiguities not unfrequently arise from this cause, which have been long felt and regretted. Is there room to hope that it is not yet too late to recommend a method of remedying this defect ? The method I would suggest is the most simple and obvious of any. It is to annex to the initial *l, n,* and *r,* in their aspirated state, the letter *h,* just as has been done to all the other consonants. The analogy of orthography would thus be maintained, the system of inflection would be more justly exhibited, and carried on by an uniform process in *Writing* as it is in *Speech*, and errors in reading and ambiguities in syntax would be avoided (*u*).

II. Another principle of authority in regulating orthography is, that each sound ought always to be represented by one and the same letter, or combination of letters. The deviations from this rule in Gaelic are extremely few. The sound of *ao* is represented sometimes by *a* alone, sometimes by *o* alone. The sound of *gh* is represented also by *dh ;* and final *c* often, though corruptly, represents the same sound with *chd*.

III. A third principle in orthography is, that no more letters ought to be employed than are necessary to represent the sound. There are probably few polished languages in which departures from this rule are not found in abundance. Reasons have been already mentioned which render it expedient to retain letters in writing many words, after the corresponding sounds have been dropped in pronouncing the same words. Quiescent letters, both vowels and consonants, are not unfrequent in Gaelic. Though these quiescent letters have no sound themselves, they are not always without effect in pronunciation, as they often determine the sound of other letters. Most, if not all, the quiescent vowels seem to have been introduced for this purpose. They ascertain the *broad* or the *small* sound of the adjoining con-

---

(*u*) Another mode, proposed by a learned correspondent, of marking the distinction in the sound of the initial Linguals, is by writing the letter double, thus ll, nn, rr, when its sound is the same with that which is represented by those double letters in the end of a syllable ; and when the sound is otherwise. to write the letter single ; as, llamh *hand*, llion *fill*, mo lamh *my hand*, lion mi *1 filled*.

It is perhaps too late, however, to urge now even so slight an alteration as this in the Orthography of the Gaelic, which ought rather to be held as fixed beyond the reach of innovation, by the happy diffusion of the Gaelic Scriptures over the Highlands.

sonants. This has been made sufficiently clear in treating
of the vowels and diphthongs separately. A consonant, as
has been shown, has its *broad* sound, both when preceded
and when followed by a broad vowel ; and in like manner
has its *small* sound, both when preceded and when followed
by a small vowel. If a consonant were preceded by a vowel
of one quality, and followed by one of a different quality,
the reader, it has been thought, might be doubtful whether
that consonant ought to be pronounced with its broad or
with its small sound. Hence this rule has long obtained in
Gaelic orthography, that in polysyllables the last vowel of
one syllable and the first vowel of the subsequent syllable
must be both of the same quality (*x*). To the extensive
application and the rigid observance of this rule it is owing
that so many diphthongs appear where one vowel is sufficient
to express the vocal sound, and that the homogeneous
vowels, when used in their quiescent capacity, are often
exchanged for each other, or written indiscriminately (*y*).
From the former of these circumstances, most of the words
in the language appear loaded with superfluous vowels ;
from the latter, the orthography of many words appears, in
some respects, arbitrary and unsettled. Even a partial
correction of these blemishes must be desirable. It may
therefore be worth while to examine this long established
canon of Gaelic orthography, with a view to discover whether
it has not been extended farther than is necessary, and
whether it ought not in many cases to be set aside.

We have seen that the Labials *b*, *m*, *f*, *p*, whether aspirated or not, have no distinction of broad and small sound.

---

(*x*) *Leathan re Leathan, is Caol re Caol.*
Of the many writers who have recorded or taken notice of this rule, I
have found none who have attempted to account for its introduction into
the Gaelic. They only tell that such a correspondence between the vowels
ought to be observed, and that it would be improper to write otherwise.
Indeed, none of them seem to have attended to the different effects of a
broad and of a small vowel on the sound of an adjacent consonant. From
this circumstance, duly considered, I have endeavoured to derive a reason
for the rule in question, the only probable one that has yet occurred to me.
(*y*) As deannibh or deannaibh *do ye*, beannuich or beannuich *bless*.

It cannot, then, be necessary to employ vowels, either prefixed or postfixed, to indicate the sound of these. Thus,
abuich *ripe*, gabhaidh *will take*, chromainn *I would bow*,
ciomaich *captives*, have been written with a 'broad vowel in
the second syllable, corresponding to the broad vowel in the
first syllable ; yet the letters abich, gabhidh, chrominn,
ciomich, fully exhibit the sound. The prepositive syllable
im, when followed by a small vowel, is written im, as in
imlich *to lick*, imcheist *perplexity*. But when the first
vowel of the following syllable is broad, it has been the
practice to insert an *o* before the *m*, as in iomlan *complete*,
iomghaoth *a whirlwind*, iomluasg *agitation*. Yet the inserted
*o* serves no purpose, either in respect of derivation, of
inflection, or of pronunciation. The unnecessary application
of the rule in question appears most unequivocally in words
derived from other languages. From the Latin words *imago
templum, liber,* are formed in Gaelic iomhaigh, teampull,
leabhar. Nothing but a servile regard to the rule under
consideration could have suggested the insertion of a broad
vowel in the first syllable of these words, where it serves
neither to guide the pronunciation, nor to point out the derivation.

Another case, in which the observation of this rule seems
to be wholly unnecessary, is when two syllables of a word
are separated by a quiescent consonant. Thus in gleidheadh
*keeping*, itheadh *eating*, buidheann *a company*, dlighecah
*lawful*, the aspirated consonants in the middle are altogether
quiescent. The vocal sound of the second syllable is
sufficiently expressed by the last vowel. No good reason,
then, appears for writing a small vowel in the second
syllable.

Thus far it is evident that the rule respecting the correspondence of vowels is wholly impertinent in the case of
syllables divided by Labials, or by quiescent consonants. If
we examine further into the application of this rule, we shall
find more cases in which it may be safely set aside.

Many of the inflections of nouns and verbs are formed by
adding one or more syllables to the root. The final con-

sonant of the root must always be considered as belonging
to the radical part, not to the adjected termination. The
sound of that consonant, whether broad or small, falls to be
determined by the quality of the vowel which precedes it in
the same syllable, not by the quality of that which follows
it in the next syllable. It seems, therefore, unnecessary to
employ any more vowels in the adjected syllable than what
are sufficient to represent its own vocal sound. The rule
under consideration has, notwithstanding, been extended to
the orthography of the oblique cases and tenses, and a
supernumerary vowel has been thrown into the termination,
whenever that was requisite to preserve the supposed
necessary correspondence with the foregoing syllable. Thus,
in forming the nominative and dative plural of many nouns,
the syllables *an* and *ibh* are added to the singular, which
letters fully express the true sound of these terminations.
If the last vowel of the nominative singular is broad, *an*
alone is added for the nominative plural; as, lamh-an *hands*,
cluas-an *ears*. But if the last vowel be small, an *e* is thrown
into the termination; as, sùil-ean *eyes*, sròin-ean *noses*. Now
if it be observed that, in the two last examples, the small
sound of the *l* and *n* in the root is determined by the preceding small vowel *i*, with which they are necessarily connected in one syllable, and that the letters *an* fully represent the sound of the termination, it must be evident that
the *e* in the final syllable is altogether superfluous. So in
forming the dative plural : if the last vowel of the root be
small, *ibh* is added ; as, sùil-ibh, sroin-ibh. But if the last
vowel of the root is broad, the termination is written *aibh ;*
as, lamh-aibh, cluas-aibh, where the *a*, for the reason already
assigned, is totally useless.

These observations apply with equal justness to the tenses
of verbs, as will be seen by comparing the following examples:
creid-idh *will believe*, stad-aidh *will stop ;* chreid-inn *I would
believe*, stad-*a*inn *I would stop ;* creid-eam *let me believe*,
stad-am *let me stop ;* creid-ibh *believe ye*, stad-*a*ibh *stop ye.*

The same observations may be further applied to derivative words, formed by adding to their primitives the syllables

*ach, achd, ag, an, ail, as;* in all which *e* has been unnecessarily introduced, when the last vowel of the preceding
syllable was small ; as, sannt-ach *covetous,* toil-each *willing;*
naomh-achd *holiness,* doimhn-eachd *depth;* sruth-an *a
rivulet,* cuil-ean *a whelp;* cauch-ag *a little cup,* cail-eag *a
girl;* fear-ail *manly,* caird-eil *friendly* (*z*); ceart-as *justice,*
caird-eas *friendship.*

The foregoing observations appear sufficient to establish
this general conclusion, that in all cases in which a vowel
serves neither to exhibit the vocal sound, nor to modify the
articulations of *the syllable to which it belongs,* it may be
reckoned nothing better than an useless incumbrance. There
seems, therefore, much room for simplifying the present system
of Gaelic Orthography, by the rejection of a considerable
number of quiescent vowels (*a*).

(*z*) It is worthy of remark that in such words as caird-eil *friendly,* slaint-
eil *salutary,* the substitution of *e* in place of *a* in the termination, both
misrepresents the sound, and disguises the derivation of the syllable.   The
sound of this termination as in fear-ail *manly,* ban-ail *womanly,* is properly
represented by *ail.*   This syllable is an abbreviation of amhuil *like,* which
is commonly written in its full form by the Irish, as fear-amhuil, &c.   It
corresponds exactly to the English termination *like,* in *soldier-like, officer-
like,* which is abridged to *ly,* as *manly, friendly.*   By writing *eil* instead
of *ail,* we almost lose sight of amhuil altogether.

(*a*) From the extracts of the oldest Irish manuscripts given by Lhuyd,
Vallancey. and others, it appears that the rule concerning the correspondence
of vowels in contiguous syllables, was by no means so generally observed
once as it is now.   It was gradually extended by the more modern Irish
writers, from whom, it is probable, it has been incautiously adopted by
the Scottish writers in its present and unwarrantable latitude.   The rule
we have been considering has been reprobated in strong terms by some of
the most judicious Irish philologers, particularly O'Brien, author of an
Irish Dictionary printed at Paris 1768, and Vallancey, author of an Irish
Grammar, and of various elaborate disquisitions concerning Irish antiquities,
from whom I quote the following passages :—" This Rule [of dividing one
syllable into two by the insertion of an aspirated consonant] together with
that of substituting small or broad vowels in the latter syllables, to correspond with the vowel immediately following the consonant in the preceding syllable, has been very destructive to the original and radical
purity of the Irish language." *Vallancey's Ir. Gram. Chap. III. letter A.*
" Another [Rule] devised in like manner by our bards and rhymers, I
mean that which is called *Caol le caol, agus Leathan le leathan,* has been
woefully destructive to the original and radical purity of the Irish
language.   This latter (much of a more modern invention than the former,
for our old manuscripts show no regard to it) imports and prescribes that

C

Almost the only quiescent consonants which occur in Gaelic are *d, f, g, s, t*, in their aspirated state. When these occur in the inflections of declinable words, serving to indicate the Root, or in derivatives, serving to point out the primitive word, the omission of them might, on the whole, be unadvisable. Even when such letters appear in their absolute form, though they have been laid aside in pronunciation, yet it would be rash to discard them in writing, as they often serve to show the affinity of the words in which they are found to others in different languages, or in different dialects of the Celtic. The aspirated form of the consonant in writing sufficiently shows that, in speaking, its articulation is either attenuated or wholly suppressed.

The writers of Gaelic seem to have carefully avoided bringing into apposition two vowels which belong to different syllables. For this purpose they have sometimes introduced a quiescent consonant into the middle of compound or of inflected words; as, gneidheil, or rather gnethail *kindly*, made up of gnè and ail; beothail *lively*, made up of beo and and ail; diathan *gods*, from the singular dia; lathaibh *days*, from the singular là, &c. It may at least bear a question, whether it would not be better to allow the vowels to denote the sound of the word by their own powers, without the intervention of quiescent consonants, as has been done in

two vowels, thus forming, or contributing to form, two different syllables, should both be of the same denomination or class of either broad or small vowels, and this without any regard to the primitive elementary structure of the word." *O'Brien's Ir. Dict. Remarks on A.* "The words *biran* and *biranach* changed sometimes into *bioran* and *bioranach* by the abusive rule of *Leathan le leathan.*" *Id. in voc.* Fear. The opinion of Lhuyd on this point, though not decisive, yet may properly be subjoined to those of Vallancey and O'Brien, as his words serve at least to show that this judicious philologer was no advocate for the Rule in question. "As for passing any censure on the rule concerning broad and small vowels, I chose rather to forbear making any remark at all upon them, by reason that old men who formerly wrote arget *silver*, instead of airgiod as we now write it, never used to change a vowel but in declining of words, &c. And I do not know that it was ever done in any other language, unless by some particular persons who, through mistake or ignorance, were guilty of it.' *Archæol. Brit. Preface to Ir. Dict. translated in Bp. Nicolson's Irish Historical Library.*

mnaibh *women*, déibh *gods*, rather than insert consonants which have nothing to do with either the radical or the superadded articulations of the word.

From the want of an established standard in orthography, the writers of Gaelic, in spelling words wherein quiescent consonants occurred, must have been often doubtful which of two or three consonants was the proper one, and may therefore have differed in their manner of spelling the same word. Accordingly we find, in many instances, the same words written by different writers, and even at different times by the same writer, with different quiescent consonants. This variation affects not indeed the pronunciation, or does it in a very slight degree. Hence, however, some who judge of the language only from its appearance in writing, have taken occasion to vilify it,' as unfixed and nonsensical (*b*). A proper attention to the affinity which the Scottish Gaelic bears to some other languages, particularly to other dialects of the Celtic, might contribute to fix the orthography in some cases where it appears doubtful, or has become variable (*c*).

IV. The last principle to be mentioned, which ought to regulate orthography, is that every sound ought to be represented by a corresponding character. From this rule there is hardly a single deviation in Gaelic, as there is no sound in the spoken language which is not, in some measure,

(*b*) Pinkerton's Inquiry into the History of Scotland.
(*c*) *E.g.*, troidh *a foot*, has been written troidh or troigh, either of which corresponds to the pronunciation, as the last consonant is quiescent. In Welsh, the articulation of the final consonant has been preserved, and the word is accordingly written troed. This authority seems sufficient to determine the proper orthography in Gaelic to be troidh and not troigh. For a like reason, perhaps, it would be proper to write tràidh *shore*, rather than tràigh, the common way of spelling the word, for we find the Irish formerly wrote tràidh, and the Welsh traeth. Claidheamh *a sword*, since the final articulation was wholly dropped, has been sometimes written claidhe. The mode of writing it still with a final labial, though quiescent, will probably be thought the more proper of the two, when it is considered that claidheamh is the cognate, or rather the same word with the Irish cloidheamh the Welsh cleddyf, and the French glaive.

exhibited in the written language. The fault of the Gaelic orthography is sometimes a redundancy, but never a deficiency of letters.

A few observations on the mode of writing some particular words, or particular parts of speech, remain to be brought forward in the sequel of this work, which it would be premature to introduce here.

The Scottish writers of Gaelic in general followed the Irish orthography, till after the middle of the last century. However that system may suit the dialect of Ireland, it certainly is not adapted to the Gaelic of this country. In the Gaelic translation of the New Testament, printed in 1767, not only were most of the Irish idioms and inflections which had been admitted into the Scottish Gaelic writings rejected, and the language adapted to the dialect of the Scottish Highlands, but the orthography also was adapted to the language. In later publications, the manner of writing the language was gradually assimilated to that pattern. The Gaelic version of the sacred Scriptures lately published has exhibited a model, both of style and orthography, still more agreeable to the purest Scottish idiom, and has a just title to be acknowledged as the standard in both. Little seems to be now wanting to confer on the orthography of the Scottish Gaelic such a degree of uniformity as may redeem its credit and ensure its stability. This, it is to be hoped, may be attained by a judicious regard to the separate, and especially the relative powers of the letters, to the most common and approved modes of pronunciation, to the affinity of the Scottish Gaelic with other branches of the Celtic tongue, to the analogy of inflection and derivation, and, above all, to the authority of some generally received standard, to which pre-eminence the late Gaelic version of the Scriptures has the only indisputable claim.

# PART II.

## OF THE PARTS OF SPEECH.

THE parts of speech in Gaelic may be conveniently divided and arranged as follows :—Article, Noun, Adjective, Pronoun, Verb, Adverb, Preposition, Conjunction, Interjection. Of these, the first five are declinable ; the other four are indeclinable.

## CHAPTER I.

### OF THE ARTICLE.

The Gaelic article an corresponds to the English definite article *the*. There is in Gaelic no indefinite article corresponding to the English a or an. The inflections of the article are but few. They depend on the gender, the number, and the case, of the noun to which it is prefixed. Hence the article is declined by gender, number, and case, as follows:

|  | Singular. | | Plural. |
|---|---|---|---|
|  | *Masc.* | *Fem.* | *Masc. & Fem.* |
| *Nom* | an, am | an, a' | na |
| *Gen.* | an, a' | na | nan, nam |
| *Dat.* | an, a,' n' | an, a,' n' | na |

In the singular, final *n* of the article is sometimes cut off, and its absence marked by an apostrophe. The same happens to the initial *a* of the dative singular.

## CHAPTER II.

### OF NOUNS.

A NOUN is the Name of any person, object, or thing whatsoever, that we have occasion to mention. In treating of this Part of Speech, we have to consider the *Gender* and the *Declension* of Nouns.


## Of Gender.

In imposing names on sensible objects, the great and obvious distinction of Sex in the animal world suggested the expediency of inventing names, not only for the particular species of animals, but also for distinguishing their Sex. Such are *vir, femina; bull, cow; coileach, cearc,* &c. To mark at once identity of species, and diversity of Sex, the same word, with a slight change on its form, was applied to both sexes: as *equus, equa; lion, lioness; oglach, banoglach.* In most languages, distinction of Sex has been marked, not only thus by the form of the noun, but further by the form of the adjective connected with the noun. Most adjectives were furnished with two forms, the one of which indicated its connection with the name of a male, the other its connection with the name of a female. The one was called by grammarians the *masculine gender,* the other the *feminine gender* of the adjective. Adjectives possessing thus a two-fold form, must necessarily have appeared under one or other of these forms, with whatever noun they happened to be conjoined. Even nouns significant of inanimate objects came thus to possess one mark of nouns discriminative of Sex, as they happened to be accompanied by an adjective of the masculine or by one of the feminine gender. If any noun was observed to be usually coupled with an adjective of the masculine gender, it was termed by grammarians a *masculine noun;* if it was found usually coupled with an adjective of the feminine gender, it was termed a *feminine noun.* Thus a distinction of nouns into masculine and feminine came to be noted, and this also was called gender.

It is observable, then, that gender, in grammar, is taken in two different acceptations. When applied to an adjective,

it signifies a certain *form*, by which *bonus* is distinguished
from *bona*. When applied to a noun, it signifies a certain
*relation* of the word to the attributives connected with it, by
which *amor* is distinguished from *cupido*. As Sex is a
natural characteristic pertaining to living objects, so gender
is a grammatical characteristic pertaining to nouns, the names
of objects whether animate or inanimate. The gender of
nouns is not, properly speaking, indicated; it is constituted
by that of the attributives conjoined with them. If there
were no distinction of gender in adjectives, participles, &c.
there could be none in nouns. When we say that *amor* is a
noun of the masculine gender, and *cupido* a noun of the
feminine gender, we do not mean to intimate any distinction
between the things signified by these nouns; we mean nothing
more than to state a grammatical fact, viz., that an adjective
connected with *amor* is always of the same form as when
joined to a noun denoting a male, and that an adjective connected with *cupido* is always of the same form as when joined
to a noun denoting a female (*d*).

(*d*) I flatter myself that all my readers, who are acquainted with any
of the ancient or the modern languages which have a distinction of gender
in their attributives, will readily perceive that the import of the term Gender,
in the grammar of those languages, is precisely what I have stated
above. The same term has been introduced into the grammar of
the English Tongue, rather improperly, because in an acceptation
different from what it bears in the grammar of all other languages.
In English there is no distinction of gender competent to Articles,
Adjectives, or Participles. When a noun is said to be of the masculine
gender, the meaning can only be that the object denoted by it is of the
male sex. Thus in the English grammars, gender signifies a quality of
the *object* named, while in other grammars it signifies a quality of the
*name* given to the object. The varieties of *who*, *which*, and *he, she, it*,
refer not to what is properly called the *gender* of the antecedent *noun*, but
to the *Sex* real or attributed, or the *absence of Sex*, of the *object* signified
by the antecedent. This is in effect acknowledged by writers on rhetoric,
who affirm that in English the pronouns *who, he, she*, imply an express
personification, or attribution of life, and consequently of Sex, to the
objects to which these pronouns refer. The same thing is still more
strikingly true of the variations on the termination of nouns, as *prince*,
*princess*; *lion*, *lioness*, which are all discriminative of Sex. It seems
therefore to be a mis-stated compliment which is usually paid to the
English, when it is said that "this is the only language which has adapted

When an adjective was to be connected with a noun that denoted an object devoid of Sex, it is not always easy to guess what views might have determined the speaker to use the adjective in one gender rather than in the other. Perhaps Sex was attributed to the object signified by the noun. Perhaps its properties were conceived to bear some resemblance to the qualities characteristic of Sex in living creatures. In many instances, the form of the noun seems to have decided the point. It must be confessed that in this mental process, the judgment has been often swayed by trivial circumstances, and guided by fanciful analogies. At least it cannot be denied that in the Gaelic, where all nouns whatever are ranked under the class of masculines or of feminines, the gender of each has been fixed by a procedure whereof the grounds cannot now be fully investigated or ascertained. Neither the natural nor artificial qualities or uses of the things named, nor the form of the names given them, furnish any invariable rule by which the gender of nouns may be known. It ought to be remembered, however, that the Gaelic is far from being singular in this respect. The oldest language with which we are acquainted, as well as some of the most polished modern tongues, stand in the same predicament.

The following observations may serve to give some idea of the analogy of gender in Gaelic nouns; though they do not furnish a complete set of rules sufficient to ascertain the gender of every noun :—

the gender of its nouns to the constitution of Nature." The fact is, that it has adapted the *Form* of some of the most common names of living creatures, and of a few of its pronouns, to the obvious distinction of *male*, and *female*, and *inanimate*, while it has left its nouns without any mark characteristic of *gender*. The same thing must necessarily happen to any language by abolishing the distinction of masculine and feminine in its attributives. If all languages had been constructed on this plan, it may confidently be affirmed that the grammatical term *gender* would never have come into use. The compliment intended, and due to the English, might have been more correctly expressed, by saying that "it is the only language that has rejected the unphilosophical distinction of gender, by making its attributives, in this respect, all indeclinable."

MASCULINES. Nouns signifying males are masculines ; as, fear *a man*, righ *a king*, sagart *a priest*, tarbh *a bull*, cu *a dog*.

Many nouns, signifying the young of animals of either Sex, are masculine, even when the individual objects they denote are mentioned as being of the female Sex ; as, laogh *a calf*, isean *a gosling*, uan *a lamb*, &c. (*e*).

Diminutives in *an ;* as, rothan *a little wheel*, dealgan *a little pin*, &c.

Derivatives in *as*, which are, for the most part, abstract nouns ; as, cairdeas *friendship*, naimhdeas *enmity*, ciuineas *calmness*, breitheamhnas *judgment*, ceartas *justice*, maitheas *goodness*, &c.

Derivatives in *air*, *ach*, *iche*, which are, for the most part, agents ; as, cealgair *a deceiver*, sealgair *a huntsman*, dorsair *a door-keeper*, marcach *a rider*, maraiche *a sailor*, coisiche *a foot traveller*, &c.

Names of such kinds of trees as are natives of Scotland ; as, darach *oak*, giuthas *fir*, uimhseann *ash*.

Most polysyllables whereof the last vowel is broad, are masculine.

FEMININES. Nouns signifying females are feminine ; as, bean *a woman*, mathair *a mother*, bo *a cow*, &c. Except bainionnach or boirionnach *a female*, mart *a cow*, capull *a horse* or *mare*, but commonly *a mare*, which are masculine, and caileann or cailinn *a damsel*, masculine or feminine. (*f*) Mark, vi. 28.

(*e*) Uan beag bainionn, 2 Sam. xii. 3. Numb. vi. 14. So leomhann boirionn, Ezek. xix. 1.

(*f*) It must appear singularly strange that any nouns which signify females exclusively should be of the masculine gender. The noun bainionnach, is derived from the adjective bainionn, *female*, which is formed from bean, the appropriate term for a *woman*. Yet this noun bainionnach, or boirionnach, *a female*, is masculine, to all grammatical intents and purposes. We say boirionnach còir, *a civil woman*, am boirionnach maiseach, *the handsome woman*.

The gender of this Noun seems to have been fixed, not by its signification, but by its determination, for most Derivatives in ach are masculines; as, oganach *a young man*, marcach *a horseman*, Albanach *a Scotsman*, &c

Some nouns denoting a species are feminine, even when the individual spoken of is characterised as a male ; as, gabhar fhirionn, *a he-goat.* Psal. l. 9.

Names of countries ; as, Albainn *Scotland*, Eirinn *Ireland.*

Names of musical instruments ; as, clarsach *a harp*, piob, *a pipe.*

Names of the heavenly bodies ; as, Grian *sun*, Gealach *moon.*

Names of diseases ; as, teasach *a fever*, a' ghriuthach *the measles*, a' bhreac *the small-pox*, a' bhuidheach *the jaundice*, a' bhuinneach, *a diarrhœa*, &c.

Collective names of trees or shrubs are feminine ; as, giuthasach *a fir wood*, iugharach *a yew copse*, seileach *a willow copse*, droighneach *a thorny brake.*

Diminutives in *ag* or *og*; as, caileag *a girl*, cuachag *a little cup.*

Derivatives in *achd*; as, iomlanachd *fulness*, doillearachd *duskiness*, doimhneachd *depth*, rioghachd *kingdom*, sinnsireachd *ancestry*, &c.

Abstract nouns formed from the genitive of adjectives ; as, doille *blindness*, gile *whiteness*, leisge *laziness*, buidhre *deafness*, &c.

Many monosyllables in *ua* followed by one or more consonants are feminine ; as, bruach *a bank*, cruach *a heap*, cuach *a cup*, cluas *an ear*, gruag *the hair of the head*, sguab *a sheaf*, tuadh *a hatchet*, tuath *peasantry.*

Almost all polysyllables, whereof the last vowel is small, except those in *air* and *iche*, already noticed, are feminine.

A few nouns are of either gender : Salm *a Psalm*, creidimh *belief*, are used as masculine nouns in some places, and feminine in others. Cruinne *the globe*, talamb *the earth*, *land*, are masculine in the nominative ; as, an cruinne-cé *the globe of the earth.* Psal. lxxxix. 11., xc. 2.—D. Buchan. 1767. p. 12. 15 ; an talamh tioram *the dry land.* Psal. xcv.

---

So in Latin, mancipium, scortum, though applied to persons, follow the gender of their termination.

5.  The same nouns are generally feminine in the genitive ;
as, gu crich na cruinne *to the extremity of the world.* Psal.
xix. 4.; aghaidh na talmhainn *the face of the earth.* Gen. i.
29. Acts xvii. 24.

OF DECLENSION.

Nouns undergo certain changes significant of Number and
of Relation.

The forms significant of Number are two : the *Singular,*
which denotes one ; and the *Plural,* which denotes any
number greater than one.

The changes expressive of Relation are made on nouns in
two ways : 1. On the beginning of the noun ; 2. On its termination.  The relations denoted by changes on the termination are different from those denoted by changes on the
beginning ; they have no necessary connection together ; the
one may take place in absence of the other.  It seems proper, therefore, to class the changes on the termination by
themselves in one division, and give it a name, and to class
the changes on the beginning also by themselves in another
division, and give it a different name.  As the changes on
the termination denote, in general, the same relations which
are denoted by the Greek and Latin cases, that seems a
sufficient reason for adopting the term case into the Gaelic
Grammar, and applying it, as in the Greek and Latin, to
signify "the changes made on the *termination* of nouns or
adjectives to mark relation" (*g*).  According to this description
of them, there are four cases in Gaelic.  These may be

(*g*) It was necessary to be thus explicit in stating the changes at the
beginning and those on the termination as unconnected independent
*accidents,* which ought to be viewed separately; because many who have
happened to turn their thoughts toward the declension of the Gaelic noun
have got a habit of conjoining these, and supposing that both contribute
their united aid toward the forming the *cases* of nouns.  This is blending
together things which are unconnected, and ought to be kept distinct.  It
has therefore appeared necessary to take a separate view of these two
*accidents* of nouns, and to limit the term *case* to those changes which
are made on the termination, excluding entirely those which take place at
the beginning.

named, like the corresponding cases in Latin, the *Nominative*, the *Genitive*, the *Dative*, and the *Vocative*. (*h*) The Nominative is used when any person or thing is mentioned as the *subject* of a proposition or question, or as the *object* of an action or affection. The Genitive corresponds to an English noun preceded by *of*. The Dative is used only after a preposition. The Vocative is employed when a person or thing is addressed.

The changes on the beginning of nouns are made by aspirating an initial consonant; that is, writing *h* after it. This may be called the *Aspirated* form of the noun. The aspirated form extends to all the cases and numbers. A noun, whereof the initial form is not changed by aspiration, is in the *Primary* form.

The *accidents* of nouns may be briefly stated thus. A noun is declined by Number, Case, and Initial form. The Numbers are two : *Singular* and *Plural*. The Cases are four : *Nominative*, *Genitive*, *Dative*, and *Vocative*. The Initial form is twofold : the *Primary form*, and the *Aspirated form* peculiar to nouns beginning with a consonant.

In declining nouns, the formation of the cases is observed to depend more on the last vowel of the nominative than on

---

(*h*) It is to be observed that these names of the cases are adopted merely because they are already familiar, not because they all denominate correctly the relations expressed by the cases to which they are respectively applied. There is no Accusative or Objective case in Gaelic different from the Nominative ; neither is there any Ablative different from the Dative. For this reason, it is not only unnecessary, but erroneous, to reckon up six Cases in Gaelic, distinguished not by the form of the Noun, but by the Prepositions prefixed. This is to depart altogether from the common and proper use of the term *Case*. And if the new use of that term is to be adopted, then the enumeration is still incomplete, for we ought to have as many Cases as there are Prepositions in the language. Thus, besides a Dative do Bhard, and an Ablative o Bhard, we should have an Impositive Case air Bhard, a Concomitative le Bard, an Insertive ann am Bard, a Precursive roimh Bhard, &c. &c. Grammarians have very correctly reckoned only five Cases in Greek, two in English, one in French [See *Moore, Murray, Buffier*, &c.] because the variations in the form of the Noun extend no further. Surely nothing but an early and inveterate prepossession in favour of the arrangements of Latin Grammar could ever have suggested the idea of Six Cases in Gaelic or in English.

the final letter. Hence the last vowel of the nominative, or in general of any declinable word, may be called the *characteristic* vowel. The division of the vowels into *broad* and *small* suggests the distribution of nouns into two Declensions, distinguished by the quality of the characteristic vowel. The first Declension comprehends those nouns whereof the *characteristic* vowel is *broad ;* the second Declension comprehends those nouns whereof the *characteristic* vowel is *small*.

The following examples are given of the inflection of nouns of the

FIRST DECLENSION.

### Bard, mas. *a Poet.*

| *Singular.* | | *Plural.* |
|---|---|---|
| *Nom.* | Bard | Baird |
| *Gen.* | Baird | Bard |
| *Dat.* | Bard | Bardaibh |
| *Voc.* | Bhaird | Bharda |

### Cluas, fem. *an Ear.*

| *Singular.* | | *Plural.* |
|---|---|---|
| *Nom.* | Cluas | Cluasan |
| *Gen.* | Cluaise | Cluas |
| *Dat.* | Cluais | Cluasaibh |
| *Voc.* | Chluas | Chluasa |

*Formation of the Cases of Nouns of the First Declension.*

*Singular Number.*

*General Rule for forming the Genitive.*—The Genitive is formed from the Nominative, by inserting *i* after the characteristic vowel, as, bàs mas. *death,* Gen. sing. bàis ; fuaran m. a *fountain,* g. s. fuarain ; clarsach f. *a harp,* g. s. clarsaich. Feminine monosyllables likewise add *a* short *e* to the Nominative ; as, cluas f. *an ear,* g. s. cluaise ; làmh *a hand,* g. s. làimhe (*i*).

(*i*) It is not improbable that anciently all feminine nouns, except a few

*Particular Rules for the Genitive.*—1 If the nominative ends in a vowel, the genitive is like the nominative; as, trà m. *a time* or *season*, g. s. trà ; so also beatha f. *life,* cro m. *a sheepfold,* cliu m. *fame,* duine *a man,* Donncha *Duncan,* a man's name, and many others. Except bo f. *a cow,* g. s. boin ; cu m. *a dog,* g. s. coin ; bru f. *the belly,* g. s. broinn or bronn.

2. Nouns ending in *chd* or *rr* have the genitive like the nominative; as, uchd m. *the breast,* sliochd m. *offspring,* feachd m. *a host,* reachd m. *statute,* cleachd m. *habit,* beachd m. *vision,* smachd m. *authority,* fuachd m. *cold,* sprochd m. *gloom,* beannachd m. *a blessing,* naomhachd f. *holiness,* earr m. *the tail,* torr m. *a heap.* Except slochd g. s. sluichd m. *a pit,* unless this word should rather be written sloc, like boc, cnoc, soc.

3. Monosyllables ending in *gh* or *th* add *a* for the genitive ; as, lagh m. *law,* g. s. lagha ; roth m. *a wheel,* g. s. rotha ; sruth m. *a stream,* g. s. srutha. Except àgh m. *felicity, grace,* or *charm,* g. s. aigh (*j*).

4. Monosyllables characterised by *io* either drop the *o* or add *a* for the genitive ; as, siol m. *seed,* g. s. sìl ; lion m. *a net,* g. s. lìn ; crioch f. *a boundary,* g. s. crìch ; cioch f. *the pap,* g. s. cìche ; fion m. *wine,* g. s. fiona, crios m. *a girdle,* g. s. criosa ; fiodh m. *timber,* g. s. fiodha. Except Criost or Criosd m. *Christ,* which has the gen. like the nominative.

5. Many monosyllables, whose characteristic vowel is *a* or *o,* change it into *u* and insert *i* after it ; as, gob m. *the bill of a bird,* g. s. guib ; crodh m. *kine,* g. s. cruidh ; bolg or balg m. *a bag,* g. s. builg ; clog or clag m. *a bell,* g. s. cluig ; lorg f. *a staff,* g. s. luirge ; long f. *a ship,* g. s. luinge ; alt m. *a*

irregular ones, added a syllable to the nominative, as *e* or *a,* in forming the genitive. The translators of the S. S. have sometimes formed the genitive of feminine polysyllables in this manner, as sionagoige from sionagog, Mark v. 36, 38. But it appears more agreeable to the analogy of inflection that such polysyllables should now be written without an *e* in the genitive.

(*j*) It is probable that this noun should rather be written àdh. See M'Farlane's Paraphrases, III. 3. also Lhuyd and O'Brien, *in loco.*

*ioint*, g. s. uilt; alld m. *a rivulet*, g. s. uilld; car m. *a turn*, g.
s. cuir; carn m. *a heap of stones*, g. s. cuirn.  So also ceol
m. *music*, g. s. ciuil; seol m. *a sail*, g. s. siuil.  Except
nouns in *on* and a few feminines, which follow the general
rule; as, bròn m. *sorrow*, g. s. bròin; lòn m. *food*, g. s. lòin;
cloch or clach f. *a stone*, g. s. cloiche; cos or cas f. *the foot*,
g. s. coise; bròg f. *a shoe*, g. s. bròige.  So also clann f.
*children*, g. s. cloinne; crann m. *a tree*, g. s. croinn.  Mac
m. *a son*, has its g. s. mic.

6. Polysyllables characterised by *ea* change *ea* into *i*; as,
fitheach m. *a raven*, g. s. fithich; cailleach f. *an old woman*,
g. s. caillich (*k*).  These two suffer a syncope, and add *e*;
buidheann f. *a company*, g. s. buidhne; sitheann f. *venison*,
g. s. sithne.

Of monosyllables characterised by *ea*, some throw away *a*
and insert *i*; as, each m. *a horse*, g. s. eich; beann f. *a peak*,
g. s. beinne: fearg f. *anger*, g. s. feirge.  Some change *ea*
into *i*; as, breac m. *a trout*, g. s. bric; fear m. *a man*, g. s.
fir; ceann m. *a head, end*, g. s. cinn; preas m. *a bush*, g. s.
pris; breac f. *the small-pox*, g. s. brice; cearc f. *a hen*, g. s.
circe; leac f. *a flag*, g. s. lice.  Gleann m. *a valley*, adds *e*, g.
s. glinne.  Some add *a* to the nominative; as, speal m. *a*
*scythe*, g. s. speala.  Dream f. *people, race*, gean m. *humour*,
have their genitive like the nominative.  Feall f. *deceit*, g. s.
foill or feill.  Geagh m. *a goose*, makes g. s. geoigh.

(*k*) Derivatives in *an* and *ag* should form their genitive according to the
general Rule, *ain*, *aig*; and in pronunciation they do so.  When the
syllable preceding the termination ends in a small vowel, the Rule of 'Caol re
caol' has introduced an *e* into the final syllable, which is then written *ean eag*.
In this case writers have been puzzled how to form the genitive.  The terminations *eain*, *eaig*, would evidently contain too many vowels for a short
syllable.  To reduce this awkward number of vowels they have commonly
thrown out the *a*, the only letter which properly expressed the vocal sound of
the syllable.  Thus from caimean m. a *mote*, they formed the gen. sing.
caimein; from cuilean m. a *whelp*, g. s. cuilein; from duileag f. a *leaf*, g. s.
duileig; from caileag f. a *girl*, g. s. caileig.  Had they not yielded too far to
the encroachments of the Rule of 'Caol re caol' they would have written both
the nom. and the gen. of these and similar nouns more simply and more
justly, thus: caiman, g.s. caimain; cuilan, g. s. cuilain; duilag, g. s. duilaig;
cailag, g. s. cailaig.

7. Nouns in *eu* followed by a liquid, change *u* into *o* and insert *i* after it; as, neul m. *a cloud*, g. s. neoil; eun m. *a bird*, g. s. eoin; feur m. *grass*, g. s. feoir; meur m. *a finger*, g. s. meoir; leus m. *a torch*, g. s. leois. Beul m. *the mouth*, g. s. beil or beoil; sgeul. m. *a tale*, g. s. sgeil or sgeoil. Other nouns characterised by *eu* add *a* for the gen., as, treud m. *a flock*, g. s. treuda; feum m. *use, need*, g. s. feuma; beum m. *a stroke*, g. s. beuma. Meud m. *bulk*, beuc m. *a roar*, freumh f. *a fibre, root*, hardly admit of *a*, but have their gen. rather like the nom.

8. Monosyllables characterised by *ia* change *ia* into *ei*; as, sliabh m. *a moor*, g. s. sleibh; fiadh m. *a deer*, g. s. feidh; biadh m. *food*, g. s. beidh or bidh; iasg m. *fish*, g. s. eifg; grian f. *the sun*, g. s. greine; sgiath f. *a wing*, g. s. sgeithe. Except Dia m. *God*, g. s. De; sgian f. *a knife*, g. s. sgine.

Piuthar f. *a sister*, has g. s. peathar; leanabh m. *a child*, g. s. leinibh; ceathramh m. *a fourth part*, g. s. ceithrimh, leabaidh or leaba f. *a bed*, g. s. leapa; talamh m. *earth*, g. s. talmhainn.

The *Dative* singular of masculine nouns is like the nominative; of feminine nouns, is like the genitive; as, tobar m. *a well*, d. s. tobar; clarsach f. *a harp*, g. s. and d. s. clarsaich; misneach f. *courage*, g. s. and d. s. misnich.

*Particular Rules for the Dative of Feminine Nouns.*—
1. If *e* was added to the nominative in forming the genitive, it is thrown away in the dative; as, slat f. *a rod*, g. s. slaite —d. s. slait; grian f. *the sun*, g. s. greine, d. s. grein.

2. If the nominative suffered a syncope in forming the genitive, or if the last vowel of the genitive is broad, the dative is like the nominative; as, buidheann f. *a company*, g. s. buidhne, d. s. buidheann; piuthar f. *a sister*, g. s. peathar, d. s. piuthar.

The *Vocative* of masc. nouns is like the genitive; of feminine nouns is like the nominative; as, bàs m. *death*, g. s. bàis, v. f. bhais; cu m. *a dog*, g. s. coin, v. s. choin; grian f. *the sun*, v. s. ghaoth.

## Plural Number.

*Nominative.*  Masculine nouns which insert *i* in the gen. sing. have their nom. plur. like the gen. sing.; as, oglach m. *a servant*, g. s. oglaich, n. p. oglaich ; fear m. *a man*, g. s. and n. p. fir.  Many of these form their nom. plur. also by adding a short *a* to the nominative singular.  Other masculine nouns, and all feminine nouns, have their nom. plural in *a*, to which *n* is added, *euphoniæ causa*, before an initial vowel (*l*).

*Particular Rules* for forming the Nom. Plur. in *a* or *an*.

1. By adding *a* to the nom. singular ; as, dubhar m. *a shadow*, n. p. dubhara ; rioghachd f. *a kingdom*, n. p, rioghachdan.  Under this Rule, some nouns suffer a syncope ; as, dorus m. *a door*, n. p. dorsa for dorusa.

2. Nouns ending in *l* or *nn*, often insert *t* before *a* ; as, reul m. *a star*, n. p. reulta ; beann f. *a pinnacle*, n. p. beannta.  So lòn m. *a marsh*, n. p. lòintean.

3. Some nouns in *ar* drop the *a*, and add to the nom. sing. the syllable *aich ;* and then the final *a* becomes *e*, to correspond to the preceding small vowel ; as, leabhar m. *a book*, n. p. leabhraiche ; tobar m. *a well*, n. p. tobraiche ; lann. f. *an enclosure*, inserts *d*, n. p. lanndaiche.  Piuthar f. *a sister*, from the g. s. peathar, has n. p. peathraiche ; so leaba f. *a bed*, g. s. leapa, n. p. leapaiche.  Bata m. *a staff*, n. p. batacha ; la or latha *a day*, n. p. lathachan or laithean.

4. Some polysyllables in *ach* add *e* or *ean* to the genitive singular ; as, mullach m. *summit*, g. s. mullaich, n. p. mullaichean ; otrach m. *a dunghill*, n. p. otraichean ; clarsach f. *a harp*, n. p. clarsaichean ; deudach f. *the jaw*, n. p. deudaichean.  So sliabh m. *a moor*, g. s. sleibh, with *t*

---

(*l*) In many instances, the Plural termination *a* is oftener written with this final *n* than without it.  When the vowel preceding the termination is small, the termination *a* or *an* is very needlessly written *e* or *ean*, to preserve the correspondence of vowels.

inserted, n. p. sleibhte. Sabhul m. *a barn*, g. s. sabhuil, n. p. saibhlean, contracted for sabhuilean.

The following Nouns form their Nominative Plural irregularly : Dia m. *God*, n. p. dée or diathan ; scian f. *a knife*, n. p. sceana or scinichean ; sluagh m. *people*, n. p. sloigh ; bo. f. *a cow*, n. p. ba.

*Genitive.* 1. Monosyllables, and nouns which form their nominative plural like the genitive singular, have the genitive plural like the nominative singular ; as, geug f. *a branch*, g. p. geug ; coimhearsnach m. *a neighbour*, g. s. and n. p. coimhearsnach.

2. Polysyllables which have their nominative plural in *a* or *an*, form the genitive like the nominative ; leabhar m. *a book*, n. p. fir, or sometimes feara, g. p. fear or feara.

Cu m. *a dog* has its g. p. con ; caora f. *a sheep*, g. p. caorach ; sluagh m. *people*, g. p. sluagh or slogh.

*Dative.* The dative plural is formed either from the nominative singular or from the nominative plural. If the nominative plural ends in a consonant, the dative plural is formed by adding *ibh* to the nominative singular ; as, crann m. *a tree*, n. p. croinn, d. p. crannaibh ; mac m. *a son*, n. p. mic, d. p. macaibh. If the nominative plural ends in a vowel, the final vowel is changed into *ibh* ; as, tobar *a well*, n. p. tobraiche, d. p. tobraichibh.

2. Monosyllables ending in an aspirated consonant, which have their nominative plural like the genitive singular, form their dative plural like the nominative plural ; as, damh *an ox*, g. s. and n. p. daimh, d. p. daimh, not damhaibh ; fiadh m. *a deer*, g. s. and n. p. and d. p. feidh. So sluagh m. *people, host*, g. s. sluaigh, n. p. and d. p. sloigh. Nouns ending in *ch*, of three or more syllables, form their dative plural like the nominative plural, rather than in *ibh* ; as, coimhearsnach m. *a neighbour*, d. p. coimhearsnaich rather than coimhearsnachaibh ; phairiseach m. *a Pharisee*, d. p. phairisich rather than phairseachaibh.

*Vocative.* The vocative plural is like the nominative plural, terminating in *a*, but seldom in *an;* as, fear m. *a man*, n. p. fir or feara, v. p. fheara ; oglach m. *a servant*, n. p. oglaich, v. p. oglacha. Except perhaps monosyllables which never form their nominative plural in *a*, nor their dative plural in *ibh;* as, damh m. *an ox*, n. p. daimh, v. p. dhaimh; a shloigh, Rom. xv. 11.

The irregular noun Bean f. *a woman*, is declined thus:

| *Singular.* | | *Plural.* |
|---|---|---|
| *Nom.* | Bean | Mnai, mnathan |
| *Gen.* | Mna | Ban |
| *Dat.* | Mnaoi | Mnathaibh |
| *Voc.* | Bhean. | Mhnathan. |

SECOND DECLENSION.

Cealgair, mas. a deceiver.

| *Singular.* | | *Plural.* |
|---|---|---|
| *Nom.* | Cealgair | Cealgaire |
| *Gen.* | Cealgair | Cealgair |
| *Dat.* | Cealgair | Cealgairibh |
| *Voc.* | Chealgair. | Chealgaire. |

Clais, fem. a gully.

| *Nom.* | Clais | Claisean |
|---|---|---|
| *Gen.* | Claise | Clais |
| *Dat.* | Clais | Claisibh |
| *Voc.* | Chlais. | Chlaise. |

*Formation of the cases of nouns of the second Declension.*

Singular Number.

*General Rule for the Genitive.* The genitive of polysyllables is like the nominative; of monosyllables is made by adding *e* to the nominative; as, caraid m. *a friend*, g. s. caraid; aimsir f. *time*, g. s. aimsir; tigh m. *a house*, g. s. tighe; ainm m. *a name*, g. s. ainme ; im m. *butter*, g. s. ime; craig f. *a rock*, g. s. craige.

*Particular Rules for the Genitive.* 1. Feminine nouns in
*ail* and *air* drop the *i* and add *ach;* if the nominative be a
polysyllable, *ai* is thrown away; as, sail f. *a beam,* g. s.
salach ; dail f. *a plain,* g. s. dalach; lair f. *a mare,* g. s. làrach ;
cathair f. *a seat,* g. s. cathrach ; nathair f. *a serpent,* g. s.
nathrach ; lasair f. *a flame,* g. s. lasrach.   To these add còir
f. *right,* g. s. còrach or còire.

2. Monosyllables characterised by *oi* drop *i* and add *a* ;
as, feoil f. *flesh,* g. s. feola ; tòin f. *bottom,* g. s. tòna ; sròin
f. *the nose,* g. s. sròine or sròna.

3. Monosyllables characterised by *ui* change *ui* into *a* or
*o,* and add *a;* as, muir f. *the sea,* g. s. mara; fuil f. *blood,*
g. s. fola or fala ; druim f. *a ridge,* g. s. droma.   Except
sùil f. *the eye,* g. s. sùla ; cuid f. *a part,* g. s. codach or
cuid.

4. A few feminine polysyllables in *eir* form their genitive like monosyllables ; as, inneir f. *dung,* g. s. inneire ;
suipeir f. *supper,* g. s. suipeire.

5. The following dissyllables seem to have formed their
genitive like monosyllables, and then suffered a contraction.
Sometimes the characteristic vowel is retained, and sometimes it is thrown away, the final *e* of the genitive being
converted into *a,* when requisite to suit an antecedent broad
vowel.

| | | |
|---|---|---|
| Amhainn, f. *a river,* | g. s. aimhne, *contracted for* amhainne |
| Aghainn ⎱ Aghann ⎰ f. *a pan,* | g. s. aighne,..............aghainne |
| Banais f. *a wedding,* | g. s. bainse,..............banaise |
| Coluinn f. *the body,* | g. s. colna, colla .........coluinne |
| Duthaich f. *a country,* | g. s. duthcha,...........duthaiche |
| Fiacail f. *a tooth,* | g. s. fiacla, ..............fiacaile |
| Gamhuinn m. *a steer,* | g. s. gamhna, ...........gamhuinne |
| Gualainn f. *the shoulder,* | g. s. guaille, ...........gualainne |
| Madainn f. *morning,* | g. s. maidne, ...........madainne |
| Obair f. *work,* | g. s. oibre, ..............obaire |
| Uilinn f. *the elbow,* | g. s. uillne,..............uilinne |

6. The following nouns form their genitive by dropping the characteristic small vowel; athair m. *a father*, g. s. athar; mathair f. *a mother*, g. s. mathair; brathair m. *a brother*, g. s. brathar; namhaid m. *an enemy*, g. s. namhad. Cnaimh m. *a bone*, g. s. cnamha; uaimh f. *a cave*, g. s. uamha. Mil f. *honey*, has g. s. meala.

7. A few monosyllables ending in a vowel have their genitive like the nominative; as, ni m. *a thing*, ti m. *a person*, ré m. *the moon;* to which add righ m. *a king*.

*Dative.* The dative singular is like the nominative; as, duine m. *a man*, d. s. duine: madainn f. *morning*, d. s. madainn.

*Vocative.* The vocative singular is like the nominative, as, caraid m. *friend*, v. s. charaid; mathair f. *mother*, v. s. mhathair.

## *Plural Number.*

*Nominative.—General Rule.* The nominative plural is formed by adding to the nominative singular *a* or *an*, written *e* or *ean* to correspond to a preceding small vowel; as, piobair m. *a piper*, n. p. piobairean; aimsir f. *time, season*, n. p. aimsirean. Some nouns suffer a contraction in the nominative plural; as, caraid m. *a friend*, n. p. càirdean; naimhaid m. *an enemy*, n. p. naimhdean; fiacail f. *a tooth*, n. p. fiaclan.

*Particular Rules.* 1. Some nouns, whose last consonant is *l* or *n*, insert *t* in the nominative plural; as, tuil f. *a flood*, n. p. tuilte; smuain f. *thought*, n. p. smuaintean; coille f. *a wood*, n. p. coilltean; àithne f. *a command*, n. p. àithnte. The *t* is aspirated in dail f. *a plain*, n. p. dailthean; sail f. *a beam*, n. p. sailthean.

2. Some nouns in *air*, chiefly such as form their genitive singular in *ach*, retain the same syllable in the nominative plural, and insert *i* after *a;* as,

| | | |
|---|---|---|
| Cathair, f. *a seat*, | g. s. cathrach, | n. p. cathraichean. |
| Lasair, f. *a flame*, | g. s. lasrach, | n. p. lasraichean. |
| Nathair, f. *a serpent*, | g. s. nathrach, | n. p. nathraichean. |

So also cuid f. *a part,* from the g. s. codach, has the n. p.
codaichean; athair m. *a father,* n. p. aithrichean; mathair f.
*a mother,* n. p. maithrichean. To which add amhainn f. *a
river,* n. p. aimhnichean; uisge m. *water,* n. p. uisgeachan;
cridhe m. *the heart,* n. p. cridheachan.

The following nouns form their nominative plural irregularly;
duine m. *a man,* n. p. daoine; righ m. *a king,* n. p. righre;
ni m. *a thing,* n. p. nithe; cliamhuinn m. *a son-in-law,* or
*brother-in-law,* n. p. cleamhna.

*Genitive.* The genitive plural of monosyllables and masculine polysyllables is twofold, like the nominative singular,
and like the nominative plural; as, righ m. *a king,* g. p. righ
or righre., The genitive plural of feminine polysyllables is
like the nominative plural only; as, amhainn f. *a river,* g. p.
aimhnichean. Suil f. *the eye,* has its g. p. sùl.

*Dative.* The dative plural is formed from the nominative
plural by changing the final vowel into *ibh;* as, coluinn f.
*the body,* n. p. coluinne, d. p. coluinnibh; cridhe m. *the
heart,* n. p. cridheacha, d. p. cridheachaibh.

*Vocative.* The vocative plural is like the nominative plural;
as, duine m. *a man,* n. p. daoine, v. p. dhaoine.

Final *a* or *e* in all the singular cases of polysyllables is occasionally cut off, especially in verse; as, leab *bed,* teang
*tongue,* coill *wood,* cridh *heart.*

## *Of the Initial form of Nouns.*

In nouns beginning with a consonant, all the cases admit
of the *aspirated form.* In the vocative singular and plural
the aspirated form alone is used, except in nouns beginning
with a lingual, which are generally in the primary form, when
preceded by a lingual; as, a sheann duine *old man.* Nouns
beginning with *s* followed by a mute consonant have no
aspirated form, because *s* in that situation does not admit of
the aspirate. In nouns beginning with *l, n, r,* a distinction
is uniformly observed in pronouncing the initial consonant,
corresponding precisely to the distinction of primary and

aspirated forms in nouns beginning with other consonants. This distinction has already been fully stated in treating of pronunciation.

The general use of the singular and plural numbers has been already mentioned. A remarkable exception occurs in the Gaelic. When the numerals fichead *twenty*, ceud *a hundred*, mile *a thousand*, are prefixed to a noun, the noun is not put in the plural, but in the singular number, and admits no variation of case. The termination of a noun preceded by da *two*, is the same with that of the dative singular, except when the noun is governed in the genitive case, and then it is put in the genitive plural (*m*); when preceded by fichead, ceud, &c., the termination is that of the nominative singular; thus da laimh *two hands*, da chluais *two ears*, dà fhear *two men*, fichead làmh *twenty hands*, ceud fear *a hundred men*, mile caora *a thousand sheep*, deich mile bliadhna *ten thousand years* (*n*).

# CHAPTER III.

## OF ADJECTIVES.

An adjective is a word used along with a noun, to express some quality of the person or thing signified by the noun.

Adjectives undergo changes which mark their relation to other words. These changes are made, like those on nouns, partly on the beginning, and partly on the termination, and may be fitly denominated by the same names. The changes on the beginning are made by aspirating an initial consonant. The numbers and cases, like those of nouns, are distinguished by changes on the termination. The gender is marked partly by the initial form, partly by the termination.

Adjectives whereof the characteristic vowel is broad, follow,

(*m*) We are informed by E. O'C. that this is the usual construction in the Irish Dialect, and it appears to be the same in the Scottish. Thus, air son mo dhà shùl, *for my two eyes*.—Judg. xvi. 28. Ir. & Scott. versions.

(*n*) So in Hebrew, we find a noun in the singular number joined with *twenty, thirty, a hundred, a thousand,* &c.

in most of their inflections, the form of nouns of the first declension, and may be termed Adjectives of the first declension. Those adjectives whereof the characteristic vowel is small, may be called Adjectives of the second declension.

### Example of Adjectives of the First Declension.

#### Mòr, great.

| | Singular. | | Plural |
|---|---|---|---|
| | *Mas.* | *Fem.* | *Com. Gend.* |
| *Nom.* | Mor, | Mhor, | Mora. |
| *Gen.* | Mhoir, | Moire, | Mora. |
| *Dat.* | Mor, | Mhoir, | Mora. |
| *Voc.* | Mhoir, | Mhor, | Mora. |

### Formation of the Cases of Adjectives of the First Declension.

#### Singular.

*Nominative.* The feminine gender is, in termination, like the masculine.

The other cases, both mas. and fem., are formed from the nominative, according to the rules already given for forming the cases of nouns of the first declension. Take the following examples in adjectives :—

*Genitive.—General rule.* Marbh *dead*, g. s. m. mhairbh, f. mairbhe ; dubh *black*, g. s. m. dhuibh, f. duibhe ; fadalach *tedious*, g. s. m. fhadalaich, f. fadalaich.

*Particular rules.* 1. Sona *happy*, g. s. m. shona, f. sona ; aosda *aged*, g. s. m. and f. aosda ; beo *alive*, g. s. m. bheo, f. beo.

2. Bochd *poor*, g. s. m. bhochd, f. bochd ; gearr *short*, g. s. m. ghearr. f. gearr.

3. Breagh *fine*, g. s. m. bhreagha, f. breagha.

4. Crion *little, diminutive*, g. s. m. chrìn, f. crìne.

5. Donn *brown*, g. s. m. dhuinn, f. duinne ; gorm *blue*, g. s. m. ghuirm, f. guirme ; lom *bare*, g. s. m. luim, f. luime.

But dall *blind*, g. s. m. dhoill, f. doille ; mall *slow*, g. s. m. mhoill, f. moille ; like the nouns crann, clann.

6. Cinnteach *certain*, g. s. m. chinntich, f. cinntich ; maiseach *beautiful*, g. s. m. mhaisich, f. maisich. Tearc *rare*, g. s. m. theirc, f. teirce ; dearg *red*, g. s. m. dheirg, f. deirge ; deas *ready*, g. s. m. dheis, f. deise. Breac *speckled*, g. s. m, bhric, f. brice ; geal *white*, g. m. ghil, f. gile.

7. Geur *sharp*, g. s. m. ghéir, f. géire ; like the nouns breug, geug.

8. Liath *hoary*, g. s. m. leith, f. léithe ; dian *keen*, g. s. m. dhéin, f. déine.

Irregulars. Odhar *pale*, g. s. m. and f. uidhir ; bodhar *deaf*, g. s. m. bhuidhir, f. buidhir.

*Dative.—General rule.* Uasal *noble*, d. s. m. uasal f. uasail ; bodhar *deaf*, d. s. m. bodhar, f. bhuidhir.

*Particular rule.* 1. Trom *heavy*, d. s. m. trom, f. thruim.

*Vocative.* Beag *small*, v. s. m. bhig, f. bheag.

## Plural.

In Monosyllables the plural, through all its cases, is formed by adding *a* to the nom. sing. ; in Polysyllables, it is like the nom. sing ; as, crom *crooked*, pl. croma ; tuirseach *melancholy*, pl. tuirseach.

A few Dissyllables form their Plural like Monosyllables, and suffer a contraction ; as, reamhar *fat*, pl. reamhra, contracted for reamhara. Gen. xli. 20.

## Adjectives of the Second Declension.

All the Cases of Adjectives of the Second Declension are formed according to the general rules for nouns of the second declension ; that is, Monosyllables add *e* for the gen. sing. fem. and for the plural cases ; Polysyllables are like the nom. sing. throughout.

In the Second Declension, as in the First, Dissyllables sometimes suffer a contraction in the plural ; as, milis *sweet*, pl. milse contracted for miliso.

### Of the Initial Form of Adjectives.

Adjectives admit the *aspirated form* through all the Numbers and Cases. In Adjectives beginning with a Labial or a Palatal, the aspirated form alone is used in the gen. and voc. sing. masc. the nom. dat. and voc. sing. feminine.

### Comparison of Adjectives.

There are in Gaelic two forms of Comparison, which may be called the *First* and the *Second Comparative*.

The *First Comparative* is formed from the gen. sing. mas. by adding *e;* as, geal *white*, g. s. m. gil, comp. gile, ghile; ciontach *guilty*, g. s. m. ciontaich, comp. ciontaiche. Some Adjectives suffer a contraction in the Comparative; as, bodhar *deaf*, comp. buidhre for buidhire; boidheach *pretty*, comp. boidhche for boidhiche.

If the last letter of the gen. be *a*, it is changed into *e*, and *i* inserted before the last consonant; as, fada *long*, g. s. m. fada, comp. faide; tana *thin*, g. s. m. tana, comp. taine.

The *Second Comparative* is formed from the first, by changing final *e* into *id ;* as, trom *heavy*, 1. comp. truime, 2. comp. truimid; tiugh *thick*, 1. comp. tiuighe, 2. comp. tiuighid. Many Adjectives, especially Polysyllables, do not admit of the Second Comparative.

Both these forms of Comparison have an *aspirated* as well as a *primary form*, but are otherwise indeclinable.

The following Adjectives are compared irregularly.

| Positive. | 1. Comp. | 2. Comp. |
|---|---|---|
| Math, maith, *good*, | fearr, | feaird. |
| Olc, *bad*, *evil*, | miosa, | misd. |
| Mòr, *great*, | mò, | mòid. |
| Beag, *small*, | lugha, | lughaid. |
| Goirid, gearr, *short*, | giorra, | giorraid. |
| Duilich, *difficult*, | dorra. | |
| Teath, *hot*, | teoithe, | teoithid. |
| Leathan, *broad*, | leatha, lèithne. | |
| Fogus, *near*, | foisge. | |

Càirdeach, *akin*,                càra.
Furas, *easy*,                    fhusa.
Toigh, *dear*,                    docha.

Ionmhuinn, *beloved*,        { annsa.
                             { ionnsa.

To these may be added the nouns—
Moran *a great number* or *quantity*, and Tuilleadh *more*.

The *Superlative*, which is but a particular mode of expressing comparison, is the same in form with the First Comparative.

An eminent degree of any quality is expressed by putting one of the particles ro, glé, before the Positive; as, ro ghlic *very wise*, glé gheal *very white*. The same effect is produced by prefixing fior *true*, sàr *exceeding*, &c., which words are, in that case, used adverbially; as, fior mhaiseach *truly beautiful*, sàr mhaith *exceedingly good*.

### Cardinal Numbers.

| | | | |
|---|---|---|---|
| 1 | Aon, a h-aon, *one*. | 40 | Dà fhichead. |
| 2 | Dà, a dhà. | 50 | Deich is dà fhichead. |
| 3 | Tri. | 60 | Tri fichead. |
| 4 | Ceithir. | 100 | Ceud. |
| 5 | Cuig. | 200 | Dà cheud. |
| 6 | Sè, sia. | 300 | Tri ceud. |
| 7 | Seachd. | 400 | Ceithir cheud. |
| 8 | Ochd. | 500 | Cuig ceud. |
| 9 | Naoi. | 1,000 | Mìle. |
| 10 | Deich. | 2,000 | Dà mhìle. |
| 11 | Aon deug. | 3,000 | Tri mìle. |
| 12 | A dhà dheug. | 10,000 | Deich mìle. |
| 13 | Tri deug. | 20,000 | Fichead mìle. |
| 20 | Fichead. | 100,000 | Ceud mìle. |
| 21 | Aon thar fhichead. | 200,000 | Dà cheud mìle. |
| 22 | Dha 'ar fhichead. | 1,000,000 | Deich ceud mìle, |
| 23 | Tri 'ar fhichead. | | Mìle de mhìltibh. |
| 30 | Deich 'ar fhichead. | | &c. &c. |
| 31 | Aon deug thar fhichead. | | |

## Cardinal Numbers joined to a Noun.

| Of the mas. gender. | Of the fem. gender. |
|---|---|
| 1 Aon fhear, *one man.* | Aon chlach, *one stone.* |
| 2 Dà fhear. | Dà chloich. |
| 3 Tri fir. | Tri clachan. |
| 10 Deich fir. | Deich clachan. |
| 11 Aon fhear deug. | Aon chlach dheug. |
| 12 Dà fhear dheug. | Dà chloich dheug. |
| 13 Tri fir dheug. | Tri clachan deug. |
| 20 Fichead fear. | Fichead clach. |
| 21 Aon fhear thar fhichead. | Aon chlach thar fhichead. |
| 22 Dà fhear thar fhichead. | Dà chloich thar fhichead. |
| 23 Tri fir fhichead. | Tri clacha fichead. |
| 30 Deich fir fhichead. | Deich clacha fichead. |
| 31 Aon fhear deug 'ar fhichead. | Aon chlach dheug thar fhichead. |
| 40 Dà fhichead fear. | Da fhichead clach. |
| 41 Fear is da fhichead. | Clach is dà fhichead. |
| 42 Dà fhear is dà fhichead. | Dà chloich is da fhichead. |
| 50 Deich is dà fhichead fear. | Deich is da fhichead clach. |
| 60 Tri fichead fear. | Tri fichead clach. |
| 70 Tri fichead fear agus deich. | Tri fichead clach agus deich. |
| 100 Ceud fear. | Ceud clach. |
| 101 Ceud fear agus a h-aon. | Ceud clach agus a h-aon. |
| 309 Tri cheud fear. | Tri cheud clach. |
| 1,000 Mìle fear. | Mìle clach. |
| 10,000 Deich mìle fear, &c. | Deich mìle clach, &c. |

## Ordinal Numbers.

1 An ceud fhear, *the first man;* a' cheud chlach, *the first*
2 An dara fear. 　　　　　　　　　　　　　　　　　　[*stone.*
3 An treas fear, an tri-amh fear.
4 An ceathramh fear.
5 An cuigeamh fear.
6 An seathamh fear.
7 An seachdamh fear.
8 An t-ochdamh fear.

9 An naothamh fear.
10 An deicheamh fear.
11 An t-aon fear deug.
12 An dara fear deug.
20 Am ficheadamh fear.
21 An t-aon fhear fichead.
22 An dara fear fichead.
31 An t-aon fhear deug thar fhichead.
40 An dà fhicheadamh fear.
60 An tri ficheadamh fear.
100 An ceudamh fear.
101 An t-aon fhear thar cheud.
200 Am ficheadamh fear thar cheud.
200 An da cheudamh fear.
1000 Am mileamh fear, &c.

The following numeral Nouns are applied only to persons :—

| | |
|---|---|
| 2. Dithis, *two persons.* | 7. Seachdnar. |
| 3. Triuir. | 8. Ochdnar. |
| 4. Ceathrar. | 9. Naoinar. |
| 5. Cuignear. | 10. Deichnar. |
| 6. Sèanar. | |

# CHAPTER IV.

## OF PRONOUNS.

The *Pronouns* are, for the most part, words used instead of nouns. They may be arranged under the following divisions : Personal, Possessive, Relative, Demonstrative, Interrogative, Indefinite, Compound.

The *Personal Pronouns* are those of the 1st, 2d, and 3d persons. They have a Singular and a Plural Number, a Simple and an Emphatic Form. They are declined thus :—

|  | Singular. |  | Plural. |  |
|---|---|---|---|---|
|  | Simple Form. | Emphat. F. | Simple F. | Emphat. |
| 1. | Mi, mhi, *I, me*, | Mise, mhise. | Sinn, *we, us*, | Sinne. |
| 2. | Tu, thu, *thou*,<br>Thu, *thee*, | Tusa, thusa. | Sibh, *ye, you*, | Sibhse. |
| 3. | E, se, *he*,<br>E, *him*, | Esan. |  |  |
|  | I, si, *she*,<br>I, *her*, | Ise. | Iad, siad, *they*<br>Iad, *them*, | Iadsan (*o*) |

The Pronoun 'sibh' *you*, of the plural number is used almost universally in addressing a single person of superior rank or of greater age; while 'tu' *thou*, of the singular number is used in addressing an inferior or an equal. But the degree of seniority or of superiority, which is understood to entitle a person to this token of respect, varies in different parts of the Highlands (*p*). The Supreme Being is always addressed by the pronoun 'tu' *thou*, of the singular number.

The *Possessive Pronouns* correspond to the Personal Pronouns, and, like them, may be called those of the 1st, 2d, and 3d persons singular, and 1st, 2d, and 3d persons plural. They have an Emphatic Form, which is made by connecting the syllable *sa* with the possessive pronoun of the 1st, 2d,

(*o*) The Pronouns tu *thou*, se *he*, si *she*, siad *they*, are not employed, like other nominatives, to denote the object after a transitive verb. Hence the incorrectness of the following expression in most editions of the Gaelic Psalms : Se chrùnas *tu* le coron graidh, Psal. ciii. 4., which translated literally signifies, *it is he whom thou wilt crown*, &c. To express the true sense, viz., *it is he who will crown thee*, it ought to have been, se chrùnas *thu* le coron graidh. So is mise an Tighearn a slanuicheas *thu*, *I am the Lord that healeth thee*, Exod. xv. 26 ; Ma ta e ann a fhreagaireas *thu*, *If there be any that will answer thee*, Job v. 1 ; Co e a bhrathas thu? *Who is he that will betray thee?* John xxi. 20., Comp. Gen. xii. 3. and xxvii. 29.

(*p*) This use of the Pronoun of the 2d person plural is probably a modern innovation, for there is nothing like it found in the more ancient Gaelic compositions, nor in the graver poetry even of the present age. As this idiom seems, however, to be employed in conversation with increasing frequency, it will probably lose by degrees its present import, and will come to be used as the common mode of addressing any individual ; in the same manner as the corresponding Pronouns are used in English, and other European languages.

and 3d persons singular, and 2d person plural ; *ne* with that
of the 1st person plural, and *san* with that of the 3d person
plural. These syllables are placed immediately after the
nouns to which the possessive pronouns are prefixed, and
connected by a hyphen.

These Pronouns are as follow :—

| *Simple.* | *Emphatic.* | *Simple.* | *Emphatic.* |
|---|---|---|---|
| *Singular.* | | *Plural.* | |
| 1. Mo, *my,* mo mhac-sa | | 1. Ar, *our,* | ar mac-ne |
| 2. Do, *thy,* do——-sa | | 2. Bhur, 'ur, *your,* bhur—sa | |
| 3. { A, *his,* a mhac-sa, san / A, *her,* a mac-sa, san } | | 3. An,am,*their,* an,am—sa san | |

If the noun be followed by an adjective, the emphatic
syllable is affixed to the adjective; as, do làmh gheal-sa
*thy white hand.*

The possessive pronouns mo, do, when followed by a
vowel, commonly lose the *o,* whose absence is marked by an
apostrophe ; as, m' ainn *my name ;* d' athair (*q*) *thy father.*
The same pronouns when preceded by the preposition ann
*in,* suffer a transposition of their letters, and are written am,
ad, one broad vowel being substituted for another ; as, ann ad
chridhe *in thy heart,* 1 Sam. xiv. 7, ann am aire *in my
thoughts.*

The possessive pronoun a *his,* is often suppressed altogether after a vowel; as, na sanntaich bean do choimh-
earsnaich, no oglach, no bhanoglach, no dhamh, no asal, *covet
not thy neighbour's wife, or his man-servant, or his maid-servant,* &c., Exod. xx. 17. In these and similar instances, as
the tense is but imperfectly expressed (especially when the
noun begins with a vowel), and cannot be gathered with cer-
tainty from any other part of the sentence, perhaps it might

(*q*) There seems hardly a sufficient reason for changing the *d* in this
situation into *t,* as has been often done, as t'oglach for d'oglach *thy servant,*
&c. The *d* corresponds sufficiently to the pronunciation, and being the
constituent consonant of the pronoun, it ought not to be changed for
another.

be an improvement to retain the pronoun, even at the expense of cutting off the final vowel of the preceding word; as, n' a oglach, n' a bhanoglaich, &c. In many cases, however, this appears hardly practicable; as, cha bheo athair *his father is not alive*, which could not with any propriety be written cha bheo a athair (*r*).

The word fein corresponding to the English words *self*, *own*, is subjoined occasionally both to the personal and possessive pronouns : thus mi fein *myself*, mise fein *I myself*, thu fein *tnyself*, thusa fein *thou thyself*, or *thy own self*, mo shluagh fein *my own people*.

The other Pronouns are as follow :—

| *Relative.* | *Demonstrative.* | *Interrogative.* |
|---|---|---|
| N.A,*who,which,that.* | So, *this, these.* | Co ? *who ?* |
| G.&D.An. | Sin, *that, those.* | Cia ? *which ?* |
| Nach, *who not, which not,* | Sud (*s*), ud, *yon.* | Ciod, creud? *what ?* |
| Na, *that which, what* (*t*). | | |

| *Indefinite.* | *Compound.* | |
|---|---|---|
| Eigin, *some.* | E so, *this one,* m. | E sud, *yon one,* m. |
| Ge b'e ⎫ *whoever* (*u*).<br>Cia b'e ⎭ | I so, *this one,* f. | I sud, *yon one,* f. |

(*r*) The Irish are not so much at a loss to avoid a *hiatus*, as they often use na for a *his ;* which the translators of the Psalms have sometimes judiciously adopted ; as,
> An talamh tioram le na laimh
> Do chruthaich e 's do dhealbh. Psal. xcv. 5.

(*s*) In the North Highlands this Pronoun is pronounced sid.

(*t*) This Pronoun occurs in such expressions as an deigh na chuala tu *after what you have heard ;* their leat na th' agad, or na bheil agad, *bring what you have.* It seems to be contracted for an ni a *the thing which.*

(*u*) There is reason to think that ge b'e is corruptly used for cia b' e. Of the former I find no satisfactory analysis. The latter cia b' e is literally *which it be,* or *which it were ;* which is just the French *qui que ce soit, qui que ce fût* expressed in English by one word *whosoever, whichsoever.* We find cia used in this sense and connection, Psal. cxxxv. 11. Glasg. 1753. Gach uile rioghachd mar an ceadn' *cia* h-iomdha bhi siad ann, *All*

Eile, *other.*  Iad so, *these.*  Iad sud, *yon,* pl.

Gach, } *each,*
Cach, } *every (x).* } E sin, *that one,* m. Cach eile, *the rest.*

Cach, *others, the rest.* Iad sin, *those.*  Cach a chéile, *each.*

Cuid, *some.*  *other (y).*

# CHAPTER V.

## OF VERBS.

A WORD that signifies to be, to do, or to suffer anything, is called a *Verb.*

The Verb in Gaelic, as in other languages, is declined by Voices, Moods, Tenses, Numbers, and Persons.

The *Voices* are two : Active and Passive.

The *Moods* are five : the Affirmative or Indicative, the Negative or Interrogative, the Subjunctive, the Imperative, and the Infinitive.  Many, but not all, Transitive Verbs have a Passive Participle.

The *Tenses* are three : the Present, the Preterite, and the Future.

The *Numbers* are two : Singular and Plural.

The *Persons* are three : First, Second, and Third.  The dis-

*kingdoms likewise, however numerous they be.* See also Gen. xliv. 9, Rom. ii. 1.

(*x*) This pronoun is found written with an initial c in Lhuyd's "Archæol. Brit." Tit. I. page 20. col. 2. ceach ; again Tit. X. voc. Bealtine ; cecha bliadna *each year.* So also O'Brien, cach *all, every,* like the French *chaque.* "Irish Dict." voc. cach.

(*y*) The pronouns *cach eile* and *cach a chéile* are hardly known in Perthshire. Instead of the former, they use the single word càch pronounced long, and declined like a noun of the singular number ; aud instead of the latter, a chéile, as in this example, choinnich iad a chéile ; thuit cuid, agus theich càch, *they met each other ; some fell, and the rest fled.* Here càch may be considered as a simple pronoun ; but the first clause, choinnich iad a cheile, *they met his fellow,* hardly admits of any satisfactory analysis. The phrases, in fact, seem to be elliptical, and to be expressed more fully, according to the practice of other districts, thus : choinnich iad cach a chiéle ; thuit, cuid, agus theich cach eile. Now, if cach be nothing else than gach *every,* (a conjecture supported by the short pronunciation of the *a,* as well as by the authorities adduced in the preceding note,) the expressions may be easily analysed : choinnich iad gach [aon] a cheile ; thuit cuid, agus theich gach [aon] eile ; *they met every* [one] *his fellow ; some fell, and every other* [one] *fled.* See 1 Thess. v. 11.

tinction of number and person takes place only in a few tenses.

The inflections of Verbs, like those of nouns, are made by changes at the beginning, and on the termination.

The changes on the termination are made according to one model, and by the same rules. But for the sake of stating some diversity in the *initial* changes, it may be convenient to arrange the verbs in two *conjugations*, whereof the first comprehends those verbs which begin with a consonant, the second, those verbs which begin with a vowel. Verbs beginning with *f*, followed by a vowel, are ranged under the second conjugation, along with verbs beginning with a vowel.

The verb Bi *be*, which is used as an auxiliary to other verbs, is declined as follows :—

Bi, *be*.

### *Affirmative* or *Indicative Mood.*

| Present. | Preterite. | Future. |
|---|---|---|
| *Sing.* | *Sing.* | *Sing.* |
| 1. Ta mi, *I am*, | Bha mi, *I was*, | Bithidh mi, *I will be*, |
| 2. Ta thu, | Bha thu, | Bithidh tu, |
| 3. Ta e ; | Bha e ; | Bithidh se ; |
| *Plur.* | *Plur.* | *Plur.* |
| 1. Ta sinn, | Bha sinn, | Bithidh sinn, |
| 2. Ta sibh, | Bha sibh, | Bithidh sibh, |
| 3. Ta iad. | Bha iad. | Bithidh siad. |

### *Negative* or *Interrogative Mood.*

| | | Present. | Preterite. |
|---|---|---|---|
| | | *Sing.* | *Sing.* |
| ni | 1 Bheil mi, *I am not*, | Robh mi, *I was not*, |
| cha | 2 Bheil thu, | Robh thu, |
| nach | 3 Bheil e; | Robh e; |
| mur, | *Plur.* | *Plur.* |
| &c. | 1 Bheil sinn, | Robh sinn, |
| | 2 Bheil sibh, | Robh sibh, |
| | 3 Bheil iad. | Robh iad. |

### Future.
*Sing.*

|        |                          |
|--------|--------------------------|
| ni     | Bi mi, *I shall not be,* |
| cha    | Bi thu,                  |
| nach   | Bi se;                   |
| mur,   | *Plur.*                  |
| &c.    | Bi sinn,                 |
|        | Bi sibh,                 |
|        | Bi siad.                 |

### Subjunctive Mood.

**Preterite or Imperfect.**
*Sing.*

1 Bhithinn, *I would be,*
2 Bhitheadh tu,
3 Bhitheadh e;
*Plur.*
1 Bhitheadheamaid,
  Bhitheadh sinn,
2 Bhitheadh sibh,
3 Bhitheadh iad.

**Future.**
*Sing.*

Ma bhitheas mi, *If I shall be,*
Bhitheas tu,
Bhitheas e;
*Plur.*
Bhitheas sinn,

Bhitheas sibh,
Bhitheas iad.

### Imperative Mood.
*Sing.*

1 Bitheam, *let me be,*
2 Bi, bi thusa,
3 Bitheadh e;
*Plur.*
1 Bitheamaid,
2 Bithibh,
3 Bitheadh iad.

### Infinitive Mood.

Bith, *being,*
do bhith, } *to be,*
a bhith, }
gu bhith, } *to be,*
gu bith, }
iar bhith, } *after being, been,*
iar bith, }
o bhith, *from being,* &c.

### Compound Tenses.

| Present. | Preterite. | Future. |
|----------|------------|---------|

### Affirmative Mood.

| *Sing.* | *Sing.* | *Sing.* |
|---------|---------|---------|
| Ta mi iar bith, | Bha mi iar bith, | Bithidh mi iar bith, |
| *I have been,* &c. | *I had been,* &c. | *I shall have been,* &c. |

*Negative Mood.*

|  | *Sing.* | *Sing.* | *Sing.* |
|---|---|---|---|
| ni, &c. { | Bheil mi iar bith, *I have not been.* | Robh mi iar bith, *I had not been.* | Bi mi air bith, *I shall not have been.* |

*Subjunctive Mood.*

Preterite or Pluperfect.                              Future.

*Sing.*               *Sing.*

1 Bhithinn iar bith, *I should*    Ma bhitheas mi iar bith, *If I*
    have been, *&c.*                shall have been, *&c.*

The present affirmative ta is often written tha.   This is one of many instances where there appears reason to complain of the propensity remarked in Part I. in those who speak the Gaelic, to attenuate its articulations by aspiration.   Another corrupt way of writing ta which has become common, is ata. This has probably taken its rise from uniting the relative to the verb ; as, an uair *ata* mi ; instead of an uair *a ta*, &c., mar *a ta*, &c.   Or perhaps it may have proceeded from a too compliant regard to a provincial pronunciation.

The pret. neg. robh appears to be made up of the verbal participle ro, the same with do, and bha, throwing away the last vowel ; ro bha, robh.

The verb and pronoun of the 1st per. sing. and 3d per. plur. are frequently incorporated into one word, and written taim *I am*, taid *they are*.

The pres. neg. loses the initial *bh* after the participle cha *not*, mur *if not*, nach *that not; n* is inserted, *euphoniae causa*, betwixt the participle cha and the verb; as, cha n 'eil, mur 'eil, nach 'eil.   This Tense is often pronounced beil after the participle am ; as, am beil e ? *is it ?*

In the North Highlands, the pret. neg. often takes the common verbal participle do before it; as, cha do robh mi, or cha d'robh mi, *I was not.*

Initial *b* of the fut. neg. is aspirated after the participle cha *not ;* as, cha bhi.

Initial *bh* of the pret. subj. loses the aspiration after the participles ni *not*, mur *if not*, nach **that not**, gu *that*, nam *if ;* as, mur bithinn, nam bitheadh tu.

The subjunct. and imper. often suffer a contraction, by changing *ithea* into *io ;* as, biodh, biom, bios, &c.

Some of the compound tenses of Bi are rarely if ever used. They are here given complete, because they correspond to the analogy of other verbs ; and show how accurately the various modifications of time may be expressed by the substantive verb itself.

Example of a verb of the First Conjugation. Buail *to strike.*

### ACTIVE VOICE.

### Simple Tenses.

### *Affirmative* or *Indicative Moods.*

| Preterite. | Future. |
|---|---|
| *Sing.* | *Sing.* |
| 1 Do bhuail mi, *I struck,* Bhuail mi, | Buailidh mi, I *will strike,* |
| 2 Bhuail thu, | Buailidh tu, |
| 3 Bhuail e ; | Buailidh se ; |
| *Plur.* | *Plur.* |
| 1 Bhuail sinn, | Buailidh sinn, |
| 2 Bhuail sibh, | Buailidh sibh, |
| 3 Bhuail iad. | Buailidh siad. |

### *Negative* or *Interrogative Mood.*

| | Preterite. | Future. |
|---|---|---|
| | *Sing.* | *Sing.* |
| | 1 Do bhuail mi, *I struck not,* | Buail mi, *I will not strike,* |
| ni | 2 Do bhuail thu, | Buail thu, |
| cha | 3 Do bhuall e ; | Buail e ; |
| nach | *Plur.* | *Plur.* |
| mur, | 1 Do bhuail sinn, | Buail sinn, |
| &c. | 2 Do bhuail sibh, | Buail sibh, |
| | 3 Do bhuail iad. | Buail iad. |

## Subjunctive Mood.

| Preterite. | Future. |
|---|---|
| *Sing.* | *Sing.* |

1 Bhuailinn, *I would strike,*    Ma bhuaileas mi, *If I shall strike,*

2 Bhuaileadh tu,    Bhuaileas tu,

3 Bhuaileadh e ;    Bhuaileas e ;

| *Plur.* | *Plur.* |
|---|---|

1 Bhuaileamaid,    Bhuaileas sinn,
Bhuaileadh sinn,

2 Bhuaileadh sibh,    Bhuaileas sinn,

3 Bhuaileadh iad.    Bhuaileas iad.

| *Imperative Mood.* | *Infinitive Mood.* |
|---|---|
| *Sing.* | Bualadh, *striking,* |

1 Buaileam, *let me strike,*    ag bualadh, *a-striking, striking,*

2 Buail,    iar bualadh, *struck,*

3 Buaileadh e ;    do bhualadh, ⎫
*Plur*    a bhualadh, ⎬ *to strike,*

1 Buaileamaid,    ri bualadh, *at striking,*

2 Buailibh,    le bualadh, *with striking,*

3 Buaileadh iad.    o bhualadh, *from striking,*
       &c.

## Compound Tenses.

### *Affirmative Mood.*

| Present. | Preterite. |
|---|---|
| 1. *Comp.* | 1. *Comp.* |
| Ta mi ag bualadh, | Bha mi ag bualadh, |
| *I am striking,* &c. | *I was striking,* &c. |

### Future.

1 *Comp.*
Bithidh mi ag bualadh.
*I will be striking,* &c.

Present.

2 *Comp.*

Ta mi iar bualadh,
*I have struck*, &c.

Preterite.

2. *Comp.*

Bha mi iar bualadh,
*I had struck*, &c.

Future.

2 *Comp.*

Bithidh mi iar bualadh,
*I will have struck*, &c.

*Negative Mood*

Present.

1. *Comp.*

Bheil mi ag bualadh,
*I am not striking*, &c.

Preterite.

1. *Comp.*

Robh mi ag bualadh,
*I was not striking*, &c.

Future.

1. *Comp.*

Bi mi ag bualadh,
*I will not be striking*, &c.

ni
cha
nach
mur,
&c.

Present.

2. *Comp.*

Bheil mi iar bualadh,
*I have not struck*, &c.

Preterite.

2. *Comp.*

Robh mi iar bualadh,
*I had not struck*, &c.

Future.

2. *Comp.*

Bi mi iar bualadh,
*I will not have struck*, &c.

*Subjunctive Mood.*

Preterite.

1. *Comp.*

Bhithinn ag bualadh,
*I would be striking*, &c.

Future.

1. *Comp.*

Ma bhitheas mi ag bualadh,
*If I shall be striking*, &c.

2. *Comp.*

Bhithinn iar bualadh,
*I would have struck*, &c.

2. *Comp.*

Ma bhitheas mi iar bualadh,
*If I shall have struck*, &c.

| *Imperative Mood.* | *Infinitive Mood.* |
|---|---|
| 1. *Comp.* | 1. *Comp.* |
| Bitheam ag bualadh, | Do bhith ag bualadh, |
| *Let me be striking,* &c. | *To be striking,* &c. |
| | Iar bith ag bualadh, |
| | *Been striking,* &c. |
| 2. *Comp.* | 2. *Comp.* |
| Bitheam iar bualadh, | Do bhith iar bualadh, |
| *Let me have struck,* &c. | *To have been striking,* &c. |

PASSIVE VOICE.

*Affirmative Mood*

Simple Tenses.

| Preterite. | Future. |
|---|---|
| *Sing.* | *Sing.* |
| 1 Do bhuaileadh mi, *I was struck.* | Buailear mi, *I shall be struck.* |
| Bhuaileadh mi, | |
| 2 Bhuaileadh thu, | Buailear thu, |
| 3 Bhuaileadh e ; | Buailear e ; |
| *Plur.* | *Plur.* |
| 1 Bhuaileadh, sinn, | Buailear sinn, |
| 2 Bhuaileadh sibh, | Buailear sibh, |
| Bhuaileadh iad. | Buailear iad. |

*Negative Mood.*

| | Preterite. | Future. |
|---|---|---|
| | *Sing.* | *Sing.* |
| | 1 Do bhuaileadh mi, *I was not struck,* | Buailear mi, *I shall not be struck,* |
| ni | 2 Do bhuaileadh thu, | Buailear thu, |
| cha | 3 Do bhuaileadh e ; | Buailear e ; |
| nach | *Plur.* | *Plur.* |
| mur, | 1 Do bhuaileadh sinn, | Buailear sinn, |
| &c. | 2 Do bhuaileadh sibh, | Buailear sibh, |
| | 3 Do bhuaileadh iad. | Buailear iad. |

## Subjunctive Mood.

| Preterite. | Future. |

### Sing.

1 Bhuailteadh mi, *I would be struck*,  Ma bhuailear mi, *If I shall be struck.*
2 Bhuailteadh thu,  Bhuailear thu,
3 Bhuailteadh e;  Bhuailear e;

### Plur.

1 Bhuailteadh sinn,  Bhuailear sinn,
2 Bhuailteadh sibh,  Bhuailear sibh,
3 Bhuailteadh iad.  Bhuailear iad.

## Imperative Mood.

### Sing.

1 Buailtear mi, *Let me be struck*,
2 Buailtear thu,
3 Buailtear e.

### Plur.

1 Buailtear sinn,
2 Buailtear sibh,
3 Buailtear iad.

## Participle.

Buailte, *struck*.

## Compound Tenses

### Affirmative Mood.

Present.  Preterite.

1. *Comp.*  1. *Comp.*

Ta mi buailte, *I am struck*, &c.  Bha mi buailte, *I was struck,* &c.

### Future.

1. *Comp.*

Bithidh mi buailte, *I shall be struck*, &c.

| Present. | Preterite. |
|---|---|
| 2. *Comp.* | 2. *Comp.* |
| *Sing.* | *Sing.* |

1 Ta mi iar mo bhualadh,    Bha mi iar mo bhualadh,
   *I have been struck,*      *I had been struck,*
2 Ta thu iar do bhualadh,   Bha thu iar do bhualadh,
3 Ta se iar a bhualadh ;     Bha se iar a bhualadh ;

    *Plur.*            *Plur.*

1 Ta sinn iar ar bualadh,   Bha sinn iar ar bualadh,
2 Ta sibh iar 'ur bualadh,   Bha sibh iar 'ur bualadh,
3 Ta siad iar am bualadh.   Bha siad iar am bualadh.

### Future.

2. *Comp.*

*Sing.*

1 Bithidh mi iar mo bhualadh,   *I shall have been struck.*
2 Bithidh tu iar do bhualadh,
3 Bithidh se iar a bhualadh;

    *Plur.*

1 Bithidh sinn iar ar bualadh,
2 Bithidh sibh iar 'ur bualadh,
3 Bithidh siad iar am bualadh.

### *Negative Mood.*

| Present. | Preterite. |
|---|---|
| 1. *Comp.* | 1. *Comp.* |
| Ni bheil mi buailte, | Ni'n robh mi buailte, |
| *I am not struck,* &c. | *I was not struck,* &c. |

### Future.

1. *Comp.*

Ni'm bi mi buailte, *I shall not be struck,* &c.

| Present. | Preterite. |
|---|---|
| 2. *Comp.* | 2. *Comp.* |
| Ni' m bheil mi iar mo bhualadh, | Ni'n robh mi iar mo bhualadh, |
| *I have not been struck,* &c. | *I had not been struck,* &c. |

Future.

2. *Comp.*

Ni'm bi mi iar mo bhualadh, *I shall not have been struck,* &c.

*Subjunctive Mood.*

Preterite.
1. *Comp.*
Bhithinn buailte,
*I would be struck,* &c.

2. *Comp.*
Bhithinn iar mo bhualadh,
*I would have been struck,* &c.

Future.
1. *Comp.*
Ma bhitheas mi buailte,
*If I shall be struck,* &c.

2. *Comp.*
Ma bhitheas mi iar mo bhualadh,
*If I shall have been struck,* &c.

*Imperative Mood.*
1. *Comp.*
Bitheam buailte,
*Let me be struck,* &c.

2. *Comp.*
Bitheam iar mo bhualadh,
*Let me have been struck,* &c.

*Infinitive Mood.*
1. *Comp.*
Do bhith buailte,
*To be struck,* &c.

2. *Comp.*
Do bhith iar mo bhualadh,
*To have been struck,* &c.

*Examples of Verbs of the Second Conjugation.*

Orduich, *to appoint.*

ACTIVE VOICE.

Simple Tenses

|  | Preterite. | Future. |
|---|---|---|
| *Affirmat.* | Dh'orduich, | Orduichidh, |
| *Negat.* | D'orduich, | Orduich, |
| *Subjunct.* | Dh'orduichinn. | Dh'orduicheas. |
| *Imperat.* | Orduicheam. | *Infinit.* Orduchadh. |

PASSIVE VOICE.

|  | | |
|---|---|---|
| *Affirmat.* | Dh'orduicheadh, | Orduichear, |
| *Negat.* | D'orduicheadh, | Orduichear, |
| *Subjunct.* | Dh'orduichteadh. | Dh'orduicheas. |
| *Imperat.* | Orduichear. | *Particip.* Orduichte. |

## Folaich, *to hide*.

ACTIVE VOICE.

|  | Preterite. | Future. |
|---|---|---|
| *Affirmat.* | Dh'fholaich, | Folaichidh, |
| *Negat.* | D'fholaich, | Folaich, |
| *Subjunct.* | Dh'fholaichinn. | Dh'fholaicheas. |
| *Imperat.* Folaicheam. | | *Infinit.* Folachadh. |

PASSIVE VOICE.

|  |  |  |
|---|---|---|
| *Affirmat.* | Dh'fholaicheadh, | Folaichear, |
| *Negat.* | D'fholaicheadh, | Folaichear, |
| *Subjunct.* | Dh'fholaichteadh. | Dh'fholaichear. |
| *Imperat.* Folaichtear. | | *Particip.* Folaichte. |

The Compound tenses may be easily learned from those of the Verb Buail in the first Conjugation, being formed exactly in the same manner.

FORMATION OF THE TENSES.

### Of the Initial Form.

An Initial Consonant is aspirated in the Preterite Tense, through all the Moods and Voices, except in the Preterite Subjunctive after the Particles ni, mur, nach, gu, an, am. An initial Consonant is occasionally aspirated in the Future Tense, and in the Infinitive and Participle, indicating their connection with the preceding word.

In the first Conjugation, do is prefixed to the Pret. Aff. and Neg. Active and Passive. However, it often is, and always may be, omitted before the Pret. Aff. It is sometimes omitted in the Pret. Neg. in verse, and in common conversation. In the second Conjugation, the same Particle do is prefixed to the Preterite through all the Moods and Voices, and to the Fut. Subj. excepting only the Subjunctive Tenses after ni, mur, nach, gu, an, am. In this

Conjugation, do always loses the *o* to avoid a *hiatus*, and the *d* is aspirated in the Affirm. and Subjunct. Moods (z).

### Of the Termination.

In all regular Verbs, the Terminations adjected to the Root are, strictly speaking, the same in Verbs characterised by a small vowel. But where the first vowel of the Termination does not correspond in quality to the last vowel of the Root, it has become the constant practice to insert in the Termination a vowel of the requisite quality, in order to produce this correspondence. Thus a variety has been introduced into the Terminations even of regular Verbs, prejudicial to the uniformity of inflection, and of no use to ascertain either the sense or the pronunciation (*a*). In the foregoing examples of regular Verbs, the common mode of Orthography has been followed, but in the following rules the simple Terminations only are specified.

ACTIVE VOICE.

### Simple Tenses.

The Theme or Root of the Verb is always found in the second Per. sing. of the imperative.

The *Preterite* Affirm. and Negat. is like the Root, and has no distinction of Number or Person. In most of the editions of the Gaelic Psalms, some inflections of the Pre-

(*z*) In the older Irish MSS. the Particle *do* appears under a variety of forms. In one MS. of high antiquity it is often written *dno*. This seems to be its oldest form. The two consonants were sometimes separated by a vowel, and the *n* being pronounced and then written *r*, (See Part I. p. 19.) the word was written doro. (See *Astle's Hist. of the Orig. and Progr. of Writing, page* 126, *Irish Specimen, No.*6.) The Consonants were sometimes transposed, suppressing the latter Vowel, and the Particle became nod (*O Brien's Ir. Dict. voc.* Sasat, Treas,) and rod *id. voc.* Ascaim. Fial.) Sometimes one of the syllables only was retained; hence no (*O'Br. voc.* No,) ro (*id. voc.* Ro,) and do in common use. Do likewise suffered a transposition of letters, and was written sometimes ad. (O'Br. *voc.* Do.)

(*a*) This correspondence of the Termination with the Root was overlooked in the older editions of the Gaelic Psalms; as pronnûdh, cuirfar, molfidh, innsam, guidham, coimhdar, sinnam, gluaisfar, &c.

terite have been admitted, with good effect, from the Irish
Verb; such as, bhuaileas *I struck*, bhuailis *thou didst strike*,
bhuaileamar *we struck*, bhuaileadar *they struck*. The Pret.
Subj. is formed by adding to the Root *inn* for the first pers.
sing., and *adh* for the other persons. The first pers. plur.
also terminates in *amaid*.

The *Future* Affirm. adds *idh* to the Root; in the Negat.
it is like the Root; and in the Subjunct. it adds *as*. A
poetic Future Tense terminating in *ann* or *onn*, is frequent in
the Gaelic Psalms; as, gairionn *will call*, seasfann *will stand*,
do bheirionn, *will give*, &c. The Future has no distinction of
Number or Person. The Termination of the Future Affirm.
and Negat. in many Verbs was formerly *fidh*, like the Irish;
of which many examples occur in the earlier editions of the
Gaelic Psalms. In later Gaelic publications, the *f* has been
uniformly set aside (*b*). The Termination of the first pers.
and third pers. plur. is often incorporated with the
corresponding Pronoun; as, seinnam cliu *I will sing praise*,
Psal. lxi. 8., Ni fuigham bàs, ach mairfam beo, *I shall not die,
but shall remain alive*, Ps. cxviii. 17., Ithfid, geillfid, innsid,
*they will eat, they will submit, they will tell*, Ps. xxii. 26, 29,
31. (*c*).

(*b*) The disposition in the Gaelic to drop articulations has, in this instance,
been rather unfortunate; as the want of the *f* weakens the sound of the
word, and often occasions a *hiatus*. There seems a propriety in retaining the *f* of the Future, after a Liquid, or an aspirated Mute; as, cuirfidh,
mairfidh, molfidh, geillfidh, pronnfidh, brisfidh, &c., for these words lose
much in sound and emphasis by being changed into caithidh, mairidh,
&c.

(*c*) The incorporation of the Verb with a Personal Pronoun is a manifest
improvement, and has gradually taken place in almost all the polished
languages. There is incomparably more beauty and force in expressing
the energy of the Verb, with its *personal* relation and concomitant circumstances, in one word, than by a periphrasis of pronouns and auxiliaries.
The latter mode may have a slight advantage in point of precision, but the
former is greatly superior in elegance and strength. The structure of the
Latin and Greek, compared with that of the English Verb, affords a striking
illustration of this common and obvious remark. Nothing can be worse
managed than the French Verb; which, though it possesses a competent
variety of *personal* inflections, yet loses all the benefit of them by the
perpetual enfeebling recurrence of the personal Pronouns.

In the *Imperative* Mood, the second pers. sing. is the Root of the Verb. The other persons are distinguished by these Terminations ; 1st pers. sing. *am*, 3d pers. sing. *adh*, 1st pers. plur. *amaid*, 2d pers. plur. *ibh*, 3d pers. plur. *adh*.

The Terminations peculiar to the 1st pers. sing. and plur. of the Pret. Subj. and of the Imperat. supply the place of the Personal Pronouns ; as does also the Termination of the 2d pers. plur. of the Imperative.

The *Infinitive* is variously formed.

*General Rule.* The Infinitive is formed by adding *adh* to the Root; as, aom *bow, incline*, Infin. aomadh ; ith *eat*, Infin. itheadh.

1. Some Verbs suffer a syncope in the penult syllable, and are commonly used in their contracted form ; as,

| *Imper.* | *Infin.* |
|---|---|
| Caomhain, *spare*, | Caomhnadh. |
| Coisin, *win*, | Coisneadh, Cosnadh. |
| Diobair, *deprive*, | Diobradh. |
| Fògair, *remove*, | Fògradh. |
| Foghain, *suffice*, | Foghnadh. |
| Fosgail, *open*, | Fosgladh. |
| Innis, *tell*, | Innseadh. |
| Iobair, *sacrifice*, | Iobradh. |
| Mosgail, *awake*, | Mosgladh. |
| Seachain, *avoid*, | Seachnadh. |
| Tionsgain, *begin*, | Tionsgnadh. |
| Togair, *desire*, | Togradh. |

Observe that Verbs which thus suffer a syncope in forming

In comparing the Scottish and Irish dialects of the Gaelic, it may be inferred that the former, having less of inflection or *incorporation* than the latter, differs less from the parent tongue, and is an older branch of the Celtic, than its sister dialect. It were unfair, however, to deny that the Irish have improved the Verb, by giving a greater variety of inflection to its *Numbers* and *Persons*, as well as by introducing a simple Present Tense. The authors of our metrical version of the Gaelic Psalms were sensible of the advantage possessed by the Irish dialect in these respects, and did not scruple to borrow an idiom which has given grace and dignity to many of their verses.

the Infinitive, suffer a like syncope in the Preterite Subjunctive, and in the Imperative Mood ; as, innis *tell*, Infin. innseadh, Pret. Subj. innsinn, innseadh, innseamaid, Imperat. innseam, innseamaid, innsibh.

2. A considerable number of Verbs have their Infinitive like the Root ; as,

| | |
|---|---|
| Caoidh, *lament.* | Ol, *drink.* |
| Dearmad, *neglect.* | Ruith, *run* |
| Fàs, *grow.* | Snamh, *swim.* |
| Gairm, *call.* | Sniomh, *twine.* |
| Meas, *estimate.* | |

3. Polysyllables in *ch*, whose characteristic Vowel is small, either throw it away, or convert it into a broad Vowel and add *adh*; as,

| | |
|---|---|
| Ceannaich, *buy,* | Ceannachadh. |
| Smuainich, *think,* | Smuaineachadh. |

Most Monosyllables in *sg*, and a few others, follow the same Rule ; as,

| *Imper.* | *Infin.* | *Imper.* | *Infin.* |
|---|---|---|---|
| Coisg, *check,* | Cosgadh. | Naisg, *bind,* | Nasgadh. |
| Fàisg, *wring,* | Fàsgadh. | Paisg, *wrap,* | Pasgadh. |
| Loisg, *burn,* | Losgadh. | Blais, *taste,* | Blasadh. |
| Luaisg, *rock.* | Luasgadh. | Buail, *strike.* | Bualadh. |

4. Many Verbs, whose characteristic Vowel is small, either throw it away, or convert it into a broad Vowel, without adding *adh* ; as,

| *Imper.* | *Infin.* | *Imper.* | *Infin.* |
|---|---|---|---|
| Amhairc, *look,* | Amharc. | Iomain, *drive,* | Ioman. |
| Amais, *reach,* | Amas. | Leighis, *curc,* | Leigheas. |
| Caill, *lose,* | Call. | Sguir, *cease,* | Sgur. |
| Ceangail, *bind,* | Ceangal. | Siubhail, *travel,* | Siubhal. |
| Cuir, *put,* | Cur. | Tachrais, *wind,* | Tachras. |
| Coimhid, *keep,* | Coimhead. | Tiondaidh, *turn,* | Tiondadh. |
| Fulaing, *suffer,* | Fulang. | Toirmisg, *forbid,* | Toirmeasg. |
| Fuirich, *stay,* | Fuireach. | Toinail, *gather,* | Toinal. |
| Guil, *weep,* | Gul. | Tiongsgail, *contrive,* | Tiongsgal. |

5. The following Verbs in *air* add *t* to the Root :—

| *Imper.* | *Infin.* |
|---|---|
| Agair, *claim,* | Agairt. |
| Bagair, *threaten,* | Bagairt. |
| Casgair, *slaughter,* | Casgairt. |
| Freagair, *answer,* | Freagairt. |
| Iomair, *use,* | Iomairt. |
| Labhair, *speak,* | Labhairt. |
| Lomair, *shear,* | Lomairt. |
| Saltair, *trample,* | Saltairt. |
| Tabhair, *give,* | Tabhairt. |
| Tachair, *meet,* | Tachairt. |

6. These Monosyllables add *sinn* to the Root :—

| | |
|---|---|
| Beir, *bear,* | Beirsinn. |
| Creid, *believe,* | Creidsinn. |
| Faic, *see,* | Faicsinn. |
| Goir, *crow,* | Goirsinn. |
| Mair, *continue,* | Mairsinn. |
| Saoil, *think,* | Saoilsinn. |
| Tréig, *forsake,* | Tréigsinn. |
| Tuig, *understand,* | Tuigsinn, or Tuigeil. |
| Ruig, *reach,* | Ruigsinn, or Ruigheachd. |

7. These Monosyllables add *tuinn* or *tinn* to the Root:—

| | |
|---|---|
| Bean, *touch,* | Beantuinn. |
| Buin, *take away,* | Buntuinn. |
| Can, *say, sing,* | Cantuinn. |
| Cinn, *grow,* | Cinntinn. |
| Cluinn, *hear,* | Cluinntinn. |
| Fan, *stay,* | Fantuinn. |
| Gin, *produce,* | Giontuinn, or Gionmhuin. |
| Lean, *follow,* | Leantuinn, or Leanmhuin. |
| Meal, *enjoy,* | Mealtuinn. |
| Pill, *return,* | Pilltinn. |
| Seall, *look,* | Sealltuinn. |

F

8. The following Monosyllables add *ail* to the Root:—

| *Imper.* | *Infin.* | *Imper.* | *Infin.* |
|---|---|---|---|
| Cum, *hold,* | Cumail. | Leag, *cast down,* | Leagail. |
| Gabh, *take,* | Gabhail. | Tog, *raise,* | Togail. |
| Fàg, *leave,* | Fàgail. | Tuig, *understand,* | Tuigeil. |

9. These Monosyllables add *amh* to the Root:—

| *Imper.* | *Infin.* |
|---|---|
| Caith, *spend,* | Caitheamh. |
| Dean, *do, make,* | Deanamh. |
| Feith, *wait,* | Feitheamh. |
| Seas, *stand,* | Seasamh. |

10. The following Verbs form the Infinitive irregularly :—

| | |
|---|---|
| Beuc, *roar,* | Beucaich. |
| Bùir, *bellow,* | Bùirich. |
| Geum, *low,* | Geumnaich. |
| Glaodh, *cry,* | Glaodhaich. |
| Caisd, *listen,* | Caisdeachd. |
| Eisd, *hearken,* | Eisdeachd. |
| Marcaich, *ride,* | Marcachd. |
| Thig, *come,* | Teachd, tighinn. |
| Faigh, *find,* | Faghail, faotainn. |
| Eirich, *rise,* | Eirigh. |
| Iarr, *request,* | Iarraidh. |
| Taisg, *lay up,* | Tasgaidh. |
| Coidil, *sleep,* | Codal. |
| Fuaigh, *sew,* | Fuaghal. |
| Gluais, *move,* | Gluasad, gluasachd. |
| Tuit, *fall,* | Tuiteam. |
| Teirig, *wear out,* | Teireachduinn. |
| Teasairg, *deliver,* | Teasairgin. |

### Compound Tenses.

The *compound Tenses of the first order* are made up of the several simple Tenses of the auxiliary verb Bi *be,* and the Infinitive preceded by the Preposition ag *at.* Between two Consonants, ag commonly loses the *g,* and is written *a ;* as,

ta iad a' deanamh *they are doing*. Between two Vowels, the
*a* is dropped, and the *g* is retained ; as, ta mi 'g iarruidh *I
am asking*. When preceded by a Consonant, and followed
by a Vowel, the Preposition is written entire ; as, ta iad ag
iarruidh *they are asking*. When preceded by a Vowel, and
followed by a Consonant, it is often suppressed altogether;
as, ta mi deanamh *I am doing* (*d*).

The *compound Tenses of the second order* are made up of
the simple Tenses of Bi and the Infinitive preceded by the
Preposition iar *after* (*e*).

### PASSIVE VOICE.

### *Simple Tenses.*

The *Preterite* Affirm. and Negat. is formed from the same
Tense in the Active, by adding *adh*. The Preter. Subj. adds
*teadh*.

The *Future* is formed from the Fut. Act. by changing the
Terminations in the Affirm. and Subj. into *ar*, (more properly
*far*, as of old) and adding the same syllable in the
Negative.

The *Imperative* is formed from the Imperat. Act. by
adding to the second pers. sing. *tar*, *thar*, or *ar*. (*f*)

(*d*) Such at least is the common practice in writing, in compliance with
the common mode of colloquial pronunciation. It might perhaps be better
to retain the full form of the Preposition, in grave pronunciation, and
always in writing. It is an object worthy of attention to preserve radical
articulations, especially in writing ; and particularly to avoid every
unnecessary use of the monosyllable *a*, which, it must be confessed, recurs
in too many senses.

(*e*) The Preposition iar has here been improperly confounded with air *on*.
I have ventured to restore it, from the Irish Grammarians. Iar is in
common use in the Irish dialect, signifying *after*. Thus, iar sin *after that*,
iar leaghadh an tshoisgeil *after reading the Gospel*, iar sleachdadh do
niomlan *after all have kneeled down*, iar seasamh suas *after standing up*,
&c. See "Irish Book of Common Prayer." Air, when applied to time, signifies not *after*, but *at* or *on*: air an am so, air an uair so *at this time*,
air an la sin *on that day*. There is therefore sufficient reason to believe
that, in the case in question, iar is the proper word ; and that it has been
corruptly supplanted by air.

(*f*) The Imperative seems to have been anciently formed by adding *tar*
to the Root. This form is still retained in Ireland, and in some parts of

The *Participle* is formed by adding *te* to the Root (*g*).

There is no distinction of Number or Person in the Tenses of the Passive Voice.

Verbs which suffer a syncope in the Infinitive, suffer a like syncope in the Pret. Aff. and Neg. throughout the Future Tense, and in the Imperative.

## Compound Tense.

The *compound Tenses of the first order* are made up of the simple Tenses of the auxiliary Bi and the Passive Participle.

Scotland, chiefly in verbs ending in a Lingual; as, buailtear, deantar. (See the Lord's Prayer in the older editions of the Gaelic Version of the Assembly's Catechism; also, the "Irish N. Test." Matt. vi. 10. Luke xi. 2.) In other verbs, the *t* seems to have been dropped in pronunciation. It was, however, retained by the Irish in writing, but with an aspiration to indicate its being quiescent ; thus, togthar, teilgthear. "Ir. N. T." Matt. xxi. 21, Mark xi. 23, crochthar, Matt. xxvii. 22. So also the "Gaelic N. T." 1767, deanthar, Matt. vi. 10, Luke xi. 2. In the later publica- tions the *t* has been omitted altogether, with what propriety may be well doubted.

(*g*) To preserve a due correspondence with the pronunciation, the Pass. Part. should always terminate in *te*, for in this part of the verb, the *t* has always its *small* sound. Yet in verbs whereof the characteristic vowel is broad, it is usual to write the termination of the Pass. Part. *ta ;* as, togta *raised*, crochta *suspended*. This is done in direct opposition to the pronunciation, merely out of regard to the Irish Rule of *Leathan ri leathan*, which in this case, as in many others, has been permitted to mar the genuine orthography.

When a verb, whose characteristic vowel is broad, terminates in a Liquid, the final consonant coalesces so closely with the *t* of the Pass. Part. that the *small* sound of the latter necessarily occasions the like sound in pronouncing the former. Accordingly the small sound of the Liquid is properly represented in writing, by an *i* inserted before it. Thus, ol *drink*, Pass. Part. òilte ; pronn *pound*, proinnte ; crann *bar*, crainnte ; sparr *ram*, spairrte ; trus *pack*, truiste. But when the verb ends in a mute, whether plain or aspirated, there is no such coalescence between its final consonant and the adjected *t* of the Participle. The final consonant if it be pronounced retains its broad sound. There is no good reason for maintaining a correspondence of vowels in the Participle, which ought therefore to be written, as it is pronounced, without regard to *Leathan ri leathan* ; as, tog *raise*, Pass. Part. togte ; croch *hang*, crochte ; sath *thrust*, sàthte ; cnamh *chew*, cnamhte.

The same observations apply, with equal force, to the Pret. Subj. in which the *t* of the termination is always pronounced with its *small* sound, and should therefore be followed by a small vowel in writing ; as, thogteadh, chrochteadh, not thogtadh, chrochtadh.

The *compound Tenses of the second order* are made up of the simple Tenses of *Bi* and the Infinitive preceded by the Preposition *iar* and the Possessive Pronoun corresponding in Person to the Pronoun, or to the Noun, which is the Nominative to the verb.

### *Use and Import of the Moods and Tenses.*

The *Affirmative* or *Indicative* Mood expresses affirmation, and is used in affirmative propositions only ; as, Do bhuail mi *I struck*, bha mi ag bualadh *I was striking.*

The *Negative* or *Interrogative* Mood is used in negative propositions and interrogative clauses, after the Particles ni *not*, cha *not*, nach *which not, that not, not ?* mur *if not;* also, gu, gur, *that*, an, am, whether used relatively or interrogatively ; as, cha d'fholaich mi *I did not hide*, mur buail sinn *if we shall not strike*, nach robh iad *that they were not*, gu robh iad *that they were ;* am buail mi? *shall I strike ?*  It is used in the Future Tense after ged *although ;* as, ged bhuail e mi, *though he strike me* (*h*).

The *Subjunctive* Mood is used in the Preterite, either with or without conjunctions ; as, bhuailinn *I would strike*, na'm, mur, nach, &c., buailinn *if, unless, &c., I should strike.*  In the Future it is used only after the conjunctions ma *if*, o, o'n *since*, and the Relative *a* expressed or understood; as, ma bhuaileas mi *if I shall strike*, am fear a bhuaileas mi *the man*

---

(*h*) In all *regular* verbs, the difference between the Affirmative and the Negative Moods, though marked but slightly and partially in the Preterite Tense, (only in the initial form of the 2d Conjugation,) yet is strongly marked in the Future Tense.  The Fut. Aff. terminates in a feeble vocal sound.  In the Fut. Neg. the voice rests on an articulation, or is cut short by a forcible aspiration.  Supposing these Tenses to be used by a speaker in reply to a command or a request ; by their very structure, the former expresses the softness of compliance ; and the latter, the abruptness of a refusal.  If a command or a request be expressed by such verbs as these, tog sin, gabh sin, ith sin, the compliant answer is expressed by togaidh, gabhaidh, ithidh ; the refusal, by the cha tog, cha ghabh, cha n-ith.  May not this peculiar variety of form in the same Tense, when denoting affirmation, and when denoting negation, be reckoned among the characteristic marks of an original language ?

*who will strike me,* or *the man whom I shall strike;* an uair a
bhuaileas mi, tra bhuaileas mi *the time* [*in*] *which I shall
strike, i. e., when I shall strike ;* c'uin [cia ùine] a bhuaileas
mi? *what* [*is*] *the time* [*in*] *which I shall strike ? i. e., when
shall I strike ?*

The *Imperative* Mood expresses desire, whether purpose,
command, or request; as, buaileam *let me strike,* buailibh
*strike ye.*

The *Infinitive* (*i*) is, in all respects, a noun, denoting the
action or energy of the verb, and commonly preceded by a
Preposition which marks the time of the action; as, ag
bualadh *at striking,* am bualadh *the striking, the threshing.*
It assumes a regular genitive case, bualadh g. s. bualaidh ;
as, urlar-bualaidh *a threshing floor.* The Infinitive sometimes loses the termination, and is regularly declined in its
abridged form ; thus, cruinnich *assemble,* inf. cruinneach-adh
per. apocop. cruinneach g. s. cruinnich ; hence, àite-cruinnich
*a place of meeting,* Acts xix. 29, 31, so, fear-criochnaich, Heb.
xii. 2, fear-cuidich, Psalm xxx. 10, liv. 4, ionad-foluich, Psalm
xxxii. 7, cxix. 114, litir-dhealaich, Matt. v. 31 (*k*).

There is no part of the Active Voice that can, strictly speak·
ing, be denominated a Participle. The Infinitive preceded
by the Preposition ag *at,* corresponds in meaning to the present Participle ; and preceded by iar *after,* it corresponds to
the participle of the past time ; as, ag bualadh *at striking,* or
*striking ;* iar bualadh *after striking,* or *struck* (*l*).

(*i*) This part of the verb, being declined and governed like a noun, bears
a closer resemblance to the Latin Gerund than to the Infinitive ; and might
have been properly named the Gerund. But as Lhuyd and all the later
Irish Grammarians have already given it the name of Infinitive, I choose
to continue the same appellation rather than change it.

(*k*) The Editor of the Gaelic Psalms printed at Glasgow, 1753, judging,
as it would seem, that cuidich was too bold a licence for cuideachaidh,
restored the gen. of the full form of the Infinitive ; but in order to reduce
it to two syllables, so as to suit the verse, he threw out the middle syllable,
and wrote cuid'idh.

(*l*) I have met with persons of superior knowledge of the Gaelic who
contended that such expressions as—ta mi deanamh *I am doing,* ta e bualadh
*he is striking* (see page 83), are complete without any Preposition under·
stood ; and that in such situations deanamh, bualadh, are not infinitives or

Many words, expressing state or action, take the Preposition *ag* before them, and may be considered as Infinitives of Verbs, whereof the other parts are not in use ; as, ag atharrais *mimicking*, ag gàireachdaich *laughing*, a' fanoid, a' maga lh *mocking, jeering.*

nouns, but real participles of the Present Tense. With much deference to such authorities, I shall here give the reasons which appear to me to support the contrary opinion.

1. The form of the supposed Participle is invariably the same with that of the Infinitive.

2. If the words deanamh, bualadh, in the phrases adduced, were real Participles, then in all similar instances, it would be not only unnecessary, but ungrammatical, to introduce the preposition ag at all. But this is far from being the case. In all verbs beginning with a vowel, the preposition ag or its unequivocal representative *g* is indispensable ; as, ta iad ag iarruidh, ta mi 'g iarruidh. Shall we say, then, that verbs beginning with a consonant have a present participle, while those that begin with a vowel have none ? But even this distinction falls to the ground, when it is considered that in many phrases which involve a verb beginning with a consonant, the preposition ag stands forth to view, and can on no account be suppressed; as, ta iad 'g a bhualadh *they are striking him*, ta e 'g ar bualadh *he is striking us.* From these particulars it may be inferred that the preposition ag must always precede the infinitive, in order to complete the phrase which corresponds to the English or Latin pres. participle ; and that in those cases where the preposition has been dropped, the omission has been owing to the rapidity or carelessness of colloquial pronunciation.

3. A still stronger argument, in support of the same conclusion, may be derived from the regimen of the phrase in question. The infinitive of a transitive verb, preceded by any preposition, always governs the noun, which is the object of the verbal action, in the genitive. This is an invariable rule of Gaelic Syntax ; thus, ta sinn a' dol a dh' iarruidh na spréidhe, *we are going to seek the cattle ;* ta iad ag iomain na spréidhe, *they are driving the cattle ;* ta iad iar cuairteachadh na spréidhe, *they have gathered the cattle.* This regimen can be accounted for on no other principle, in Gaelic, than that the governing word is a noun, as the infinitive is confessed to be. Now, it happens that the supposed participle has the very same regimen, and governs the genitive as uniformly as the same word would have done, when the presence of a preposition demonstrated it to be a noun ; so, ta mi bualadh an doruis, *I am knocking the door ;* ta thu deanamh an uilc, *you are doing mischief.* The inference is, that even in these situations, the words—bualadh, deanamh, though accompanied with no preposition, are still genuine nouns, and are nothing else than the infinitives of their respective verbs, with the preposition ag understood before each of them.

4 The practice in other dialects of the Celtic, and the authority of respectable grammarians, affords collateral support to the opinion here defended. Gen. Vallancey, the most copious writer on Irish grammar, though he gives the name of participle to a certain part of the Gaelic verb,

The *Participle* passive is an adjective, denoting the completion of the action or energy expressed by the verb; as, arbhar buailte *threshed corn*.

The *Simple Tenses* which belong to all verbs are the Preterite or Future, besides which the verb Bi to *be*, and the defective verb Is I *am*, have a Present Tense (*m*).

The *Present* expresses present existence, state, or energy.

The *Preterite Affirmative* and *Negative* expresses past time indefinitely. The *Preterite Subjunctive* corresponds to the English Tenses formed by the auxiliaries *would*, *could*, &c. In general it denotes that the action or energy of the verb takes place eventually or conditionally. The Pret. Aff. or

because it corresponds, in signification, to a part of the Latin verb which has obtained that name, yet constantly exhibits this participle, not as a single word, but a composite expression ; made up of a preposition and that part of the verb which is here called the infinitive. The phrase is fully and justly exhibited, but it is wrong named ; unless it be allowed to extend the name of Participle to such phrases as *inter ambulandum*, εν τῳ περιπατειν.—Lhuyd, in his Cornish Grammar, informs us, with his usual accuracy, that the Infinitive Mood, as in the other dialects of the British, sometimes serves as a Substantive, as in the Latin ; and by the help of the participle *a* [the Gaelic ag] before it, it supplies the room of the participle of the present tense, &c. Archæol. Brit." page 245, col. 3. This observation is strictly applicable to the Gaelic verb. The infinitive, with the particle. *ag* before it, *supplies the room of the present Participle*. The same judicious writer repeats this observation in his "Introduction to the Irish or Ancient Scottish Language": The Participle of the Present Tense is *supplied* by the Participle *ag* before the Infinitive Mood ; as, *ag radh* saying, *ag cainnt* talking, *ag teagasg* teaching, *ag dul* going, &c. " Arch. Brit." page 303, col. 2.

(*m*) It may appear a strange defect in the Gaelic, that its Verbs, excepting the substantive verbs Bi, Is, have no *simple* Present Tense. Yet this is manifestly the case in the Scottish, Welsh, and Cornish dialects (see "Arch. Brit." page 246, col. 1, and page 247, col. 1.); to which may be added the Manks. Creidim *I believe*, guidheam *I pray*, with perhaps one or two more Present Tenses, now used in Scotland, seem to have been imported from Ireland, for their paucity evinces that they belong not to our dialect. The want of the simple Present Tense is a striking point of resemblance between the Gaelic and the Hebrew verb.

I am indebted to a learned and ingenious correspondent for the following important remark ; that the want of the simple Present Tense in all the British dialects of the Celtic, in common with the Hebrew, while the Irish has assumed that Tense, furnishes a strong presumption that the Irish is a dialect of later growth ; that the British Gaelic is its parent tongue ; and consequently that Britain is the mother country of Ireland.

Neg. is used sometimes in this sense, like the English, when the Pret. Subj. occurred in the preceding clause of a sentence , as, na'm biodh tus' an so, cha d' fhuair mo bhrathair bàs, *if thou hadst been here, my brother had not [would not have] died ;* mur bitheamaid air deanamh moille bha sinn a nis air pilltinn air ar n-ais, *if we had not lingered, we had [should have] now returned,* Gen. xliii. 10.

The *Future* makes future time indefinitely. This Tense is used in a peculiar sense in Gaelic, to signify that an action or event takes place uniformly, habitually, according to ordinary practice, or the course of nature. Thus ; Blessed is he that *considereth* the poor, expressed according to the Gaelic idiom, would be, Blessed is he that *will consider,* &c. A wise son *maketh* a glad father, in Gaelic would run, A wise son *will make,* &c. Your patient, I am told, is in a bad way; he neither *enjoys* rest, nor *takes* medicine. Nay, his situation is worse than you know of ; yesterday, he became delirious, and is now almost unmanageable; he *tosses* his arms, and *endeavours* to beat every one within his reach. In Gaelic, *will enjoy —will take—will toss—will endeavour.* In like manner, a great many Gaelic Proverbs express a general truth by means of the Future tense ; *e.g.,* bithidh dùil ri fear feachd, ach cha bhi dùil ri fear lic, *There* is *hope that a man may return from war, but there* is *no hope that a man may return from the grave ;* literally, there *will be* hope—there *will be* no hope. Teirgidh gach ni r' a chaitheamh, *every thing* wears *out in the using* literally,—*will wear* out (*n*).

The *Compound Tenses* mark different modifications of time,

---

(*n*) From observing the same thing happen repeatedly or habitually it is naturally inferred that it will happen again. When an event is predicted it is supposed that the speaker, if no other cause of his foreknowledge appears, infers the future happening of the event from its having already happened in many instances. Thus the Future Tense, which simply fore-tells, conveys to the hearer an intimation that the thing foretold has already taken place frequently and habitually. In Hebrew, the Future Tense is used with precisely the same effect. In the law of Jehovah he *will* medi-tate ; *i.e.,* he *does* meditate habitually. Psal. i. 2. See also Psal. xlii. 1 : Job ix. 11, xxiii. 8, 9, &c., *passim.*

which will be easily understood by analysing their component parts.

In the *Active Voice*, the compound tenses of the first order denote that the action is going on, but not completed at the time specified by the auxiliary verb, or its adjuncts; as, ta mi ag bualadh, *I am at striking*, i.e., *I am striking ;* bha mi ag buaiadh an dé, *I was striking yesterday.*

Those of the second order denote that the action is newly completed and past, at the time marked by the auxiliary verb; ta mi iar bualadh, *I am after striking*, i.e., *I have struck*, *Je viens de frapper ;* Bha mi iar bualadh, *I was striking*, i.e., *I had struck.*

In the *Passive Voice*, the compound tenses of the first order denote that the action is *finished* at the time marked by the auxiliary verb; ta mi buailte, *I am struck.*

Those of the second order denote that the action is *newly finished* at the time marked by the auxiliary (*o*) ; ta mi iar mo bhualadh, *I am after my striking*, or, *I am after the striking of me*, which has always a passive signification ; that is, it is always understood, from this form of expression, that *striking* is the action of some agent different from the person struck. It is equivalent to *I have been struck*, *Je viens d'etre frappé.*

A set of Compound Tenses, of a structure similar to these last, having the preposition ag, in place of iar, is sometimes used, and in a passive sense, denoting that the action is *going on* at the time marked by the auxiliary; as, tha 'n tigh 'g a thogail, *the house is at its building*, i.e., *a-building ;* sea bliadhna agus da fhichead bha 'n teampull 'g a thogail, *forty and six years was this temple in building.* John ii. 20, 1 Kings vi. 7. Bha an crodh 'g an leigeadh, *the cows were a-milking ;* bidh deudaichean 'g an rusgadh. " Gillies' Collect." p. 82. So

---

(*o*) Though this be the precise import of the Compound Tenses of the second order, yet they are not strictly confined to the point of time stated above ; but are often used to denote past time indefinitely. In this way, they supply the place of the Compound Tenses of the first order in those verbs which have no passive participle.

in English, the book is a-printing; the deed's a-doing now,
" Douglas," Act 1.

The following scheme shows the different modifications of
time, as expressed by the several Tenses of the Gaelic Verb,
brought together into one view, and compared with the corresponding Tenses of the Greek Verb in Moor's Greek Grammar.

### ACTIVE VOICE.

*Indicative or Affirmative Mood.*

#### Present Tense.

| Ta mi ag bualadh, | τυπτω, | I strike, or am striking. |

#### Imperfect.

| Bha mi ag bualadh, | ἐτυπτον, | I was striking. |

#### Future.

| Buailidh mi Bithidh mi ag bual-adh, | τυψω, | I will strike, or be strik-ing. |

#### Aorist or Preterite.

| Bhuail mi, | ἐτυψα, | I struck. |

#### Perfect.

| Ta mi iar bualadh | τετυφα, | I have struck. |

#### Pluperfect.

| Bha mi iar bualadh, | ἐτετυφειν, | I had struck. |

*Interrogative or Negative Mood.*

#### Present.

Am bheil mi ag bualadh?　　　　Am I striking?

#### Imperfect.

An robh mi ag bualadh?　　　　Was I striking?

#### Future.

Am buail mi?　　　　Shall I strike?

Aorist or Preterite.

An do bhuail mi?                     Did I strike?

Perfect.

Am bheil mi iar bualadh?            Have I struck?

Pluperfect.

An robh mi iar bualadh?             Had I struck?

*Subjunctive Mood.*

Imperfect.

Bhuailinn,            } ἐτυπτον ἀν,   I would strike.
Bhithinn ag bualadh, }

Future.

Ma bhuaileas mi,                    If I shall strike.

Pluperfect.

Bhithinn iar bualadh,  ἐτυψα ἀν,   I would have struck

*Imperative Mood.*

Buaileam,                           Let me strike.
Buail,               τυπτε,         Strike.

*Infinitive Mood.*

Am bualadh,      το τυπτειν,     The striking.
A' bhualaidh,    του τυπτειν,    Of the striking.
Ag bualadh,      ἐν τῳ τυπτειν,  A-striking.

PASSIVE VOICE.

*Indicative or Affirmative Mood.*

Present.

Ta mi 'g am bhualadh,  τυπτομαι,   I am in striking (*p*).

Imperfect.

Bha mi 'g am bhualadh,  ετυπτομην,   I was in striking.

(*p*) See Moor. So tha 'n tigh 'g a thogail, *the house is in building.*

### Future.

Buailear mi,
Bithidh mi buailte,     } τυφθησομαι   I shall be struck.

### Aorist or Preterite.

Bhuaileadh mi,     ἐτυφθην,     I was struck.

### Perfect.

Ta mi buailte,
Ta mi iar mo bhual-  } τετυμμενος εἰμι,  } I have been struck.
adh,

### Pluperfect.

Bha mi buailte,
Bha mi iar mo bhual-  } τετυμμενος ἠν,  } I had been struck.
adh,

### Interrogative or Negative Mood.

#### Future.

Am buailear mi?     Shall I be struck?

#### Aorist or Preterite.

An do bhuaileadh mi?     Was I struck?

#### Perfect.

Am bheil mi buailte?
Am bheil mi iar mo bhualadh?  } Have I been struck?

#### Pluperfect.

An robh mi buailte?
An robh mi iar mo bhualadh?  } Had I been struck?

### Subjunctive Mood.

#### Imperfect.

Bhuailteadh mi,     ἐτυπτομην ἀν, I should be struck.

#### Future.

Ma bhuailtear mi,     If I shall be struck.

Pluperfect.

Bhithinn buailte,⎫                    ⎧ I   should   have   been
Bhithinn   iar   mo ⎬ ἐτυφθην ἀν, ⎨ struck.
   bhualadh,      ⎭                    ⎩

*Imperative Mood.*

Buailtear mi,                              Let me be struck.
Buailtear thu,          τυπτου,            Be thou struck.
      &c.
                      Participle.
Buailte,               τετυμμενος   Struck.

It will afford satisfaction to the grammatical reader, to see
how correctly the various modifications of time, as distinguished and arranged by Mr Harris, are expressed in the
Gaelic verb, by the auxiliaries, bi *be*, and dol *going*   See
*Hermes B.* I. *c.* 7.

                  Aorist of the Present.
Τυπτω,            I strike,            ⸺⸺⸺⸺

                  Aorist of the Past.
Ετυψα,            I struck,            Bhuail mi.

                  Aorist of the Future.
Τυψω,             I shall strike,      Buailidh mi.

                  Inceptive Present.
Μελλω τυπτειν,    I am going to strike, Ta mi dol a bhualadh.

                Middle or extended Present.
Τυγχανω τυπτων,   I am striking,       Ta mi ag bualadh.

                  Completive Present.
Τετυφα,           I have struck,       Ta mi iar bualadh.

                      ⸺⸺⸺⸺

                  Inceptive Past.
Ευελλον τυπτειν,  I was going to strike, Bha mi dol a bhualadh.

Middle or extended Past.

Ετυπτον,            I was striking,      Bha mi ag bualadh.

Completive Past.

Ετετυφειν,          I had struck,        Bha mi iar bualadh

------

Inceptive Future.

Μελλησω τυπτειν,   I shall be going to Bithidh   mi   dol   a
                    strike,              bhualadh.

Middle or extended Future.

Εσομαι τυπτων,      I shall be striking, Bithidh  mi  ag  bual-
                                         adh.

Completive Future.

Εσομαι τετυφως,     I shall have struck, Bithidh  mi  iar  bual-
                                         adh.


IRREGULAR VERBS OF THE FIRST CONJUGATION.

Beir, *bear.*

ACTIVE VOICE.

Preterite.                    Future.
*Affirm.*  Do rug,            Beiridh.
*Negat.*   D' rug,            Beir.
*Subjunct.* Bheirinn,         Bheireas.
   *Imperat.* Beiream.   *Infin.* Beirsinn, breith.

PASSIVE VOICE.

*Affirm.*  Do rugadh,         Beirear.
*Negat.*   D' rugadh,         Beirear.
*Subjunct.* Bheirteadh,       Bheirear.
   *Imperat.* Beirthear

## Cluinn, *hear.*

### ACTIVE VOICE.

Preterite.            Future.

*Affirm.* Do chuala,      Cluinnidh.
*Negat.* Cuala,         Cluinn.
*Subjunct.* Chluinnin,      Chluinneas.
*Imperat.* Cluinneam. *Infin.* Cluinntinn.

### PASSIVE VOICE.

*Affirm.* Do Chualadh,     Cluinnear.
*Negat.* Cualadh,        Cluinnear.
*Subjunct.* Chluinnteadh,    Chluinneal.
*Imperat.* Cluinntear.

## Dean, *do* or *make.*

### ACTIVE VOICE.

Preterite.            Future.

*Affirm.* Do rinn,        Ni.
*Negat.* D' rinn,         Dean.
*Subjunct.* Dheanainn,     Ni.
*Imperat.* Deanam.    *Infin.* Deanamh.

### PASSIVE VOICE.

*Affirm.* Do rinneadh,      Nithear.
*Negat.* D' rinneadh,      Deanar.
*Subjunct.* Dheantadh,      Nithear.
*Imperat.* Deantar.   *Particip.* Deanta.

## Rach, *go.*

### ACTIVE VOICE.

Preterite.            Future.

*Affirm.* Do chaidh,       Théid.
*Negat.* Deachaidh,      Téid (*q*).
*Subjunct.* Rachainn,      Théid.
*Imperat.* Racham.    *Infin.* Dol.

(*q*) Teid the Fut. Negat. of Rach to *go*, has been generally written

## Ruig, *reach.*

### ACTIVE VOICE.

Preterite.            Future.

*Affirm.*   Do rainig,      Ruigidh.
*Negat.*    D' rainig,       Ruig.
*Subjunct.* Ruiginn,       Ruigeas.
     *Imperat.* Ruigeam.    *Infin.* Ruigsinn, ruigheachd.

## Tabhair, (*r*) *give.*

### ACTIVE VOICE.

Preterite.            Future.

*Affirm.*   Do thug,       Bheir.
*Negat.*    D' thug,        Tabhair.
*Subjunct.* Bheirinn, tabhairinn,    Bheir.
     *Imperat.* Tabhaiream, thugam.    *Infin.* Tabhairt.

### PASSIVE VOICE.

*Affirm.*   Do thugadh,      Bheirear.
*Negat.*    D' thugadh,       Tabhairear.
*Subjunct.* Bheirteadh, tugtadh.    Bheirear.
     *Imperat.* Thugthar.

## Thig, *come.*

### ACTIVE VOICE.

Preterite.            Future.

*Affirm.*   Do thainig,      Thig.
*Negat.*    D' thainig,       Tig (*s*).
*Subjunct.* Thiginn,        Thig.
     *Imperat.* Thigeam.    *Infin.* Tighinn, teachd.

d'theid; from an opinion, it would seem, that the full form of that Tense
is do théid. Yet as the participle *do* is never found prefixed to the Future
Negative of any regular verb, it appears more agreeable to the analogy of
conjugation to write this tense in its simplest form téid. See " Gael. New
Test." 1767, and 1796, Mat. xiii. 28. xiv. 15. A different mode of writing
this tense has been adopted in the edition of the "Gael. Bible," Edin. 1807,
where we uniformly find dthéid, dthoir, dthig.

    (*r*) Throughout the verb tabhair, the syllables *abhair* are often contracted
into *oir ;* as, toir, toirinn, &c. Acts xviii. 10. Sometimes written d'thoir,
d'thoirinn; rather improperly. See the last note (*q*).

    (*s*) Tig rather than d'thig. See the last note (*q*).

### IRREGULAR VERBS OF THE SECOND CONJUGATION.

### Abair, (*t*) *say.*

#### ACTIVE VOICE.

Preterite.                              Future.

*Affirm.* Thubhairt, dubhairt,    Their.
*Negat.* Dubhairt,                Abair.
*Subjunct.* Theirinn, abairinn,   Their.
*Imperat.* Abaiream.    *Infin.* Radh.

#### PASSIVE VOICE.

*Affirm.* Dubhradh,               Theirear.
*Negat.* Dubhradh,                Abairear.
*Subjunct.* Theirteadh, abairteadh, Theirear.
*Imperat.* Abairear (*u*).

### Faic, *see.*

#### ACTIVE VOICE.

Preterite.                              Future.

*Affirm.* Do chunnaic,            Chi.
*Negat.* Faca,                    Faic.
*Subjunct.* Chithinn, faicinn,    Chi.
*Imperat.* Faiceam.    *Infin.* Faicsinn.

#### PASSIVE VOICE.

*Affirm.* Do chunnacadh,          Chithear.
*Negat.* Facadh,                  Faicear.
*Subjunct.* Chiteadh, faicteadh,  Chithear.
*Imperat.* Faicthear.    *Infin.* Faicsinn.

(*t*) A Pres. Aff. of this Verb, borrowed from the Irish, is often used in the G. SS. Deiream *I say*, deir e *he saith*, deir iad *they say.*

(*u*) Dubhairt, dubhradh, are contracted for do thubhairt, &c. Abairinn, abaiream, abairear, are often contracted into abrainn, abram, abrar.

Faigh, *get.*

ACTIVE VOICE.

Preterite.                          Future.

*Affirm.*   Fhuair,                 Gheibh.
*Negat.*    D'fhuair,               Faigh.
*Subjunct.* Gheibhinn, faighinn,    Gheibh.
    *Imperat.* Faigheam.   *Infin.* Faghail, faotainn.

PASSIVE VOICE.

*Affirm.*   Fhuaradh,               Gheibhear.
*Negat.*    D' fhuaradh,            Faighear.
*Subjunct.* Gheibhteadh, faighteadh, Gheibhear.
    *Imperat.* Faightear.

The verbs Tabhair, Abair, Faic, Faigh, have a double Preterite Subjunctive. The latter form of it, which is derived regularly from the Root, is used after the same particles which are prefixed to the Negative Mood, *viz.* ni, cha, nach, mur, gu, an, am.

———

Of Defective Verbs.

The following defective verbs are in common use.

Arsa *said, quoth,* indeclinable; used only in the Pret. Aff. through all the persons; arsa Donull, *quoth Donald.*

Tiucainn *come along,* tiucainnibh *come ye along,* used only in the 2d pers. sing. and plur. of the Imperative.

Theab mi *I was near to, I had almost;* used through all the persons of the Pret. Aff. and Neg.; as, theab iad bhith caillte *they had nearly perished.*

Is mi *I am,* used in the Pres. and Pret. Tenses, which are declined as follows:—

### Affirmative Mood.

| Present. | Preterite. |
|---|---|
| *Sing.* | *Sing.* |
| 1 Is mi, *I am, it is I.* | Bu mhi, *I was, it was I.* |
| 2 Is tu. | Bu tu. |
| 3 Is e. | B' e. |
| *Plur.* | *Plur.* |
| 1 Is sinn. | Bu sinn. |
| 2 Is sibh. | Bu sibh. |
| 3 Is iad. | B' iad. |

### Negative Mood.

| | | *Sing.* | *Sing.* |
|---|---|---|---|
| ni, | 1 | mi, *I am not, &c.* | Bu mhi, *I was not, &c.* |
| cha, | 2 | tu. | Bu tu. |
| nach, | 3 | e. | B' e. |
| &c. | | *Plur.* | *Plur.* |
| | 1 | sinn. | Bu sinn. |
| | 2 | sibh. | Bu sibh. |
| | 3 | iad. | B' iad. |

### Subjunctive Mood.

| *Sing.* | *Sing.* |
|---|---|
| 1 Ma 's mi, *If I be, it be I.* | Nam bu mhi, *If I were, it were I.* |
| 2 's tu. | Bu tu. |
| 3 's e. | B' e. |
| *Plur.* | *Plur.* |
| 1 's sinn. | Bu sinn. |
| 2 's sibh. | Bu sibh. |
| 3 's iad. | B' iad. |

The only varieties of form which this Verb admits of, are the two syllables *is* and *bu.* Each of these syllables commonly loses the vowel when it comes in apposition with another vowel.

It is remarkable, that in the Pres. Neg. the Verb disappears altogether, and the preceding Particle, ni, cha, nach, gur, &c., and the subsequent Pronoun, or Noun, are always understood to convey a proposition, or a question, as unequivocally as though a Verb had been expressed ; as, cha tu *thou art not,* nach e ? *is he not ?* is it not he ? am mise e ? *is it I ?* cha luchd-brathaidh sinn *we are not spies,* Gen. xlii. 31. Am mò thusa na Abraham? *Art thou greater than Abraham ?* gur còir urnuigh a dheanamh *that it is proper to pray,* Luke xviii. 1 (*x*).

(*x*) It may appear an odd peculiarity in the Gaelic, that in many of the most common phrases, a proposition or question should thus be expressed without the least trace of a Verb. It can hardly be said that the Substantive Verb is *understood,* for then there would be no impropriety in express-ing it. But the fact is, that it would be completely contrary to the idiom and usage of the language, to introduce a Substantive Verb in these phrases. It will diminish our surprise at this peculiarity to observe that in the ancient languages numerous examples occur of sentences, or clauses of sentences, in which the Substantive Verb is omitted, without occasioning any obscurity or ambiguity ; and this in Prose as well as in Verse. Thus in Hebrew ; Gen. xlii. 11, 13, 14. We [are] all one man's sons—we [are] true men—thy servants [are] twelve brethren—the youngest [is] with his father—ye [are] spies—&c.

'Ουκ ἀγαθον πολυκοιρανιη.—*Iliad,* B. 204.
κακα κερδεα ἰσ' ἀτησι.—*Hes.* E. και H. d.
ἐγω δε τισου ταχυπειθης.—*Theoc. Idyl.* 7.
Et mî genus ab Jove summo.—*Virg. Æn.* VI. 123.
Varium et mutabile semper Femina.—*Æn.* IV. 569.

Omnia semper suspecta atque sollicita ; nullus locus amicitiæ. *Cic. de Amic.* 15.

Fennis mira feritas, foeda paupertas ; non arma, non equi, non penates ; victui herba, vestitui pelles, cubile humus ; sola in sagittis spes, &c.—*Tacit. de. mor. Germ. Cap. ult.* In these and the like examples, the Substantive Verb might have been expressed, if with less elegance, yet without grammatical impropriety. What has been frequently done in other languages, seems, in Gaelic, to have been adopted, in certain phrases, as an invariable mode of speech.

The omission of the Substantive Verb is not unknown in English ; as,

" In winter awful thou."—*Thomson.*
" A ministering angel thou."—*Scott.*
" A cruel sister she."—*Mallet.*

OF THE RECIPROCATING STATE OF VERBS.

Any transitive Verb may be so combined with a Pronoun, either Personal or Possessive, that it shall denote the agent to be also the object of the action. This may be called the *reciprocating state* of the Verb. It is declined as follows:—

Buail thu fein, *strike thyself.*

### ACTIVE VOICE.

### Simple Tenses.

#### *Affirmative Mood.*

| Preterite. | Future. |
|---|---|
| *Sing.* | *Sing.* |
| 1 Do bhuail mi mi fein, | Buailidh mi mi fein, |
| Bhuail mi mi fein, | *I will strike myself.* |
| *I struck myself.* | |
| 2 Do bhuail thu thu fein, | Buailidh tu thu fein. |
| 3 Do bhuail se e fein ; | Buailidh se e fein. |

| *Plur.* | *Plur.* |
|---|---|
| 1 Do bhuail sinn sinn fein, | Buailidh sinn sinn fein. |
| 2 Do bhuail sibh sibh fein, | Buailidh sibh sibh fein. |
| 3 Do bhuail siad iad fein. | Buailidh siad iad fein. |

#### *Negative Mood.*

| Preterite. | Future. |
|---|---|
| *Sing.* | *Sing.* |
| cha, { 1 Do bhuail mi mi fein, | Bhuail mi mi fein, |
| &c. { *I struck not myself.* | *I shall not strike myself.* |

#### *Subjunctive Mood.*

| *Sing.* | *Sing.* |
|---|---|
| 1 Bhuailinn mi fein, | 1 Bhuaileas mi mi fein, |
| *I would strike myself.* | *I shall strike myself.* |

*Imperative Mood.*

*Sing.*            *Plur.*

1 Buaileam mi fein,      Buaileamaid sinn fein.
    *Let me strike myself.*
2 Buail thu fein.         Buailibh sibh fein.
3 Buaileadh e e fein.     Buaileadh iad iad fein.

*Infinitive Mood.*

'g am bhualadh fein, *striking myself.*
'g ad bhualadh fein, *striking thyself.*
'g a bhualadh fein, *striking himself.*
'g ar bualadh fein, *striking ourselves.*
'g 'ur bualadh fein, *striking yourselves.*
'g am bualadh fein, *striking themselves.*
iar mo bhualadh fein, *after striking myself, &c.*
gu mo bhualadh fein, *to strike myself, &c.*

Compound Tenses.

*Affirmative Mood.*

Present.          Preterite.

1. *Comp.*          1. *Comp.*

Ta mi 'g am bhualadh fein,    Bha mi 'g am bhualadh fein,
*I am striking myself.*      *I was striking myself.*

Future.

1. *Comp.*

Bidh mi 'g am bhualadh fein,
*I will be striking myself.*

Present.          Preterite.

2. *Comp.*          2. *Comp.*

Ta mi iar mo, &c.      Bha mi iar mo, &c.
*I have struck myself.*     *I had struck myself.*

Future.

2. *Comp.*

Bidh mi iar mo, &c.
*I shall have struck, &c.*

### Negative Mood.

| Present. | Preterite. |
|---|---|
| 1. *Comp.* | 1. *Comp.* |
| Ni bheil mi 'g am, &c. | Ni robh mi 'g am, &c. |
| *I am not striking myself.* | *I was not striking myself.* |

Future.

1. *Comp.*

Ni'm bi mi 'g am bhualadh fein.
*I shall not be striking myself.*

| Present. | Preterite. |
|---|---|
| 2. *Comp.* | 2. *Comp.* |
| Ni bheil mi iar mo, &c. | Ni robh mi iar mo, &c. |
| *I have not struck myself.* | *I had not struck myself.* |

Future.

2. *Comp.*

Ni'm bi mi iar mo, &c.
*I shall not have struck myself.*

### Subjunctive Mood.

| Preterite. | Future. |
|---|---|
| 1. *Comp.* | 1. *Comp.* |
| Bhithinn 'g am, &c. | Ma bhitheas mi 'g am, |
| *I would be striking, &c.* | *If I shall be striking, &c.* |
| 2. *Comp.* | 2. *Comp.* |
| Bhithinn iar mo, &c. | Ma bhitheas mi iar mo, &c. |
| *I would have struck, &c.* | *If I shall have struck, &c.* |

| *Imperative Mood.* | *Infinitive Mood.* |
|---|---|

1. *Comp.*               Do bhith 'g am bhualadh fein,
                          *To be striking myself.*
Bitheam 'g am bhualadh fein, Iar bith 'g am bhualadh fein.
*Let me be striking myself.*   *To have been striking myself.*

From the foregoing example it appears that the Verb, in its reciprocating state, retains its original form throughout its several Moods, Tenses, and Persons. In the *simple Tenses*, the Personal Pronoun immediately following the Verb is the Nominative to the Verb. The same pronoun repeated is to be understood as in the objective state. The word fein, corresponding to the English *self*, accompanies the last Pronoun.

In the *compound Tenses*, the auxiliary Verb, as usual, is placed first; then follows the Personal Pronoun as its Nominative; then the Prep. *ag* abridged to *'g* in the compound Tenses of the first order, iar in those of the second order ; after which follows the Possessive Pronoun, corresponding in Person to that which is the Nominative to the Verb ; and lastly the Infinitive, which is the' noun to the Possessive Pronoun. Mo and do are here changed, by Metathesis and the substitution of one broad vowel for another, into am and ad. Ta mi 'g am bhualadh fein, rendered literally, is, *I am at my own striking, i.e., I am at the striking of myself*, equivalent to, *I am striking myself.* The reciprocal fein is sometimes omitted in the compound Tenses, but is generally retained in the 3d Persons, to prevent their being mistaken for the same persons when used without reciprocation : ta e 'g a bhualadh, *he is striking him*, ta e 'g a bhualadh fein, *he is striking himself.*

### OF THE IMPERSONAL USE OF VERBS.

Intransitive Verbs, though they do not regularly admit of a Passive Voice, yet are used *impersonally* in the 3d Pers. Sing. of the Passive Tenses. This impersonal use of the Passive of intransitive Verbs is founded on the same principle with the Latin Impersonals *concurritur, pugnatum est,*

&c., which are equivalent to *concursus fit, pugna facta est.*
So in Gælic, gluaisfear leam, *I will move,* Psal. cxvi. 9;
gluaisfear leo, *they will move,* Psal. cxix. 3; ghuileadh leinn,
*we did weep,* flebatur a nobis, Psal. cxxxvii. 1, Edit. Edinb.
1787; cha bhithear saor o pheacadh, *there wanteth not sin,*
Prov. x. 19.

To the class of Impersonals ought to be referred a certain
part of the Verb which has not yet been mentioned. It
resembles in form the Fut. Negat. Passive; buailear, faicear,
faighear, &c. In signification, it is Active, Present, and
Affirmative. In the course of a narrative, when the speaker
wishes to enliven his style by representing the occurrences
narrated as present, and passing actually in view, instead of
the Preterite Tenses, he adopts the Part of the Verb now
described, employing it in an impersonal acceptation, without a Nominative to it expressed. One or two examples
will serve to exhibit the use and effect of this anomalous
Tense:—Shuidh an òg bhean air sgeir, is a sùil air an lear.—
Chunnaic i long a' teachd air barraibh nan tonn. Dh'
aithnich i aogas a leannain, is chlisg a cridhe 'n a com. Gun
mhoille gun tamh, *buailear* dh' fhios na traighe; agus *faighear*
an laoch, 's a dhaoine m' a thimchioll. In English thus: The
young woman sat on a rock, and her eye on the sea. She
spied a ship coming on the tops of the waves. She perceived the likeness of her lover, and her heart bounded in
her breast. Without delay or stop, she *hastens* to the shore;
and *finds* the hero, with his men around him. Again:
Mar sin chuir sinn an oidhche tharuinn. 'S a' mhadainn dh'
imich sinn air ar turus. O bha sinn 'n ar coigrich anns an tìr,
*gabhar* suas gu mullach an t-sleibh, *direar* an tulach gu grad,
agus *seallar* mu 'n cuairt air gach toabh. *Faicear* thall fa 'r
comhair sruth cas ag ruith le gleann cumhann, &c. Thus
we passed the night. In the morning we pursued our
journey. As we were strangers in the land, we *strike* up to
the top of the moor, *ascend* the hill with speed, and *look*
around us on every side. We *see* over against us a rapid
stream, rushing down a narrow valley, &c.

The scrupulons chastenesss of style maintained in the
Gaelic version of the Sacred Scriptures, has totally excluded
this form of expression.   It is, however, universally known
and acknowledged, as an established idiora of the Gaelic,
very common in the mouths of those who speak it, and in
animated narration almost indispensable (*y*).

## Of Auxiliary Verbs.

It has been already shown how bi *be*, is used as an
Auxiliary in the declension of all verbs.   There are two
other verbs which are occasionally employed in a similar
capacity ; the one with an Active the other with a Passive
effect.   These are dean to *do* or *make*, and rach to *go*.

The simple tenses of dean combined with the Infinitive
of any verb, correspond to the English auxiliary *do, did*.   It
sometimes adds to the emphasis, but not to the sense.   The
following are examples of this Auxiliary combined with the
Infinitive of an *Intransitive* verb:—Rinn  e seasamh *he made
standing*, i.e., *he did stand ;* dean suidhe *make sitting*, i.e.,
*sit down ;* dheanainn gul agus caoidh *I would make weeping*

(*y*) The effect of this Tense in narration seems to be very nearly, if not
precisely, the same with that of the Present of the Infinitive in Latin ; as
in these passages :

"——misere discedere quaerens,
*Ire* modo ocius ; interdum *consistere ;* in aurem
*Dicere* nescio quid puero."          *Hor. Sat.* 1. 8. *v.* 9.

" At Danaum proceres, Agamemnoniæque phalanges
Ingenti *trepidare* metu ; pars *vertere* terga,
Ceu quondam petiêre rates ; pars *tollere* vocem."
*Æneid. VI.* 492.

"  ——nihil illi *tendere* contra ;
Sed *celerare* fugam  in sylvas, et *fidere* nocti.'
*Æneid. IX.* 378.

" Tarquinius *fateri* amorem, *orare, miscere* precibus minas, *versare* in
omnes partes muliebrem animum."—*Liv. I.* 58.

" Neque post id locorum Jugurthæ dies aut nox ulla quieta fuere : neque
loco, neque mortali cuiquam, aut tempori satis *credere ;* cives, hostes, juxta
*metuere ; circumspectare* omnia, et omni strepitu *pavescere ;* alio atque alio
loco, saepe contra decus regium, noctu *requiescere ;* interdum somno excitus,
arreptis armis, tumultum *facere ;* ita formidine quasi vecordia *exagitari.*"
—*Sall. Bell. Jugur.* 72.

*and lamentation*, i.e., *I would weep and lament.* The same arrangement takes place when the Auxiliary is combined with the Infinitive of a *Transitive* verb, accompanied by a possessive pronoun ; as, rinn e mo bhualadh *he made my striking*, i.e., *he made [or caused] the striking of me*, or, *he did strike me ;* cha dean mi do mholadh, *I will not make your praising*, i.e., *I will not praise you ;* dean do gharadh, *make your warming*, dean do gharadh fein, *make your own warming*, i.e., *warm yourself.*

The Simple Tenses of rach, combined with the Infinitive of a transitive verb, correspond to the Passive Voice of the verb ; as, chaidh mo bhualadh *my striking went*, i.e., *came to pass*, or *happened*, equivalent to *I was struck;* rachadh do mharbhadh *your killing would happen*, i.e., *you would be killed.*

In phrases where either of the auxiliaries dean or rach is combined with a transitive verb, as above, the possessive pronoun may be exchanged for the corresponding personal pronoun in the emphatic form, followed by the preposition *do* before the Infinitive. The preposition in this case is attenuated into *a*, which, before a verb of the second conjugation is dropped altogether. Thus, rinn e mo bhualadh *he struck me*, rinn e mis' a bhualadh *he struck* ME, chaidh mo bhualadh *I was struck*, chaidh mis' a bhualadh *I myself was struck.* In like manner, a noun, or a demonstrative pronoun, may occupy the place of this personal pronoun; as, chaidh an ceannard a mharbhadh (*z*), agus na daoine chur san ruaig, *the leader was killed, and the men put to flight ;* theid am buachaill a bhualadh, agus an treud a sgapadh, *the shepherd will be smitten, and the sheep scattered ;* is math a chaidh sin innseadh dhuit, *that was well told you.*

(*z*) "An ceannard a mharbhadh " may be considered as the nominative to the verb chaidh ; and so in similar phrases ; much in the same way as we find in Latin, an Infinitive with an accusative before it, become the nominative to a verb; as,"*hominem* hominis incommodo suum *augere* commodum *est* contra naturam." *Cic. de. Offic.* III. 5. " Turpe *est eos* qui bene nati sunt turpiter *vivere.*"

# CHAPTER VI.

## OF ADVERBS.

An Adverb, considered as a separate part of speech, is a single indeclinable word, significant of time, place, or any other circumstance or modification of an action or attribute. The number of simple Adverbs in Gaelic is but small. Adverbial phrases, made up of two or more words, are sufficiently numerous. Any adjective may be converted into an adverbial expression, by prefixing to it the preposition gu *to;* as, fìrinneach *true,* gu fìrinneach [*corresponding*] *to* [*what is*] *true,* κατα το αληθες, i.e., *truly.* Adverbs of this form need not be enumerated. It may be useful, however, to give a list of other adverbs and adverbial phrases, most commonly in use; subjoining, where it can be done, a literal translation of their component parts, and also the English expression which corresponds most nearly to the sense of the Gaelic phrase.

### *Adverbs of Time.*

A cheana ; already, truly.

A chianamh ; a little while ago.

A chlisge ; quickly, in a trice.

A choidhche,
Choidh; } for ever.

A nis,
Nise ; } now.

A ris,
Rithist ; } again.

Ainmic,
Ainmeach ; } seldom.

Air ball ; *on* [*the*] *spot,* immediately.

Air dheireadh ; hindmost.

Air thoiseach ; foremost.

Air tùs ; in the beginning, at first.

Air uairibh ; *at times,* sometimes.

Am bliadhna ; this year.

Am feadh ; whilst.

Am feasd ; for ever.

Am màireach ; to-morrow.

An ceart uair ; *the very hour*, presently.

An comhnuidh ; *in continuation*, continually.

An dé ; yesterday.

An deigh laimh ; *behind hand*, afterwards.

An diugh ; *the [present] day*, to-day (*a*).

An ear-thrath, } *the after time*, the day after to-morrow.
An iar-thraith ;

An nochd ; *the [present] night*, to-night.

An raoir, } yesternight.
An reidhr ,

An sin ; *in that [time]*, then.

An trath ; *the time*, when.

An tràth so, } *this time*, at present.
An tràs' ;

An uair ; *the time*, when.

An uiridh ; last year.

Aon uair ; *one time*, once.

Cia fhada ; how long.

Cia minic, } how often.
Cia tric ;

C'uine ; *what time*, when.

Do la, } by day (*b*)
A la ;

Dh' oidhche ; by night (*b*).

Do ghnàth ; *[according] to custom*, always.

Fa dheoidh ; *at the end*, at last.

Fathast, } yet, still.
Fòs ;

(*a*) So in Hebrew, the article prefixed to the nouns *day, night*, imports the present day or night.   See Exod. xiv. 13.

(*b*) Perhaps the proper Prep. in these phrases is *de*, not *do*—see the Prepositions in the next Chap.—as we find the same Prep. similarly applied in other languages ; de nuit *by night*, John iii. 2 ; de nocte, Hor. Epis. 1. 2, 32; de tertia vigilia, Cæs. B. G.

Gu bràth (c),  } to the general conflagration, for ever.
Gu la bhràth ; }

Gu dìlinn (c); to the expiration of time, or till the deluge, for ever.

Gu minic ; often.

Gu siorruidh ; to ever-flowing, for ever.

Gu suthainn ; for ever.

Gu tric ; often.

Idir ; at all.

Mar tha ; as it is, already.

Mu dheireadh ; at last.

O cheann tamuill ; a while ago.

O chian ; from far, of old, long ago.

Rè seal,       } for a time.
Rè tamuill ;  }

Riamh ; ever, said of past time only.

Roimh làimh ; before hand.

Uair eigin ; some time.

### Adverbs of Place.

A bhos,   } on this side, here below.
Bhos ;    }

A leth taobh ; to one side, aside.

A mach,   } without, out.
A muigh ; }

A mhàn (d) ; downwards, down.

An aird ; to the height, upwards, up.

A nall,  } to this side.
Nall ;   }

A nuas ; from above, down hither.

A null,        } to the other side.
Null, nunn ;  }

(c) These expressions are affirmed, not without reason, to refer to the supposed destruction of the world by fire, or by water ; events which were considered as immeasurably remote. (See Smith's "Gal. Antiq." pp. 59. 60). Another explanation has been given of dìlinn, as being compounded of dith, want, failure, and linn an age ; qu. absumptio sæculi.

(d) Perhaps am fàn, from fàn or fànadh a descent. (See Lhuyd's "Arch. Brit." tit. x. in loco.)

A thaobh ; aside.

Air aghaidh, ⎫
Air adhart ;  ⎬ *on* [*the*] *face*, forward.

Air ais ; backwards.

Air dheireadh ; hindmost,

Air thoiseach ; foremost.

Am fad,  ⎫
An céin ; ⎬ afar.

An gar ; close to.

An laimh ; in hand, in custody.

An sin ; *in that* [*place*], there.

An so ; *in this* [*place*], here.

An sud ; *in yon* [*place*], yonder.

An taice ; close adjoining, in contact.

Asteach, ⎫
Astigh ;  ⎬ (*e*) within, in.

C' àite ; *what place*, where.

Cia an taobh ; *what side*, whither.

C' ionadh ; *what place*, whither.

Fad as ; afar off.

Fad air astar ; far away.

Far ; where,—relatively.

Fogus,   ⎫
Am fogus ; ⎬ near.

H-uig' agus uaith ; to and fro.

Iolar, ⎫
Ioras ; ⎬ below there, below yonder.

Le leathad ; *by a descent*, downwards.

Leis ; *along with it*, down a stream, declivity, &c.

Mu 'n cuairt ; *by the circuit*, around.

Ri bruthach ; *to an ascent*, upwards.

Ris ; in an exposed state, bare, uncovered.

Seachad ; past, aside.

Sios, a sios ; downwards.

Suas, a suas ; upwards.

---

(*e*) *i.e.* anns an teach, anns an tigh, *in the house.* So in Hebrew, מבית *within*, Gen. vi. 14.

Shios ; below there, below yonder.
Shuas ; above there, above yonder.
Tarsuing ; across.
Thairis ; over.
Thall ; on the other side.
Uthard ; above there, above yonder.

Deas (*f*) ; south.
Gu deas ; southward.
A deas ; from the south.

Iar (*g*),   } west.
Siar ;     }
Gus an aird an iar ; westward.
O'n iar ; from the west.

Tuath ; north.
Gu tuath ; northward.
A tuath ; from the north.

Ear, Oir, Soir ; east.
Gus an aird an ear ; eastward.
O'n ear ; from the east.

### Adverbs of Manner.

Air achd ; in a manner.
Air a' chuthach,   } distracted, mad.
Air boile ;       }
Air chall ; lost.
Air chòir ; aright.
Air chor ; in a manner.
Air chor eigin ; in some manner, somehow.
Air chuairt ; sojourning.
Air chuimhne ; in remembrance.
Air éigin ; with difficulty, scarcely.
Air fogradh ; in exile, in a fugitive state.

(*r*) Deas, applied to the hand, signifies the *right hand*. So in Hebrew, ימין signifies the *right hand* and the *South*.

(*g*) Iar, as a Preposition, signifies *after* or *behind*. In like manner in Hebrew, אחר signifies *after*, or the *West*.

Air ghleus; in trim.

Air iomadan; adrift.

Air iomroll; astray.

Air iunndrain; amissing.

Air lagh; { trimmed for action, as a bow bent, a firelock cocked, &c.

Air leth; apart, separately.

Air seacharan; astray.

Air sgeul; found, not lost.

Amhàin; only.

Amhuil,
Amhludh; } like as.

Am bidheantas; customarily, habitually.

Am feabhas; convalescent, improving.

An coinnimh a chinn; headlong.

An coinnimh a chùil; backwards.

An deidh,
An geall; } desirous, enamoured.

An nasgaidh; for nothing, gratis.

An tòir; in pursuit.

Araon; together.

As an aghaidh; *out of the face*, to the face, outright.

As a chéile; loosened, disjointed.

Car air char; rolling, tumbling over and over.

Cia mar; *as how*, how.

C' arson; *on account of what*, why, wherefore.

C' ionnas; *what manner*, how.

Cha, cho; not.

Comhla (*h*), mar chomhla,
Cuideachd; } together, in company.

C'uime; for what, why.

Do dheoin, a dheoin; spontaneously, intentionally.

Dh' aindeoin; against one's will.

Do dhìth, a dhìth; a-wanting.

Do rìreadh; really, actually, indeed.

(*h*) Probably co luath *equally quick, with equal pace.*

Fa leth ; severally, individually.

Gle ; very.

Gu beachd ; *to observation*, evidently, clearly.

Gu buileach ; *to effect*, thoroughly, wholly.

Gu dearbh ; *to conviction*, truly, certainly.

Gu deimhin ; *to assurance*, assuredly, verily.

Gu leir ; altogether.

Gu leor ; *to sufficiency*, enough.

Gun amharus ; *without doubt*, doubtless.

Gun chàird ; *without rest*, incessantly, without hesitation.

Leth mar leth ; half and half.

Le chéile ; *with each other*, together.

Maraon ; *as one*, together, in concert.

Mar an ceudna ; in like manner, likewise.

Mar sin ; *as that*, in that manner.

Mar so ; *as this*, thus.

Mar sud ; *as yon*, in yon manner.

Mu seach ; in return, alternately.

Na, Nar ; let not,—used optatively, or imperatively.

Nach ; that not, who not, not?

Ni ; not.

Ni h-eadh (*i*) ; it is not so.

Os àird ; openly.

Os barr ; *on top*, besides.

Os iosal ; secretly, covertly.

Ro ; very.

Roimh a cheile ; prematurely, too hastily.

Seadh (*i*) ; it is so.

Thar a chéile, ⎫
Troimh a chéile ; ⎭ in disorder, in confusion, stirred about.

Theagamh ; perhaps.

Uidh air 'n uidh ; *stage by stage*, gradually.

(*i*) The probable analysis of seadh is, is *é*, *it is*, pronounced in one syllable, 's e. When this syllable was used as a responsive, and not followed by any other word ; the voice, resting on the final sound, formed a faint articulation. This was represented in writing by the gentle aspirate *dh ;* and so the word came to be written as we find it. In like manner ni h-eadh is probably nothing else than a substitute for ni he, *it is not.*

# CHAPTER VII.

## OF PREPOSITIONS.

THE Prepositions, strictly so called, are single words, most of them monosyllables, employed to mark relation. Relation is also expressed by combinations of words which often correspond to simple prepositions in other languages. These combinations are, not improperly, ranked among the prepositions. The following lists contain first the Prepositions properly so called, which are all simple; secondly, improper Prepositions, which, with one or two exceptions, seem all to be made up of a simple Preposition and a Noun.

### Proper Prepositions.

| | | |
|---|---|---|
| Aig, Ag, *at.* | Gu, Gus, *to.* | Roimh, *before.* |
| Air, *on.* | Gun, *without.* | Tar, Thar, *over, accross.* |
| Ann, *in.* | Iar, *after.* | Tre, |
| As, A, *out of.* | Le, Leis, *with, by.* | Troimh, } *through.* |
| De, *of.* | Mar, *like to.* | Throimh, |
| Do, *to.* | Mu, *about.* | Seach, *past, in compari-* |
| Eadar, *between.* | O, Ua, *from.* | [*son with.* |
| Fa, *upon.* | Os, *above.* | |
| Fuidh, Fo, *under.* | Re, Ri, Ris, *to.* | |

The Preposition ann is often written double, ann an eolas, *in knowledge;* ann an gliocas, *in wisdom.* The final *n* or *nn* is changed into *m* before a labial; as, am measg, *among;* ann am meadhon, *in midst.* Before the Article or the Relative, this Preposition is written anns; as, anns an toiseach, *in the beginning;* an cor anns am bheil e, *the condition in which he is;* and in this situation the letters *ann* are often dropped, and the *s* alone retained, 's an toiseach, *in the beginning.*

De, so far as I know, is found in no Scottish publications. The reasons which have induced me to assign it a place among the prepositions will be mentioned in treating of the combinations of the Proper Prepositions with the Personal Pronouns.

The Preposition *do,* like the verbal particle, and the Possessive Pronoun of the same sound, loses the *o* before a vowel, and the consonant is aspirated; thus, dh' Albainn, *to Scot-*

*land.*  It is also preceded sometimes by the vowel *a* when it
follows a final consonant ; as, dol a dh' Eirin, *going to Ireland.*
This *a* seems to be nothing else than the vowel of *do* transposed ; just as the letters of the pronouns mo, do, are in certain
situations transposed, and become am, ad.    In this situation,
perhaps it would be advisible to join the *a*, in writing, to the
*dh* thus, dol adh Eirin.    This would rid us of one superfluous
*a* appearing as a separate inexplicable word.    The same remarks
apply to the prep. *de* ; *e.g.*, armailt mhòr de dhaoinibh agus *a*
*dh* eachaibh, *a great army of men and of horses*, lan do [de]
reubainn agus a dh' aingidheachd, *full of ravining and wicked-*
*ness*, Luke xi. 39.   Do, as has been already observed, often loses
the *d* altogether, and is written *a;* as, dol a Dhuneidin, *going*
*to Edinburgh.*    When the preposition is thus robbed of its articulation, and only a feeble obscure vowel sound is left, another
corruption very naturally follows, and this vowel, as well as the
consonant, is discarded, not only in speaking, but even in
writing; as, chaidh e Dhuneidin,  *he went to Edinburgh;*
chaidh e thìr eile, *he went to another land;* where the nouns appear in their aspirated form, without any word to govern them.

Fa has been improperly confounded with fuidh or fo.
That fa signifies *upon*, is manifest from such phrases as fa
'n bhord, *upon the board*, said of a dead body stretched upon
a board; leigeader fa làr, *dropped on the ground*, Carswell : fa
'n adhbhar ud, *on that account*, equivalent to air an adhbhar
ud. see Psal. cvi. 42, and xlv. 2, metr. version.  •

The reason for admitting iar *after*, has been already given
in treating of the Compound Tenses of Verbs in Chap. V.

The manner of combining these prepositions with nouns
will be shown in treating of Syntax.    The manner of combining them with the personal pronouns must be explained in
this place, because in that connection they appear in a form
somewhat different from their radical form.    A Proper Preposition is joined to a Personal Pronoun by incorporating
both into one word, commonly with some change on the
Preposition, or on the Pronoun, or on both.

The following are the Prepositions which admit of this kind of
combination, incorporated with the several Personal Pronouns :

| Prep. | Singular. | | |
|---|---|---|---|
| | *1st Pers.* | *2d Pers.* | *3d Pers.* |
| Aig, } *at.* <br> Ag; | agam, <br> *at me,* | agad, <br> *at thee.* | m. aige, <br> *at him;* <br> f. aice, <br> *at her.* |
| Air; | orm, | ort. | m. air. <br> f. oirre. <br> uirre. <br> orra. |
| Ann; | annam, | annad, | m. ann. <br> f. innte. |
| As; | asam, | asad, | m. as. <br> f. aisde. |
| De; | dhiom, | dhiot, | m. dheth. <br> f. dh'i. |
| Do; | { dhomh, <br> dhom, } | dhuit, | m. dha. <br> f. dh'i. |
| Eadar; | ... | ... | ... |
| Fo, Fuidh; | fodham, | fodhad, | m. fodha. <br> f. fuidhpe |
| Gu; | h-ugam, | h-ugad, | m. h-uige. <br> f. h-uice. |
| Le; | leam, | leat, | m. leis. <br> f. leatha. |
| Mu; | umam, | umad, | m. uime. <br> f. uimpe. |
| O, Ua; | uam, | uait, | m. uaith. <br> f. uaipe. |
| Re, Ri; | rium, | riut, | m. ris. <br> f. rithe. |
| Roimh; | romham, | romhad, | m. roimhe. <br> f. roimpe. |
| Thar; | tharam, | tharad, | f. thairte. |
| Troimh; | tromham, | tromhad, | m. troimhe. <br> f. troimpe. |

**Plural.**

| 1st Pers. | 2d Pers. | 3d Pers. |
|---|---|---|
| againn, *at us.* | agaibh, *at you.* | aca, *at them.* |
| oirnn, | oirbh, | orra. |
| annainn, | annaibh, | annta. |
| asainn, | asaibh, | asda. |
| dhinn, | dhibh, | dhiu. |
| dhuinn, | dhuibh, | dhoibh. |
| eadarainn, | eadaraibh, | eatorra. |
| fodhainn, | fodhaibh. | fodhpa. |
| h-ugainn, | h-ugaibh, | h-uca. |
| leinn, | leibh, | leo. |
| umainn, | umaibh, | umpa. |
| uainn, | uaibh, | uapa. |
| ruinn, | ribh, | riu. |
| romhainn, | romhaibh, | rompa. |
| tharuinn, | tharuibh, | tharta. |
| tromhainn, | tromhaibh, | trompa. |

In most of these compound terms, the fragments of the Pronouns which enter into their composition, especially those of the first and second Persons, are very conspicuous (*j*). These fragments take after them occasionally the emphatic syllables *sa, san, ne,* in the same manner as the Personal Pronouns themselves do: as, agamsa *at ME,* aigesan *at HIM,* uainne *from US.*

The two prepositions *de* and *do* have long been confounded together, both being written *do.* It can hardly be supposed that the composite words dhiom, dhiot, &c. would have been distinguished from dhomh, dhuit, &c., by orthography, pronunciation, and signification, if the Prepositions, as well as the Pronouns, which enter into the composition of these words, had been originally the same. In dhiom, &c., the initial Consonant is always followed by a small vowel. In dhomh, &c., with one exception, it is followed by a broad vowel. Hence it is presumable that the Preposition which is the root of dhiom, &c., must have had a small vowel after *d,* whereas the root of dhomh, &c., has a broad vowel after *d.* *De* is a preposition preserved in Latin (a language which has many marks of affinity with the Gaelic), in the same sense which must have belonged to the root of dhiom, &c., in Gaelic. The preposition in question itself occurs in Irish, in the name given to a Colony which is supposed to have settled in Ireland, A.M. 2540, called Tuath de Danann. (See Lh. "Arch. Brit." tit. x. *voc.* Tuath; also Miss Brooke's "Reliques of Irish Poetry," p. 102.) These facts afford more than a presumption that the true root of the Composite dhiom, &c., is *de,* and that it signifies *of.* It has therefore appeared proper to separate it from *do,* and to assign to each its appropriate meaning (*k*).

(*j*) This mode of incorporating the Prepositions with the personal pronouns will remind the Orientalist of the Pronominal Affixes, common in Hebrew and other Eastern languages. The close resemblance between the Gaelic and many of the Asiatic tongues, in this particular, is of itself an almost conclusive proof that the Gaelic bears a much closer affinity to the parent stock than any other living European language.

(*k*) " In corroboration of this (Mr. S.'s) hypothesis, I have frequently met

Dhiom, dhiot, &c., and dhomh, dhuit, &c., are written with a *plain* d after a Lingual; diom, domh, &c.

Eadar is not incorporated with the pronouns of the singular number, but written separately; eadar mis agus thusa, *between me and thee.*

In combining *gu* and *mu* with the pronouns, the letters of the Prepositions suffer a transposition, and are written *ug*, *um*. The former of these was long written with *ch* prefixed, thus chugam, &c. The translators of the Scriptures, observing that *ch* neither corresponded to the pronunciation, nor made part of the radical Preposition, exchanged it for *th*, and wrote thugam. The *th*, being no more than a simple aspiration, corresponds indeed to the common mode of pronouncing the word. Yet it may well be questioned whether the *t*, even though aspirated, ought to have a place, if *g* be the only radical consonant belonging to the Preposition. The component parts of the word might be exhibited with less disguise, and the common pronunciation (whether correct or not), also represented, by retaining the *h* alone, and connecting it with the Preposition by a hyphen, as when written before a Noun; thus h-ugam, h-ugaibh, &c.

### Improper Prepositions.

Air cheann; *at* [*the*] *end*, against a certain time.

Air feadh, } throughout, during.
Air fad;

Air muin; *on the back*, mounted on.

Air sgàth; for the sake, on pretence.

Air son ; on account.

Air tòir ; in pursuit.

Air beulaobh; *on the fore side*, before.

Air culaobh ; *on the back side*, behind.

Am fochair ; *in presence.*

Am measg ; *in the mixture*, amidst, among.

---

*de* in old MSS. I have therefore adopted it in its proper place."—E. O'C.'s "Grammar of the Irish Gaelic." Dublin, 1808.

An aghaidh, *in the face*, against, in opposition.

An ceann ; *in the end*, at the expiration.

An comhail,  
An coinnimh ; } *in meeting*, to meet.

An cois,  
A chois ; } *at the foot*, near to, hard by.

An dàil ; *in the rencounter*, to meet.

An diaigh,  
An deigh,  
An deaghaidh, } probably for an deireadh; } in the end, after.  
An déis,

An eiric ; in return, in requital.

Am fianuis,  
An lathair ; } in presence.

An lorg ; *in the track*, in consequence.

As eugais,  
As easbhuidh ; } *in want*, without.

As leth ; in behalf, for the sake.

A los ; in order to, with the intention of.

Car ; during.

Do bhrigh, a bhrigh ; *by virtue*, because.

Do chòir, a chòir; *to the presence*, near, implying motion.

Do chum, a chum (*l*) ; to, towards, in order to.

Do dhìth, a dhìth,  
Dh' easbhuidh ; } for want.

Dh' fhios ; *to the knowledge*, to.

Dh' ionnsuidh, *to the approach*, or *onset*, toward.

Do réir, a réir ; according to.

Do thaobh, a thaobh ; *on the side*, with respect, concerning.

Fa chùis ; by reason, because.

Fa chomhair ; opposite.

Mu choinnimh ; opposite, over against.

Mu thimchoill, timchioll ; *by the circuit*, around.

O bharr, bharr ; *from the top*, off.

Os ceann ; *on the top*, above, atop.

(*l*) In many places, this Prep. is pronounced **hun.**

Ré; *duration*, during.
Taréis; *after (m)*.
Trid; through, by means.

It is evident, from inspection, that almost all these improper Prepositions are compounded; and comprehend, as one of their component parts, a Noun, which is preceded by a simple or Proper Preposition; like the English, *on account, with respect*, &c. The words ceann, aghaidh, lorg, barr, taobh, &c., are known to be real Nouns, because they are employed in that capacity in other connections, as well as in the phrases here enumerated. The case is not so clear with regard to son, cum, or cun, reir, which occur only in the above phrases; but it is probable that these are nouns likewise, and that, when combined with simple Prepositions, they constitute phrases of precisely the same structure with the rest of the foregoing list *(n)*. Comhair is probably comh-aire *mutual attention*. Dàil and còir, in the sense of proximity, are found in their compounds comh-dhail and fochair [fa chòir.] Tòir, in like manner, in its derivative tòireachd, *the act of pursuing*. Dh' fhios, *to the knowledge*, must have been originally applied to persons only. So it is used in many Gaelic songs: beir mo shoiridh le dùrachd dh' fhios na cailinn, &c., *bear my good wishes with cordiality to the knowledge of the maid*, &c., i.e., *present my affectionate regards*, &c. This appropriate meaning and use of the phrase came by degrees to be overlooked; and it was employed, promiscuously with do chum and dh' ionnsuidh, to signify *unto* in a more general sense. If this analysis of the expression be just, then ghios *(o)* must be deemed only a different, and a corrupt manner of writing dh' fhios.

In the improper preposition os ceann, the noun has almost

---

*(m)* Tar éis, on the track or footstep. See O'Brien's " Ir. Dict." *voc.* éis.
*(n)* On consulting O'Brien's " Ir. Dict." we find son translated *profit advantage*, cum *a fight, combat*, réir *will, desire*. From these significations the common meaning of air son, do chum, do réir, may perhaps be derived without much violence.
*(o)* See Gaelic Poems published by Doctor Smith, pp. 8, 9, 178, 291.

always been written cionn. Yet in all other situations, the
same noun is uniformly written ceann. Whence has arisen
this diversity in the orthography of a simple monosyllable ?
And is it maintained upon just grounds ? It must have
proceeded either from a persuasion that there are two distinct
nouns signifying *top*, one of which is to be written ceann,
and the other cionn (*p*) ; or from an opinion that, granting
the two words to be the same individual noun, yet it is
proper to distinguish its meaning when used in the capacity
of a preposition, from its meaning in other situations, by
spelling it in different ways. I know of no good argument
in support of the former of these two opinions ; nor has it
probably been ever maintained. The latter opinion, which
seems to be the real one, is founded on a principle subversive
of the analogy and stability of written language, namely,
that the various significations of the same word are to be
distinguished in writing, by changing its letters, the constituent elements of the word. The variation in question,
instead of serving to point out the meaning of a word or
phrase in one place, from its known meaning in another
connection, tends directly to disguise it; and to mislead the
reader into a belief that the words, which are thus presented
to him under different forms, are themselves radically and
essentially different. If the same word has been employed
to denote several things somewhat different from each other,
that does by no means appear a sufficient reason why the
writers of the language should make as many words of one
(*q*).

(*p*) There is in Gaelic a Noun cion or cionn, signifying *cause ;* which
occurs in the expressions a chionn gu *because that,* cion-fàth *a reason* or
*ground.* But this word is entirely different from ceann *end* or *top.*

(*q*) Some confusion has been introduced into the Grammar of the Latin
language, by imposing different grammatical names on words, according to
the connection in which they stood, while they retained their form and
their signification unchanged ; as in calling *quod* at one time a Relative
Pronoun, at another time a Conjunction ; *post* in one situation a Preposition,
in another, an Adverb. An expedient was thought requisite for distinguishing, in such instances, the one part of speech from the other. Accordingly
an accent, or some such mark, was, in writing or printing, placed over the

The use of the *proper Prepositions* has been already shown
in the composition of adverbial phrases, and of the *improper
Prepositions*. The following examples show the further use
of them in connection with Nouns and Verbs, and in some
idiomatic expressions which do not always admit of being
literally rendered in English.

### Ag, aig.

*At:* aig an dorus, *at the door;* aig an tigh, *at the house, at
    home.*

*By reason of:* aig ro mheud aighir's a shòlais, *by reason of his
    great joy and satisfaction,* Smith's *Seann dàna*, p. 9;
    ag meud a mhiann *through intense desire,* Psal.
    lxxxiv. 2, metr. vers.; ag lionmhoireachd, Psal. xl.
    5.

Signifying possession: tha tuill aig na sionnaich, *the foxes
    have holes;* bha aig duine araidh dithis mhac, *a
    certain man had two sons;* cha n'eil fhios agam, *I
    have not the knowledge of it, I do not know it.*

Chaidh agam air, *I have prevailed over him,* Psal. xiii. 4, metr.
    vers.

Joined to the Infinitive of Verbs: ag imeachd, *a-walking,
    walking.*

### Air.

On, upon: air an làr, *on the ground;* air an là sin, *on that
    day;* air an adhbhar sin, *on that account, for that
    reason.*

the last vowel of the word, when employed in what was reckoned its
secondary use; while, in its primary use, it was written without any
distinguishing mark. So the conjunction *quòd* was distinguished from the
relative *quod*; and the adverb *post* from the preposition *pòst*. The distinction was erroneous; but the expedient employed to mark it was, at least,
harmless. The word was left unaltered and undisguised; and thus succeed-
ing grammarians had it the more in their power to prove that the relative
*quod* and the conjunction *quòd* are, and have ever been, in reality, one
and the same part of speech. It would have been justly thought a bold
and unwarrantable step, had the older grammarians gone so far as to alter
the letters of the word, in order to mark a distinction of their own
creation.

Denoting claim of debt : ioc dhomh na bheil agam ort, *pay me what thou owest me*, Matt. xviii. 28 ; cia meud ata aig mo thighearn ortsa ? *how much owest thou unto my lord ?* Luke xvi. 57. (*r*)

Denoting an oath: air m' fhocal, *upon my word ;* air làimh d' athar 's do sheanathar, *by the hand of your father and grandfather.*

Tha eagal, mulad, sglos, ocras, &c., air, *he is afraid, sad, fatigued, hungry,* &c.

Thig mo bheul air do cheartas, is air do chliù, *my mouth shall speak of thy justice and thy praise*, Psal. xxxv. 28. metr.; thig mo bheul air gliocas, *my mouth shall speak of wisdom*, Psal. xlix. 3, metr. v.; sin cùis air am bheil mi nis a' teachd, *that is the matter of which I am now to treat.*

Tog ort, *rouse thyself, bestir thyself*, Psal. lxxiv. 22, metr. v.

Chaidh agam air, *I prevailed over him*, Psal. xiii. 4.; metr.; 'S ann ormsa chaidh, *it was I that was worsted.*

Thug e am monadh air, *he betook himself to the mountain.*

*In respect of* : cha 'n fhaca mi an samhuil air olcas, *I never saw their like for badness*, Gen. xli. 19; air a lughad, *however small it be.*

*Joined with, accompanied by:* mòran iarruinn air bheag faobhar, *much iron with little edge*, M'Intyre's Songs. Oidhche bha mi 'n a theach, air mhòran bidh 's air bheagan eudaich, *I was a night in his house, with plenty of*

(*r*) From this use of the preposition *air* arises the *equivoque* so humorously turned against Mr James Macpherson by Maccodrum the poet, as related in the Report of the Committee of the Highland Society of Scotland on the authenticity of Osian's Poems, Append. p. 95. Macpherson asked Maccodrum, "Am bheil dad agad air an Fhéinn ?" literally, "Have you anything on the Fingalians ?" intending to inquire whether the latter had any poems in his possession *on* the subject of the Fingalian history and exploits. The expression partakes much more of the English than of the Gaelic idiom. Indeed, it can hardly be understood in Gaelic, in the sense that the querist intended. Maccodrum, catching up the expression in its true Gaelic acceptation, answered, with affected surprise, "Bheil dad agam air an Fhéinn ? Ma bha dad riamh agam orra, is fad o chaill mi na còirichean." "Have I any claim on the Fingalians ? If ever I had, it is long since I lost my voucher."

*food, but scanty clothing ;* air leth laimh, *having but one hand.*

Denoting measure or dimension : dà throidh air àirde, *two feet in height.*

Olc air mhath leat e, *whether you take it well or ill.*

### Ann, ann an, anns.

*In.* : Anns an tigh, *in the house;* anns an oidhche, *in the night ;* ann an dòchas, *in hope ;* anns a' bharail sin, *of that opinion.*

Denoting existence : ta abhainn ann, *there is a river,* Psal. xlvi. 4, metr. ; nach bithinn ann ni 's mò, *that I should not be any more ;* b' fhearr a bhi marbh na ann, *it were better to be dead than to be alive ;* ciod a th' ann? *what is it ?* is mise th' ann, *it is I ;* mar gu b' ann, *as it were ;* tha e 'n a dhuine ionraic, *he is a just man ;* tha i 'n a bantraich, *she is a widow* (*s*).

Marking emphasis : is ann air eigin a thàr e as, *it was with difficulty he got off ;* an àite seasamh is ann a theich iad, *instead of standing (keeping their ground) they fled ;* nach freagair thu? fhreagair mi ann, *will you not answer ? I have answered.*

### As.

*Out of :* as an dúthaich, *out of the country.*

Denoting extinction : tha an solus, no an teine, air dol as, *the light, or the fire, is gone out.*

As an alt, *out of joint;* as a' ghualainn, as a' chruachainn, as an uilinn, &c., *dislocated in the shoulder, hip, elbow-joint.*

---

(*s*) This use of the preposition *ann* in conjunction with a possessive Pronoun, is nearly akin to that of the Hebrew ל, [for] in such expressions as these : ' He hath made me [for] a father to Pharaoh, and [for] lord of all his house ;" *rinn e mi 'n am athair do Pharaoh, agus 'n am thighearn os ceann a thighe uile,* Gen. xlv. 8. ' Thou hast taken the wife of Uriah to be [for] thy wife ;' *ghabh thu bean Uriah gu bi 'n a mnaoi dhuit fein.* 2 Sam. xii. 10

Chaidh e as, *he escaped.*
Cuir as da, *destroy him,* or *it.*
Chaidh as da, *he is perished, undone.*
Thug e na buinn as, *he scampered off.*
Dubh as, *blot out.*

### De.

*Of:* Armailt mhòr de dhaoinibh agus a dh' eachaibh, *a great army of men and horses.*

*Off:* Bha na geugan air an sgathadh dheth, *the branches were lopped off;* thug iad an ceann deth, *they beheaded him.*

Dh aon rùn, *with one consent, with one purpose ;* dh' aon bharail, *with one mind, judgment.*

A là agus a dh' oidhche, *i.e.,* de là agus de oidhche, *by day and by night.* Lat. *de nocte,* Hor.

Saidhbhreas mór d'a mheud, *riches however great.* Psal. cxix. 14, metr.

### Do.

*To:* Tabhair dhomh, *give to me, give me*; thug sinn a bos mìn do Dhearg, *we gave her soft hand to Dargo.*

Dh' eirich sud dha gu h-obann, *that befell him suddenly.* Mar sin duinne gu latha, *so it fared with us till day, so we passed the night;* ma 's olc dhomh, cha n-fhearr dhoibh, *if it goes ill with me, they fare no better.*

Latha dhomhsa siubhal bheann, *one day as I travelled the hills ;* latha dhuinn air machair Alba, *one day when we were in the lowlands of Scotland ; on Scotia's plains.*

### Eadar.

*Between :* eadar an dorus agus an ursainn, *between the door and the post.*

Dh' eirich eadar mi agus mo choimhearsnach, *a quarrel arose betwixt me and my neighbour.*

Eadar mhòr agus bheag, *both great and small*, Psal.
xlix. 2, metr.; Rev. xix. 5, eadar bhochd agus nochd,
*both the poor and the naked.*

## Fa.

*Upon:* Fa 'n bhòrd, *upon the board;* leigeadar fa làr, *was
dropped on the ground, omitted, neglected.* Carswel.
Fa 'n adhbhar ud, *on that account;* creud fa 'n abradh
iad? *wherefore should they say?*
Fa sheachd, *seven times*, Psal. vii. 6, metr.; fa cheud,
*a hundred times*, Psal. lxii. 9, metr.

## Fuidh, fo.

*Under:* Fuidh 'n bhòrd, *under the board;* fuidh bhlàth *in
blossom;* tha an t-arbhar fo dhéis, *the corn is in the
ear;* fuidh smuairean, *under concern;* fo ghruaim,
*gloomy;* fo mhi-ghean, *in bad humour;* fuidh mhi-
chliu, *under bad report.*
Denoting intention or purpose: air bhi fuidhe, *it
being his purpose*, Acts xx. 7; tha tighinn fodham,
*it is my intention or inclination*

## Gu, Gus.

*To:* O thigh gu tigh, *from house to house;* gu crìch mo
shaoghail fein, *to the end of my life;* gus an crion
gu luaithre a' chlach, *until the stone shall crumble
to dust.* Sm. Seann dàna.
A' bhliadhna gus an àm so, *this time twelvemonth,
a year ago;* a sheachduin gus an dé, *yesterday se'en-
night.*
Mile gu leth, *a mile and a half;* bliadhna gu leth,
*a year and a half.*

## Gun.

*Without:* Gun amharus, *without doubt;* gun bhrogan, *without
shoes;* gun fhios, *without knowledge, unwittingly;*
gun fhios nach faic thu e, *in case you may see him,*

I

*if perhaps you may see him;* gun fhios am faic
thu e, *if perhaps you may not see him.* Gun
chomas aig air, *without his being able to prevent it,
or avoid it; involuntarily.* Gniomh gun chomain,
*an unmerited, or unprovoked deed.* Dh' àithn e dha
gun sin a dheanamh, *he ordered him not to do that.*
Fhuair iad rabhadh gun iad a philltinn, *they were
warned not to return.*

## Iar.

*After:* Iar sin, *after that;* iar leughadh an t-Soisgeil, *after
the reading of the Gospel;* iar tuiteam sios da aig
a chosaibh, *having fallen down at his feet;* bha mi
iar mo mhealladh, *I was received.*

## Le, leis.

*With:* Chaidh mi leis a' chuideachd mhòir, *I went with the
multitude.*
Denoting the instrument : mharbh e Eoin leis a'
chlaidheamh, *he killed John with the sword.*
Denoting the agent: thomhaiseadh le Diarmid an torc,
*the boar was measured by Diarmid.*
Denoting possession : is le Donull an leabhar, *the
book is Donald's;* cha leis e, *it is not his.*
Denoting opinion or feeling : is fada leam an là gu
h-oidhche, *I think the day long, or tedious, till night
come;* is cruaidh leam do chor, *I think your case a
hard one;* is dòcha leam, *I think it probable;* is
doilich leam, *I am sorry;* is aithreach leis, *he repents.*
*Along:* leis an t-sruth *along the stream;* leis an leathad,
*down the declivity.*
Leig leam, *let me alone;* leig leis, *let him alone.*

## Mu.

*About :* ag iadhadh mu a cheann, *winding about his head;*
labhair e mu Iudas, *he spoke about Judas;* nuair
smachduichear duine leat mu 'lochd, *when thou cor-*

*rectest a man for his sin,* Psal. xxxix. 11, metr. ;
sud am fàth mu'n goir a' chorr, *that is the reason of
the heron's cry.* Seann dàna. Sud fàth mu 'n
guidheann ort na naoimh, *for this reason will the
saints make supplication to Thee.*

## O.

*From :* O bhaile gu baile, *from town to town ;* o mhadainn
gu feasgar, *from morning to evening ;* o 'n là thainig mi dhachaidh, *from the day that I came home ;*
o 'n là, is often abridged into la; as, la thainig mi
dhachaidh, *since I came home.*

*Since, because :* thugamaid uil' oirnn a' bhanais, o fhuair
sinn cuireadh dhol ann, *let us all to the wedding,
since we have been bidden to it.*

Denoting want in opposition to possession, denoted
by *aig :* na tha uainn 's a b' fheairrd sinn againn,
*what we want and should be the better for having.*

Implying desire: ciod tha uait? *what would you have?*
Tha claidheamh uam, *I want a sword.*

## Os.

*Above :* Mar togam os m' uil' aoibhneas àrd cathair Ierusaleim,
*if I prefer not Jerusalem above my chief joy,* Psal.
cxxxvii. 6, metr. ; os mo cheann, *above me, over me.*

## Ri, ris.

*To :* cosmhuil ri mac righ, *like to the son of a king ;* chuir
iad teine ris an tigh, *they set fire to the house.*

Maille ri, *together with.*

Laimh ris a' bhalla, *nigh to the wall*

Ri là gaoithe, *on a day of wind ;* ri fad mo ré 's mo
là, *during all the days of my life ;* ri linn Righ
Uilliam, *in the reign of King William.*

Na bi rium, *don't molest me.*

Feuch ris, *try it.*

Cuir ris, *ply your work, exert yourself ;* cuirear na

nithe so ribh, *these things shall be added unto you,*
Matt. vi. 33. Tha an Spiorad ag cur ruinn na saorsa,
*the Spirit applieth to us the redemption,* Assemb.
Sh. Catech.

*Exposed :* tha an craicionn ris, *the skin is exposed, or bare;* leig
ris, *expose or make manifest.·*

### Roimh.

*Before:* roimh 'n charbad, *before the chariot;* roimh 'n chamh-
air, *before the dawn;* roimh na h-uile nithibh, *before,
in preference to, all things ;* chuir mi romham, *I set
before me, purposed, intended.*

Imich romhad, *go forward;* dh' fhalbh e roimhe, *he
went his way, he went off.*

### Seach.

*Past :* chaidh e seach an dorus, *he passed by the door.*
*In comparison with :* is trom a' chlach seach a' chlòineag, *the
stone is heavy compared with the down.*

### Tar, thar.

*Over, across :* chaidh e thar an amhainn, thar a' mhonadh, *he
went over the river, over the mountain ;* tha sin thar
m' eolas, thar mo bheachd, &c., *that is beyond my
knowledge, beyond my comprehension,* &c.

### Tre, troimh, throimh.

*Through :* tre uisge is tre theine, *through water and through
fire.*

#### Of Inseparable Prepositions.

The following initial syllables, used only in composition,
are prefixed to nouns, adjectives, or verbs, to modify or alter
their signification :—

An (*t*), Di, Ao, ea, eu, eas, Mi, Neo:—Privative syllables
signifying *not*, or serving to change the signification
of the words to which they are prefixed into its contrary; as, socair *ease*, anshocair *distress, uneasiness;*
ciontach *guilty*, dichiontach *innocent;* treabh *to
cultivate*, dithreabh *an uncultivated place, a desert;*
dionach *tight, close*, aodionach *leaky;* còir *justice,*
eucoir *injustice;* slàn *whole, in health*, easlan *sick;*
caraid *a friend*, eascaraid *an enemy;* buidheachas
*gratitude*, mibhuidheachas *ingratitude;* claon *awry,*
neochlaon *unbiassed, impartial;* duine *a man.*
neodhuine *a worthless unnatural creature.*

An, ain, intensive, denoting an immoderate degree, or
' faulty excess; as, tighearnas *dominion*, aintighearn-
as *tyranny;* tromaich *to make heavy*, antromaich
*to make very heavy, to aggravate;* teas *heat*, ainteas
*excessive heat;* miann *desire*, ainmhiann *inordinate
desire, lust.*

Ais, ath, *again, back;* as, eirigh *rising*, aiseirigh *resurrec-
tion;* beachd *view*, ath-bheachd *retrospect;* fàs
*growth*, ath-fhàs *after-growth.*

Bith, *continually;* as, bithdheanamh *doing continually, busy;*
am bithdheantas *incessantly.*

Co, com, comh, con, *together, equally, mutually;* as,
gleacadh *fighting*, co-ghleacadh *fighting together;*
lion *to fill*, colion *to fulfil, accomplish;* ith *to eat,*
comith *eating together;* radh *saying*, comhradh
*conversation, speech;* trom *weight*, cothrom *equal
weight, equity;* aois *age*, comhaois *a contemporary.*

Im, *about, round, entire;* as, làn *full*, iomlan *quite complete;*
gaoth *wind*, iomghaoth *a whirlwind;* slainte *health*,
iom-shlainte *perfect health.*

---

(*t*) This syllable assumes various forms. Before a broad vowel or consonant *an*, as, anshocair; before a small vowel or consonant *ain*, as,
aineolach *ignorant*, aindeoin *unwillingness;* before a labial *am* or *aim*, as,
aimbeartach *poor;* sometimes with the *m* aspirated, as, aimhleas *detriment*,
ruin, aimh-leathan *narrow.*

In, or ion, *worthy*; as, ion-mholta *worthy to be praised ;* ion-roghnuidh *worthy to be chosen,* Psal. xxv. 12, metr. vers.

So, *easily, gently ;* as, faicsin *seeing,* so-fhaicsin *easily seen ;* sion *weather,* soinion [so-shion] *calm weather ;* sgeul *a tale,* soisgeul *a good tale, gospel.*

Do, *with difficulty, evil ;* as, tuigsin *understanding,* do-thuigsin *difficult to be understood ;* doinion *stormy weather ;* beart *deed, exploit,* do-bheart *evil deed.*

## CHAPTER VIII.

### OF CONJUNCTIONS.

Under this class of words, it is proper to enumerate not only those single Particles which are usually denominated Conjunctions; but also the most common phrases which are used as Conjunctions to connect either words or sentences.

Ach ; but.

Agus, is ; and.

A chionn gu ; because that.

A chum as gu ; in order that.

A chum as nach ; that not.

Air chor as gu ; so that.

Air eagal gu,
D' eagal gu ; } *for fear that,* lest.

Air son gu,
Du bhrigh gu; } by reason that

Bheil fhios, 'l fhois? *is there knowledge?* is it known? an expression of curiosity, or desire to know.

Co ; as.

Ged, giodh ; although (*u*).

(*u*) The conjunction ged loses the *d* when written before an adjective of a personal pronoun ; as, ge binn do ghuth, *though your voice be sweet ;* ge h-àrd Jehovah, Psal. cxxxviii. 6.

The translators of the Scriptures appear to have erred in supposing ge to be the entire Conjunction, and that *d* is the verbal particle do. This has led them to write ge d' or ge do in situations in which do alters the sense

Ged tha, ge ta ; *though it be*, notwithstanding.

Gidheadh ; yet, nevertheless.

Gu, gur ; that.

Gun fhios ; *without knowledge*, it being uncertain whether
or not, in case not.

Ionnas gu ; insomuch that, so that.

from what was intended, or is totally inadmissible. Ge do ghluais mi,
Deut. xxix. 19, is given as the translation of *though I walk*, i.e. *though
I shall walk ;* but in reality it signifies *though I did walk*, for do ghluais
is past tense. It ought to be ged ghluais mi. So also ge do ghleidh thu
mi, Judg. xiii. 16, *though you detain me*, ought rather to be ged ghleidh
thu mi. Ge do ghlaodhas iad rium, Jer. xi. 11, *though they cry to me*, is
not agreeable to the Gaelic idiom. It ought rather to be ged ghlaodh iad
rium, as in Hosea, xi. 7. Ge do dh fheudainnse muinghin bhi agam,
Phil. iii. 4, *though I might have confidence.* Here the verbal particle is
doubled unnecessarily, and surely not according to classical precision.
Let it be written ged dh fheudainnse, and the phrase is correct. Ge do 's
eigin domh am bas fhulang, Mark xiv. 31, *though I must suffer death :* ge
do tha aireamh chloinn Israel, &c., Rom. ix. 27, *though the number
of the children of Israel be*, &c. The present tenses is and tha
never take the do before them. Ged is eigin, ged tha, is liable to no
objection. At other times, when the do appeared indisputably out of place,
the *d* has been dismissed altogether, contrary to usual mode of pronunciation ; as, ge nach eil, Acts xvii. 27, 2 Cor. xii. 11, where the common
pronunciation requires ged nach eil. So, ged' nach duin' an t-aodach, &c.
ge d' nach biodh ann ach an righ &c. (M'Intosh's "Gael. Prov." pp. 35, 36),
where the *d* is retained even before nach, because such is the constant way
of pronouncing the phrase.

These faulty expressions which, without intending to derogate from the
high regard due to such respectable authorities, I have thus freely ventured
to point out, seemed to have proceeded from mistaking the constituent
letters of the conjunction in question. It would appear that *d* was
originally a radical letter of the word ; that through time it came, like
many other consonants, to be aspirated ; and by degrees became, in some
situations, quiescent. In Irish it is written giodh. This manner of writing
the word is adopted by the translator of Baxter's "Call." One of its compounds is always written gidheadh. In these, the *d* is preserved, though
in its aspirated state. In Scotland it is still pronounced, in most situations,
ged, without aspirating the *d* at all. These circumstances put together
seem to prove the final *d* is a radical constituent letter of this Conjunction.

I have the satisfaction to say that the very accurate Author of the Gaelic
Translation of the Scriptures has, with great candour, acknowledged the
justice of the criticism contained in the foregoing note. It is judged
expedient to retain it in this edition of the Grammar, lest the authority of
that excellent Translation might perpetuate a form of speech which is
confessed to be faulty.

Ma ; if.
Mar ; as, like as.
Mar sud agus ; so also.
Ma seadh, ⎱
Ma ta ;       ⎰ *if so, if it be so, then.*
Mur ; if not.
Mur bhiodh gu ; were it not that.
Mus an, mu 'n ; before that, lest.
Na ; than.
Nach ; that not.
Na'n, na'm ; if.
No ; or.
O ; since, because.
Oir ; for.
Os barr ; moreover.
Sol, suil ; before that.
Tuille eile ; further.
Uime sin ; therefore.

## CHAPTER IX.

### OF INTERJECTIONS.

THE syllables or sounds, employed as expressions of various emotions or sensations, are numerous in Gaelic, but for the most part provincial, and arbitrary. Only one or two single vocables, and a few phrases, require to be noticed under this division.

Och ! Ochan ! alas !
Ochan nan och ! *alas* and *well-a-day !*
Fire faire ! what a pother !
Mo thruaighe ! *my misery !* ⎫
Mo chreachadh ! *my despoiling!* ⎬ woe's me !
Mo nàire ! *my shame*, for shame ! fy !
H-ugad, *at you*, take care of yourself, *gardez-vous.*
Feuch ! behold ! lo !

# PART III.

## OF SYNTAX.

SYNTAX treats of the connection of words with each other in a sentence; and teaches the proper method of expressing their connection by the *Collection* and the *Form* of the words. Gaelic Syntax may be conveniently enough explained under the common divisions of Concord and Government.

# CHAPTER I.

## OF CONCORD.

Under Concord is to be considered the agreement of the Article with its Noun;—of an Adjective with its Noun;— of a Pronoun with its Antecedent;—of a Verb with its Nominative;—and of one Noun with another.

### SECTION I.

#### OF THE AGREEMENT OF THE ARTICLE WITH A NOUN.

##### *Collocation.*

The article is always placed before its Noun, and next to it, unless when an Adjective intervenes.

##### *Form.*

The article agrees with its Noun in Gender, Number, and Case. Final *n* is changed into *m* before a plain Labial; as, am baile *the town*, am fear *the man.* It is usually cut off before an aspirated Palatal, or Labial, excepting *fh ;* as, a' chaora *the sheep*, a' mhuc *the sow*, a' choin *of the dog.* In the Dat. Sing. initial *a* is cut off after a Preposition ending in a Vowel; as, do 'n chloich *to the stone* (*v*).

*(v)* To avoid, as far as may be, the too frequent use of *a* by itself, perhaps it would be better always to write the article full, an or am : and to apply

A Noun, when immediately preceded by the Article, suffers some changes in Initial Form :—1. With regard to Nouns beginning with a Consonant, the *aspirated* form is assumed by a mas. Noun in the gen. and dat. singular ; by a fem. noun in the nom. and dat. singular. If the Noun begins with *s* followed by a vowel or by a Liquid, instead of having the *s* aspirated, *t* is inserted between the Article and the Noun, in the foresaid cases ; and the *s* becomes entirely quiescent (*w*). 2. With regard to Nouns beginning with a Vowel, *t* or *h* is inserted between the Article and the Noun in certain Cases, viz. *t* in the Nom. sing. of mas. Nouns, *h* in the gen. sing. of fem. Nouns, and *h* in the nom. and dat. plur. of Nouns of either gender. Throughout the other sing. and plur. Cases, all Nouns retain their Primary form.

The following examples show all the varieties that take place in declining a Noun with the Article.

*Nouns beginning with a Labial or a Palatal.*

### Bard, mas. *a Poet.*

| *Sing.* | *Plur.* |
|---|---|
| *N.* am Bard, | na Baird, |
| *G.* a' Bhaird, | nam Bard, |
| *D.* a', 'n Bhard (*x*). | na Bardaibh. |

### Cluas, fem. *an Ear.*

| *Sing.* | *Plur.* |
|---|---|
| *N.* a' Chluas, | na Cluasan, |
| *G.* na Cluaise, | nan Cluas, |
| *D.* a', 'n Chluais. | na Cluasaibh. |

the above rules, about the elision of its letters, only to regulate the pronunciation. Irish books, and our earlier Scottish publications, have the article written almost always full, in situations where, according to the latest mode of Orthography, it is mutilated.

(*w*) The practice of suppressing the sound of an initial consonant in certain situations, and supplying its place by another of a softer sound, is carried to a much greater extent in the Irish dialect. It is termed *eclipsis* by the Irish grammarians, and is an evidence of a nice attention to *euphonia*.

(*x*) The Dat. case is always preceded by a Preposition, ris a' bhard, do 'n bhard, aig na bardaibh ; in declining a Noun with the article, any *Proper Preposition* may be supplied before the Dative case.

*Nouns beginning with f.*

Fleasgach, m. *a Bachelor.*

| *Sing.* | *Plur.* |
|---|---|
| *N.* am Fleasgach, | na Fleasgaich, |
| *G.* an Fhleasgaich, | nam Fleasgach, |
| *D.* an, 'n Fhleasgach. | na Fleasgaich. |

Fòid. f. *a Turf.*

| *Sing.* | *Plur.* |
|---|---|
| *N.* an Fhòid, | na Foidean, |
| *G.* na Fòide, | nam Fòid, |
| *D.* an, 'n Fhòid. | na Foidibh. |

*Nouns beginning with a Lingual.*

Dorus, m. *a Door.*

| *Sing.* | *Plur.* |
|---|---|
| *N.* an Dorus, | na Dorsan, |
| *G.* An Doruis, | nan Dorsa, |
| *D.* an, 'n Dorus, | na Dorsaibh. |

Teasach, f. *a Fever.*

| *Sing.* | *Plur.* |
|---|---|
| *N.* an Teasach, | na Teasaichean, |
| *G.* na Teasaich, | nan Teasach, |
| *D.* an, 'n Teasaich. | na Teasaichibh. |

*Nouns beginning with s.*

Sloc, mas. *a Pit.*

| *Sing.* | *Plur.* |
|---|---|
| *N.* an Sloc, | na Sluic, |
| *G.* an t-Sluic, | nan Sloc, |
| *D.* an, 'n t-Sloc. | na Slocaibh. |

Sùil, fem. *an Eye.*

| *Sing.* | *Plur.* |
|---|---|
| *N.* an t-Sùil, | na Suilean, |
| *G.* na Sùla | nan Sùl, |
| *D.* an, 'n t-Sùil. | na Suilibh. |

*Nouns beginning with a Vowel.*

Iasg, m. *a Fish.*

| *Sing.* | *Plur.* |
|---|---|
| *N.* an t-Iasg, | na h-Iasga, |
| *G.* an Eisg, | nan Iasg, |
| *D.* an, 'n Iasg. | na h-Iasgaibh. |

Adharc, f. *a Horn.*

| *Sing.* | *Plur.* |
|---|---|
| *N.* an Adharc, | na h-Adhaircean, |
| *G.* na h-Adhairc, | nan Adharc, |
| *D.* an, 'n Adhairc. | na h-Adhaircibh. |

The initial Form of Adjectives immediately preceded by the Article, follows the same rules with the initial Form of Nouns.

Besides the common use of the Article as a Definitive to ascertain individual objects, it is used in Gaelic—

1. Before a Noun followed by the Pronouns *so, sin,* or *ud;* as, am fear so, *this man;* an tigh ud, *yon house.*

2. Before a Noun preceded by the Verb *is* and an Adjective; as, is maith an sealgair e, *he is a good huntsman;* bu luath an coisiche e, *he was a swift footman.*

3. Before some names of countries; as, righ na Spainne, *the king of Spain;* chaidh e do 'n Fhrainc, *he went to France;* but righ Bhreatain, *the king of Britain;* chaidh e dh' Eirin, *he went to Ireland,* without the Article.

## Section II.

### Of the Agreement of an Adjective with a Noun.

*Collocation.*

When an Adjective and the Noun which it qualifies are in the same clause or member of a sentence, the Adjective is usually placed after its Noun ; as, ceann liath, *a hoary head;* duine ro ghlic, *a very wise man.* If they be in different clauses, or if the one be in the subject, and the other in the predicate of a proposition, this rule does not apply ; as, is glic an duine sin, *that is a wise man;* cha truagh leam do chor, *I do not think your case unfortunate.*

1. Numerals, whether Cardinal or Ordinal, to which add, iomadh *many,* gach *every,* are placed before their Nouns; as, tri lathan, *three days;* an treas latha, *the third day;* iomadh duine, *many a man;* gach eun g' a nead, *every bird to its nest.* —Except such instances as the following : Righ Tearlach a h-Aon, *King Charles the First;* Righ Seumas a Cuig, *King James the Fifth.*

2. The possessive pronouns mo, do, &c., are always placed before their nouns ; as, mo lamh, *my hand.* The interrogatives co, cia, &c., are placed before their nouns, with the article intervening ; as, cia am fear? *which man ?*

3. Some adjectives of one syllable are usually placed before their Nouns; as, deadh dhuine, *a good man;* droch ghniomh, *a bad action;* seann sluagh, *old people.* Such Adjectives, placed before their Nouns, often combine with them, so as to represent one complex idea, rather than two distinct ones ; and the adjective and noun, in that situation, may rather be considered as one complex term, than as two distinct words, and written accordingly; as, oigfhear, *a young man;* ogbhean, *a young woman;* garbhchriochan, *rude regions* (y).

(y) So in English, *Grandfather, Highlands, sometimes ;* in Latin, *Respublica, Decemviri ;* in Italian, *Primavera;* in French, *Bonheur, Malheur,*

*Form.*

Though a Gaelic Adjective possesses a variety of Forms, yet its Form is not always determined by the Noun whose signification it modifies. The Form of the Adjective depends on its Noun, when it immediately follows the Noun, or only with the intervention of an intensitive Particle, ro, gle, &c., and when both the Noun and the Adjective are in the Subject or both in the Predicate, or in the same clause or member of a sentence. In all other situations, the form of the Adjective does in no respect depend on the Noun ; or, in other words, the Adjective does not agree with the Noun (z).

To illustrate this rule, let the following examples be attentively considered :—Is beag orm a' ghaoth fhuar, *I dislike the cold wind ;* is beag orm fuaim na gaoithe fuaire, *I dislike the sound of the cold wind ;* is beag orm seasamh anns a' ghaoith fhuair, *I dislike standing in the cold wind.* In these examples, the Adjective and the Noun are both in the same clause or member of a sentence, and therefore they must agree together. In the following examples the Adjective and the Noun do not necessarily agree together :—Is fuar a' ghaoth á tuath, *cold is the wind from the north;* is tric leis a' ghaoith á tuath bhi fuar, *it is usual for the wind from the north to be cold.* In these examples, the Noun is in the Subject, and the Adjective in the Predicate of the proposition.

&c. from being an adjective and a noun, came to be considered as a single complex term, or a compound word, and to be written accordingly.

A close analogy may be traced between the Gaelic and the French in the collocation of the Adjective. In both languages, the Adjective is ordinarily placed after its Noun. If it be placed before its Noun, it is by a kind of poetical inversion ; dorchadas tiugh, *des tenebres epaisses ;* by inversion, tiugh dhorchadas, *d' epaisses tenebres ;* fear mòr, *un homme grand ;* by inversion, in a metaphorical sense, mòr fhear, *un grand homme.* A Numeral Adjective, in both languages, is placed before its Noun ; as also iomadh, *plusieurs ;* except when joined to a proper name, where the Cardinal is used for the Ordinal ; Seumas a Ceithir, *Jaques Quatre.*

(z) The same seems to be the case in the Cornish Language. See Lhuyd's "Arch. Brit." p. 243, col. 3.

When an Adjective precedes its Noun, it undergoes no change of termination ; as, thig an Tighearn a nuas le ard iolaich, *the Lord will descend with a great shout,* 1 Thes. iv. 16; mar ghuth mor shluaigh, *as the voice of a great multitude,* Rev. xix. 6.

The grammatical distinction observable in the following examples is agreeable to the strictest philosophical propriety:— Rinn mis an scian gheur, *I made the sharp knife:* here the Adjective agrees with the Noun, for it modifies the Noun, distinguishing that knife from others. Rinn mis an scian geur, *I made the knife sharp:* here the Adjective does not agree with the Noun, for it modifies not the Noun but the Verb. It does not characterize the *object* on which the operation is performed, but it combines with the Verb in specifying the *nature of the operation* performed. The expression is equivalent to gheuraich mi an scian, *I sharpened the knife.* So also, mhothaich mi a' ghaoth fhuar, *I felt the cold wind;* but mhothaich mi a' ghaoth fuar, *I felt the wind cold.* In the former of these examples the Adjective modifies the Noun, and agrees with it; in the latter it does not agree with the Noun, for its use is to modify the Verb, or to specify the nature of the sensation felt. In like manner, dh' fhàg iad an obair criochnaichte, *they left the work finished;* fhuaradh an òigh sìnte, marbh, *the maid was found stretched out dead.* And so in other similar instances.

1. When an Adjective and Noun are so situated and related, that an agreement takes place between them, then the Adjective agrees with its noun in Gender, Number, and Case. A Noun preceded by the Numeral da *two,* though it be in the Singular Number, [see conclusion of Part II. Chap I.] takes an Adjective in the Plural; as, da iasg bheaga, *two small fishes,* John, vi. 9. The Initial Form of the Adjective depends partly on the Gender of the Noun, partly on its Termination, and partly on its being preceded by the Article.

The following examples of an Adjective declined along with its Noun, exhibit the varieties in the Initial Form, as well as in the Termination of the Adjective :—

## MONOSYLLABLES.

### Fear mòr, mas. *a Great Man.*

#### *Without the Article.*

| *Sing.* | *Plur.* |
| --- | --- |
| *N.* Fear mòr, | Fir mhòra, |
| *G.* Fir mhòir, | Fheara mòra, |
| *D.* Fear mòr, | Fearaibh mora, |
| *V.* Fhir mhòir. | Fheara mora. |

#### *With the Article.*

| | |
| --- | --- |
| *N.* Am Fear mòr, | Na Fir mhòra, |
| *G.* An Fhir mhòir, | Nam Fear mòra. |
| *D.* An Fhear mhòr. | Na Fearaibh mòra. |

### Slat gheal, fem. *a white rod.*

#### *Without the Article.*

| | |
| --- | --- |
| *N.* Slat gheal, | Slatan geala, |
| *G.* Slaite gile, | Shlatan geala, |
| *D.* Slait ghil, | Slataibh geala, |
| *V.* Shlat gheal. | Shlata geala. |

#### *With the Article.*

| | |
| --- | --- |
| *N.* An t-Slat gheal, | Na Slatan geala, |
| *G.* Na Slaite gile, | Nan Slata geala, |
| *D.* An t-Slait ghil. | Na Slataibh geala. |

## POLYSYLLABLES.

### Oglach dileas, m. *a Faithful Servant.*

#### *Without the Article.*

| | |
| --- | --- |
| *N.* Oglach dileas, | Oglaich dhileas, |
| *G.* Oglaich dhilis, | Oglach dileas, |
| *D.* Oglach dileas, | Oglachaibh dileas, |
| *V.* Oglaich dhilis. | Oglacha dileas. |

### With the Article.

| | |
|---|---|
| *N.* An t-Oglach dileas, | Na h-Oglaich dhileas. |
| *G.* An Oglaich dhilis, | Nan Oglach dileas. |
| *D.* An Oglach dhileas, | Na h-Oglachaibh dileas. |

Clarsach fhonnmhor, f. *a Tuneful Harp.*

### Without the Article.

| | |
|---|---|
| *N.* Clarsach fhonnmhor, | Clarsaichean fonnmhor. |
| *G.* Clarsaich fonnmhoir, | Chlarsach fonnmhor. |
| *D.* Clarsaich fhonnmhoir, | Clarsaichibh fonnmhor. |
| *V.* Chlarsach fhonnmhor, | Chlarsaiche fonnmhor. |

### With the Article.

| | |
|---|---|
| *N.* A' Chlarsach fhonnmhor, | Na Clarsaichean fonnmhor. |
| *G.* Na Clarsaich fonnmhoir, | Nan Clarsach fonnmhor. |
| *D.* A', 'n Chlarsaich fhonnoir, | Na Clarsaichibh fonnmhor. |

An Adjective, beginning with a Lingual, and preceded by a Noun terminating in a Lingual, retains its primary Form in all the Singular cases; for the sake, it would seem, of preserving the agreeable sound arising from the coalescence of the two Linguals; as, nighean donn *a brown maid,* instead of nighean dhonn; a' choin duibh *of the black dog,* instead of a' choin dhuibh; air a' chois deis *on his right foot,* instead of air a chois dheis.

II. A Noun preceded by an Adjective assumes the aspirated Form; as, ard bheann *a high hill,* cruaidh dheuchainn *a hard trial.*

1. A Noun preceded by a Numeral is in the primary Form; as, tri meoir *three fingers;* to which add iomadh *many,* gach *every;* as, iomadh fear *many a man;* gach craobh *every tree.* —Except aon *one,* da *two;* ceud *first;* as, aon fhear *one man,* da chraoibh *two trees.*

2. A Noun preceded by any of the following Possessive Pronouns, a *her,* ar *our,* bhur *your,* an *their,* is in the primary

K

Form; as, a mathair *her mother*, ar brathair *our brother*.
When the Possessive Pronoun a *her*, precedes a Noun or an
Adjective beginning with a vowel, *h* is inserted between them;
as, a h-athair, *her father*, a h-aon mhac *her only son*. The
Possessive Pronouns ar *our*, bhur *your*, usually take *n* between
them and the following Noun or Adjective beginning with a
vowel; as, ar n-athair *our father*, bhur n-aran *your bread*.
Perhaps a distinction ought to made, by inserting *n* only
after ar, and not after bhur (*d*). This would serve often to
distinguish the one word from the other in speaking, where
they are ready to be confounded by bhur being pronounced
ur.

3. A Noun beginning with a Lingual, preceded by an
Adjective ending in *n*, is in the primary Form; as, aon duine
*one man*, seann sluagh *old people*.

## Section III.

### Of the Agreement of a Pronoun with its Antecedent.

The Personal and Possessive Pronouns follow the *Number*
of their Antecedents, *i.e.* of the Nouns which they represent.
Those of the 3d Pers. Sing. follow also the Gender of their
antecedent; as, sheas a' bhean aig *a* chosaibh, agus thoisich *i air
am* fliuchadh leis *a* deuraibh, agus thiormaich *i iad* le gruaig
*a* cinn, *the woman stood at his feet, and she began to wet them
with her tears, and she wiped them with the hair of her head*,
Luke vii. 38. They follow, however, not the Gender of the
Antecedent, but the sex of the creature signified by the
Antecedent, in those words in which Sex and Gender disagree,
as, an gobhlan-gaoithe mar an ceudn' do sholair nead dh'i fein
*the swallow too hath provided a nest for herself*, Psal. lxxxiv.
3. Gobhlan-gaoithe *a swallow*, is a mas. Noun, as appears
by the mas. Article : but as it is the dam that is spoken of,
the reference is made by the Personal Pronoun of the fem.
gender. Ta gliocas air a fireanachadh leis a cloinn *Wisdom*

(*d*) Thus, bhur inntinn *your mind*, Acts xv. 24.

*is justified by her children*, Matt. xi. 19.  Gliocas is a mas.
noun; but as Wisdom is here personified as a female, the
regimen of the Possessive Pronoun is adapted to that idea
(*e*).  See also Prov. ix. 1–3.  In this sentence Och nach b'
i mhaduinn e, Deut. xxviii. 67, the former pronoun *i* is correctly put in the fem. gender, as referring to the fem. noun
*maduinn;* while the latter pron. *e* is put in the mas. gend.
because referring to no expressed antecedent.

If the Antecedent be a sentence, or clause of a sentence,
the Pronoun is of the 3d Pers. Sing. masculine; as, dh' ith na
bà caola suas na bà reamhra, agus cha n-aithnichteadh orra *e*,
*the lean cattle ate up the fat cattle, and could not be known by
them.*

If the Antecedent be a collective Noun, the Pronoun is of
the 3d Pers. Plur. as, thoir àithne do 'n t-sluagh, d' eagal gu m
bris *iad* asteach *charge the people lest they break in*, Exod. xix.
21.

An Interrogative combined with a Personal Pronoun, asks
a question without the intervention of the Substantive verb;
as, co mise? *who* [*am*] *I?* co iad na daoine sin? *who* [*are*]
*those men?* cia i a' cheud àithne? *which* [*is*] *the first commandment?*  In interrogations of this form, the noun is sometimes preceded by the Personal Pronoun, and sometimes not;
as, co e am fear? *who* [*is*] *the man?* co am fear? *what
man?*  Co am fear? is evidently an incomplete sentence,
like *what man?* in English.  The ellipsis may be
supplied thus; co e am fear a ta thu ciallachadh? *who is the
man whom you mean?*  This example may be abridged into
another common interrogation, in which the Interrogative is
immediately followed by the Relative; as, co a ta thu ciallachadh? *who* [*is he*] *whom you mean?* ciod a ta thu faicinn?
*what* [*is it*] *that you see?*

In an interrogative sentence including a Personal Pronoun
and a Noun, as, co e am fear sin? if the Noun be restricted in

(*e*) This, however, does not happen invariably.  Where the *Sex*, though
specified, is overlooked as of small importance, the Personal or Possessive
Pronouns follow the *Gender* of the Antecedent.  See 2 Sam. xii. 3.

its signification by some other words connected with it, such
as the Article, an Adjective, another Noun in the Genitive,
or a relative clause, then the Pronoun usually follows the
Gender of the Noun, or the Sex of the object signified by the
Noun, if the Gender does not correspond to it; as, co *e* am
fear a theid a suas? *who is the man that shall ascend ?* co *i*
am boirionnach sin? *who is that woman ?* cia *i* a' cheud àithne?
*which is the first commandment ?*   If the Noun be not *so restricted*, the Pronoun is of the masculine gender ; as, ciod e
uchdmhacachd? *what is adoption ?* ciod e urnuigh? *what is
prayer ? (f)*

(f) I am aware of the singularity of asserting the grammatical propriety
of such expressions as ciod e Uchdmhacachd? ciod e Urnuigh? as, the
nouns uchdmhacachd, urnuigh are known to be of the feminine Gender ; and
as this assertion stands opposed to the respectable authority of the Editor
of the Assembly's Catechism in Gaelic, Edin. 1792, where we read, Ciod i
urnuigh? &c.   The following defence of it is offered to the attentive
reader.

In every question the words which convey the interrogation must refer
to some higher genus or species than the words which express the subject
of the query.   It is in the choice of the speaker to make that reference to
any genus or species he pleases.   If I ask 'Who was Alexander?' the
Interrogative *who* refers to the species *man*, of which *Alexander*, the subject
of the query, is understood to have been an individual.   The question is
equivalent to 'What man was Alexander?'   If I ask 'What is Man?' the
Interrogative *what* refers to the genus of Existence or Being, of which Man
is considered as a subordinate genus or species.   The question is the
same with 'What Being is Man?'   1 may also ask 'What was
Alexander?'   Here the Interrogative *what* refers to some genus or species
of which Alexander is conceived to have been an individual, though the
particular genus intended by the querist is left to be gathered from the
tenor of the preceding discourse.   It would be improper, however, to say
'Who is man?' as the Interrogative refers to no higher genus than that
expressed by the word *Man*.   It is the same as if one should ask 'What
man is Man?'

In the question 'What is Prayer?' the object of the querist is to learn
the meaning of the term *Prayer*.   The Interrogative *what* refers to the
genus of Existence, as in the question 'What is Man?' not to the word
*Prayer*, which is the subject of the query.   It is equivalent to 'What is
[that thing which is named] Prayer?'   In those languages where a variety
of gender is prevalent, this reference of the Interrogative is more con-
spicuously marked.   A Latin writer would say '*Quid* est Oratio*?' A
Frenchman, 'Qu' est-ce que la Prière ?'   These questions, in a complete

* See a short Latin Catechism at the end of Mr Ruddiman's Latin Rudiments,
where many similar expressions occur; as Quid est fides?   'Quid est Lex?   Quid est
Baptismus?   'Quid Sacramenta?  &c.'

## SECTION IV.

### OF THE AGREEMENT OF A VERB WITH ITS NOMINATIVE.

As the Verb has no variation of *form* corresponding to the Person or Number of its Nominative, the connection between a Verb and its Nominative can be marked only by its *collocation*. Little variety therefore is allowed in this respect. The Nominative, whether Noun or Pronoun, is ordinarily placed after the Verb; as, ta mi *I am*, rugadh duine-cloinne *a man-child is born* (*g*). The Article or an Adjective, is frequently

form, would run thus ; 'Quid est [id quod dicitur] Oratio ?' 'Qu' est-ce que [l'on appelle] la Prière ?' On the same principle, and in the same sense, a Gaelic writer must say, 'Ciod e urnuigh ?' the Interrogative Ciod e referring not to urnuigh but to some higher genus. The expression, when completed, is ' Ciod e [sin de 'n goirear] urnuigh ?'

Is there then no case in which the Interrogative may follow the gender of the subject ? If the subject of the query be expressed, as it often is, by *a general term, limited in its signification* by a noun, adjective, relative clause, &c.; the reference of the Interrogative is often, though not always not necessarily, made to *that term* in its general acceptation, and consequently be 'What is the Lord's Prayer ?' Here the subject of the query is not *Prayer*, but an individual of that species, denoted by the term *prayer* limited in its signification by another noun. The Interrogative *what* may refer, as in the former examples, to the genus of Existence ; or it may refer to the species *Prayer*, of which the subject of the query is an individual. That is, I may be understood to ask either 'What is that *thing* which is called the Lord's Prayer ?' or 'What is that *prayer* which is called the Lord's Prayer ?' A Latin writer would say, in the former sense, ' Quid est Oratio Dominica* ?' in the latter sense, 'Quaenam est Oratio Dominica ?' The former of these expressions is resolvable into ' Quid est [id quod dicitur] Oratio Dominica ? 'the latter into 'Quaenam [oratio] est Oratio Dominica?' The same diversity of expression would be used in French : ' Qu' est-ce que l'Oraison Dominicale?' and 'Quelle est l'Oraison Dominicale ?' The former resolvable into ' Qu' est-ce que [l'on appelle] l'Oraison Dominicale? the latter into 'Quelle [oraison] est l'Oraison Dominicale ! So also in Gaelic, ' Ciod e Urnuigh an Tighearna?' equivalent to ' Ciod e [sin de'n goirear] Urnuigh an Tighearna ?' or, which will occur oftener, ' Ciod i Urnuigh an Tighearna?' equivalent to ' Ciod i [an urnuigh sin de 'n goirear] Urnuigh an Tighearna !'

(*g*) The same arrangement obtains pretty uniformly in Hebrew, and seems the natural and ordinary collocation of the Verb and its Noun in that language. When the Noun in Hebrew is placed before the Verb, it will generally be found that the Noun does not immediately connect with the Verb as the Nominative to it, but rather stands in an absolute state;

* So Ruddiman, 'Quid est Sacra Coena?'

placed between the Verb and its Nominative; as, thainig an uair, *the hour is come;* aithrisear iomadh droch sgeul, *many an evil tale will be told.* Sometimes, but more rarely, circumstances are expressed beween the Verb and its Nominative; as, rugadh dhuinne, an diugh, ann am baile Dhaibhi, an Slanuighear, *there is born to us, this day, in David's town, the Saviour.*

The word denoting the object of the verbal action, can never, even in poetry, he placed between the Verb and its Nominative, without altering the sense. Hence the arrangement in the following passages is incorrect:—Ghabh domblas agus fiongeur iad, *they took gall and vinegar.* "Buch. Gael. Poems," Edin. 1767. p. 14. The collocation should have been ghabh iad domblas, &c. Do chual e 'n cruinne-cé, *the world heard it,* id. p. 15, ought to have been, do chual an cruinne-cé e. So also, do ghabh truaighe, Iosa dhoibh, *Jesus took pity*

and that it is brought forward in that state by itself to excite attention, and denotes some kind of emphasis, or opposition to another Noun. Take the following examples for illustration : Gen. i. 1, 5. 'In the beginning God created [בָּרָא אֱלֹהִים in the natural order] the Heaven and the Earth.' וְהָאָרֶץ הָיְתָה; not and the Earth was, &c., but 'and with respect to the Earth, it was without form,' &c. Thus expressed in Gaelic : 'agus an talamh bha e gun dealbh,' &c. Gen. xviii. 33. 'And the Lord went his way [וַיֵּלֶךְ יְהוָה in the natural order] as soon as he had left communing with Abraham ;' וְאַבְרָהָם שָׁב, not simply 'and Abraham returned,' &c., but and Abraham—he too returned to his place.' In Gaelic, ' agus Abraham, phill esan g' aite fein.' See also Num. xxiv. 25.—Gen. iii. 12. 'And the man said, the woman whom thou gavest to be with me, הוּא נָתְנָה לִּי *she* it was that gave me of the tree, and I did eat.' Gen. iii. 13. 'And the woman said, הַנָּחָשׁ הִשִּׁיאָנִי, not merely 'the Serpent beguiled me,' but '*the Serpent* was the cause ; it beguiled me, and I did eat.' Exod. xiv. 14. ' *Jehovah*—he will fight for you ; but as for *you*, ye shall hold your peace.' This kind of emphasis is correctly expressed in the Eng. translation of Psal. lx. 12, 'for he *it is that* shall tread, down our enemies.' Without multiplying examples, I shall only observe that it must be difficult for the English reader to conceive that the Noun denoting the subject of a proposition, when placed after its Verb, should be in the natural order ; and when placed before its Verb, should be in an inverted order of the words. To a person well aquainted with the Gaelic, this idiom is familiar ; and therefore it is the easier for him to apprehend the effect of such an arrangement in any other language. For want of attending to this peculiarity in the structure of the Hebrew, much of that force and emphasis, which in other languages would be expressed by various particles, but in Hebrew depend on the collocation alone, must pass unobserved and unfelt.

*on them.* Matt. xx. 34, Irish vers.  It ought to have been, do ghabh Iosa truaighe, &c. (*h*).

The Relatives a *who*, nach *who not*, are always put before the verb; as, am fear a thuit, *the man who fell;* am fear nach dean beud, *the man who will not commit a fault.*

In poetry, or poetical style, where inversion is allowed, the Nominative is sometimes placed before the Verb; as doimhneachd na talmhain ta 'n a laimh, *in his hand is the depth of the earth.*  Psal. xcv. 4.

> Oigh cha tig le clàr 'n an comhdhail,
> *No virgin with harp will come to meet them.*
>                 Smith's "Ant. Gal. Poems," p. 285.

> Gach doire, gach coire, 's gach eas,
> Bheir a' m' chuimhne cneas mo Ghraidh.

*Each grove, each dell, and each water-fall, will bring to my remembrance the form of my love.*  Id. p. 30.

> An la sin cha tigh gu bràth,
> A bheir dearrsa mo ghraidh gu tuath.

*That day shall never come, which shall bring the sun-beam of my love to the North.*  Fingal II. 192.

> Am focail geilleam do Mhorlamh;
> Mo lann do neach beo cha gheill.

*In words I yield to Morla; my sword to no living man shall yield.*  Fing II. 203.  This inversion is never admitted into plain discourse or unimpassioned narrative.

In those Persons of the Verb in which the terminations supply the place of the Personal Pronouns, no Nominative is expressed along with the Verb.  In all the other Persons of the Verb, a Noun or a Pronoun is commonly expressed as its Nominative.  In sentences of a poetical structure, the Nominative is sometimes, though rarely, omitted; as, am fear nach

---

(*h*) I am happy to be put right, in my stricture on the above passage, by E. O'C., author of a Gaelic Grammar, Dublin, 1808, who informs us that *truaighe* is here the Nominative, and *Iosa* the Accusative case ; and that the meaning is not *Jesus took pity on them,* but *pity seized Jesus for them.*

gabh 'nuair gheibh, cha 'n fhaigh 'nuair 's aill, *the man who will not take when [he] can get, will not get when [he] wishes.*

A Gharna, cuim a sheas? a Ghuill, cuim a thuit?
*Garno, why stoodst ? Gaul, why didst fall ?*
Smith's " Ant. Gal. Poems," p. 153.

The Infinitive often takes before it the Nominative of the Agent ; in which case the Preposition *do* is either expressed or understood before the Infinitive ; as, feuch, cia meud a mhaith, braithre do bhi 'n an comhnuidh ann sith ! *behold how great a good it is, that brethren dwell in peace!* Psal. cxxxiii, 1. Is e mi dh' fhantuinn 's an fheoil, a 's feumaile dhuibhse, *my abiding in the flesh is more needful for you,* Phil. i. 24, Cha n'eil e iomchuidh sinne dh' fhagail focail Dé, agus a fhrithealadh do bhordaibh, *it is not meet that we should leave the word of God, and serve tables,* Acts vi. 2. The Preposition *do,* being softened as usual into *a,* readily disappears after a Vowel ; as, air son mi bhi a rìs a lathàir maille ribh, *by my being again present with you,* Phil. i. 26 (*i*).

## SECTION V.

### OF THE AGREEMENT OF ONE NOUN WITH ANOTHER.

When in the same sentence two or more Nouns, applied as names to the same object, stand in the same grammatical relation to other words, it should naturally be expected that their Form, in so far as it depends on that relation, should be the same; in other words, that Nouns denoting the same object, and related alike to the governing word, should agree in Case. This accordingly happens in Greek and Latin. In Gaelic, where a variety of form gives room for the application of the same rule, it has been followed in some instances; as, Doncha mac Chailain mhic Dhonuil, *Duncan the son of*

---

(*i*) This construction resembles that of the Latin Infinitive preceded by the Accusative of the Agent.

—— Mene desistere victam,<br>
Nec posse Italia Teucrorum avertere regem ?
I. Ænid 28.

*Colin the son of Donald;* where the words Chailain and mhic
denoting the same person, and being alike related to the preceding Noun mac are on that account both in the same Case.
It must be acknowledged, however, that this rule, obvious
and natural as it is, has not been uniformly observed by the
speakers of Gaelic.   For example; instead of mac Ioseiph an
t-saoir, *the son of Joseph the carpenter,* many would more
readily say, mac Ioseiph an saor; instead of thuit e le laimh
Oscair an laoich chruadalaich, *he fell by the hand of Oscar
the bold hero,* it would rather be said, thuit e le laimh Oscair
an laoch cruadalach.   The latter of these two modes of
expression may perhaps be defended on the ground of its
being elliptical; and the ellipsis may be supplied thus: mac
Ioseiph [is e sin] an saor; laimh Oscair [neach is e] an laoch
cruadalach.   Still it must be allowed, in favour of the rule
in question, that the observance of it serves to mark the
relation of the Nouns to each other, which would otherwise
remain, in many instances, doubtful.   Thus in one of the
foregoing examples, if we should reject the rule, and write
mac Ioseiph an saor; it would be impossible to know, from
the form of the words, whether Joseph or his son were the
carpenter.

The translators of the Scriptures into Gaelic, induced probably by the reasonableness and utility of the rule under
consideration, by the example of the most polished Tongues,
and by the usage of the Gaelic itself in some phrases, have
uniformly adhered to this rule when the leading Noun was
in the Genitive; as, do mhacaibh Bharsillai a' Ghileadaich,
1 Kings ii. 7; righ-chathair Dhaibhi athar, 1 Kings ii. 12;
do thaobh Bheniamin am brathar, Judg. xxi. 6; ag gabhail
nan clar chloiche, eadhon chlar a' cho-cheangail, Deut. ix. 9.
The rule seems to have been disregarded when the leading
Noun was in the Dative.   See 1 Kings i. 25, Ruth iv. 5
Acts xiii. 33.

## CHAPTER II.

### OF GOVERNMENT.

UNDER this head is to be explained the Government of Nouns, of Adjectives, of Verbs, of Prepositions, and of Conjunctions.

### SECTION I.

#### OF THE GOVERNMENT OF NOUNS.

One Noun governs another in the Genitive. The Noun governed is always placed after that which governs it; as, ceann tighe, *the head of a house or family;* solus na gréine, *light of the sun;* bainne ghabhar *milk of goats.*

The Infinitives of Transitive Verbs, being themselves Nouns, (See Part II. Chap. V. p. 86.) govern in like manner the Genitive of their object; as, ag cur sìl, *sowing seed;* a dh' fhaicinn an t-sluaigh, *to see the people;* iar leughadh an t-soisgeil, *after reading the gospel* (k).

Although no good reason appears why this rule, which is common to the Gaelic with many other languages, should ever be set aside, yet it has been set aside in speaking, and sometimes in writing Gaelic.

1. When the Noun governed does in its turn govern another Noun in the Genitive, the former is often put in the Nominative instead of the Genitive case. The following instances of this anomaly occur in the Gaelic Scriptures:—Guth briathran an t-sluaigh, instead of, bhriathran, *the voice of the words of the people,* Deut. v. 28; do mheas craobhan a'gharaidh, instead of, chraobhan, *of the fruit of the trees of the garden,*

---

(k) So in English, the Infinitive of a Transitive Verb is sometimes used instead of the Present Participle, and followed by the Preposition *of;* as, 'the woman was there gathering of sticks.' 1 Kings xvii. 10.

———— some sad drops
Wept at completing of the mortal sin.
                    "Parad. Lost."

See more examples, Num. xiii. 25, 2 Sam. ii. 21, 2 Chron. xx. 25, xxxv. 14. Ezek. xxxix. 12.

Gen. iii. 2; ag itheadh tighean bhantrach, for thighean, *devour-ing widows' houses*, Matt. xxiii. 14; ag nochdadh obair an lagha, for oibre, *showing the work of the law*, Rom. ii. 15; ag cuimhn-eachadh gun sgur obair bhur creidimh, agus saothair bhur graidh, for oibre, saoithreach, *remembering without ceasing your work of faith, and labour of love*, 1 Thess. i. 3; trid fuil is fearta Chriost, *through the blood and merits of Christ*, Gael. Paraph. 1787, p. 381, for trid fola Chriost, as in Eph. ii. 13; ag àiteach sliabh Shioin, for sleibh, *inhabiting the hill of Zion*, Psal. ix. 11. metr; air son obair Chriosd, Phil. ii. 30, 1767, according to the usage of the language, but changed to oibre, in Edit. 1796, to suit the Grammatical Rule (*l*). For the most part, however, the general rule, even in these circum-stances, is followed; as, guth fola do bhrathar, *the voice of thy brother's blood*, Gen. iv. 10; amhainn duthcha cloinne a shluaigh *the river of the land of the children of his people*, Numb. xxii. 5; a'nigheadh chos sheirbhiseach mo thighearna, *to wash the feet of the servants of my lord*, 1 Sam. xxv. 41.

2. Such expressions as the following seem to be exceptions to the rule:—Dithis mac, 2 Sam. xv. 27, 36; ceathrar mac, 1 Chron. xxi. 20; leanabaibh mac, Matt. ii. 16. In the following similar instances, the rule is observed:—Dithis mhac, Gen. xli. 50; dithis fhear, 2 Sam. xii. 1; ceathrar fhear, Acts xxi. 23; ceathrar mhaighdiona, Acts xxi. 9.

The same anomaly takes place in the regimen of the infinitive, as in that of other Nouns. Though an Infinitive be in that grammatical relation to a preceding Noun which would require its being put in the Genitive, yet when itself also governs another noun in the Genitive, it often retains the form of the Nominative. The Infinitives naomhhachadh, gnathachadh, briseadh, admit of a regular Genitive, naomh-achaidh, gnathachaidh, brisidh. In the following examples,

(*l*) On the same principle it is that in some compound words, composed of two Nouns whereof the former governs the latter in the Genitive, the former Noun is seldom itself put in the Genitive case. Thus, ainm bean-na-bainse, *the bride's name;* it would sound extremely harsh to say ainm mna-na-bainse; clach ceann-an-teine, not clach cinn-an-teine, the stone which supports a hearth fire.

these Infinitives, because they govern a subsequent Noun in
the Genitive, are themselves in the Nominative, though their
relation to the preceding word naturally requires their being
put in the Genitive Case. Tha an treas àithne a' toirmeasg
mi-naomhach*adh* no mi-ghnathach*adh* ni sam bith, &c., *the
third commandment forbids the profaning or the abusing of
any thing*, &c. Assem. Cat. Gael. Edin. 1792, Answer to Q.
55. Ged fheud luchdbris*eadh* na h-aithne so dol as, &c., id.
Q. 56., *though the transgressors of this commandment may
escape*, &c. Cuis crath*adh* cinn is cas*adh* béil, Psal. xxii. 7,
as it is in the older edition of the Gaelic Psalms. An deigh
leugh*adh* an lagha, *after the reading of the Law*, Acts. xiii. 15;
luchd cum*adh* uilc, Rom. i. 30 (*m*).

The Infinitive is not put in the Genitive, when preceded

(*m*) These examples suggest, and seem to authorise a special use of this
idiom of Gaelic Syntax, which, if uniformly observed, might contribute
much to the perspicuity and precision of many common expressions. When
a compound term occurs, made up of a Noun and an Infinite governed by
that Noun, it often happens that this term itself governs another Noun in
the Genitive. Let the two parts of the compound term be viewed separately.
If it appear that the subsequent Noun is governed by the *former* part of
the compound word, then the latter part should remain regularly in the
Genitive Case. But if the subsequent Noun be governed by the *latter* part
of the compound word, then, agreeably to the construction exemplified in
the above passages, that latter part, which is here supposed to be an Infinitive, should fall back into the Nominative Case. Thus tigh-coimhíd an
Righ, *the King's store house*, where the Noun Righ is governed by tigh, the
former term of the compound word ; but tigh comhead an ionmhais, Johu
viii. 20, *the house for keeping the treasure*, where ionmhais is governed by
coimhead, which is therefore put in the Nominative instead of the Genitive.
So luchd-coimhíd, Matt. xxviii. 4, when no other Noun is governed ; but
fear-coimhead a' phriosuin, Acts, xvi. 27, 36, where the last Noun is
governed in the Genitive by coimhead, which is therefore put in the Nominative. So also fear-coimhíd, Psal. cxxi. 3, but fear-coimhead Israeil, Psal.
cxxi. 4. Edin. 1799. Tigh-bearraidh nam buachaillean, *the shearing-house
belonging to the shepherds*, 2 King, x. 12, but tigh-bearradh nan caorach,
*the house for shearing the sheep*. Luchd-brathaidh an Righ *the King's
spies ;* but luchd-brathadh an Righ, *the betrayers of the King.* Luchd-
mort-aidh Heroid, *assassins employed by Herod ;* but luchd-mortadh Eoin,
*the murderers of John.*

I am aware that this distinction has been little regarded by the translators of the Scriptures. It appeared, however, worthy of being suggested,
on account of its evident utility in point of precision, and because it is
supported by the genius and practice of the Gaelic language.

by a Possessive Pronoun, because it is in the same limited
state as if it governed a Noun in the Genitive Case ; as, a
chum am marbhadh 's na beanntaibh, *to kill them in the
mountains,* Exod. xxxii., not marbha*idh,* which is the Case
regularly governed by chum. Co tha 'g iarraidh do mharbhadh?
John vii. 20, not do mharbha*idh.* Thug iad leo e chum a
cheusa*dh.* Matt. xxvii. 31. Chum an cruinneacha*dh* gu cath.
Rev. xx. 8 (*n*).

This coincidence in the Regimen of the Infinitive in two
similar situations, viz., when limited by a Possessive Pronoun,
and when limited by a subsequent Noun, furnishes no slight
argument in support of the construction defended above, of
putting the Infin. in the Nom. case when itself governs a
Noun in the Genitive; for we find the Infin. is invariably
put in the Nom. when limited in its signification by a Possess.
Pronoun.

When one Noun governs another in the Genitive, the
Article is never joined to both, even though each be limited
in its signification; as, mac an righ, *the son of the king,* not
am mac an righ; taobh deas a' bhaile, *the south side of the
town,* not an taobh deas a' bhaile (*o*). For the most part, the
Article is thus joined to the latter Noun. Sometimes it is
joined to the former Noun; as, an ceann tighe, *the head of
the family;* an ceann iuil, *the pilot;* but in such instances the
two Nouns figure as one complex term, like *paterfamilias,*
rather than as two terms. The following examples, in which
the Article is joined to both Nouns, seem to be totally repug-
nant to the Gaelic idiom : cuimhneachadh *nan* cùig aran *nan*
cùig mile, Matt. xvi. 9 ; *nan* seachd aran *nan* ceithir mìle,
Matt. xvi. 10 (*p*).

(*n*) For this reason, there seems to be an impropriety in writing chum a
losgaidh, 1 Cor. xiii. 3, instead of chum a losgadh.

(*o*) The same peculiarity in the use of the Article takes place in Hebrew.
and constitutes a striking point of analogy in the structure of the two
languages. See *Buxt. Thes. Gram. Heb. Lib. II. Cap. V.*

(*p*) This solecism is found in the Irish as well as in the Scottish Gaelic
translation. The Manks translation has avoided it. In the Irish version
and in the Scottish Gaelic version of 1767, a similar instance occurs in

A Possessive Pronoun joined to the Noun governed ex-
cludes, in like manner, the Article from the Noun governing;
as, barr-iall a bhròige, *the latchet of his shoe*, not am barr-iall
a bhròige; obair bhur lamh, *the work of your hands*, not an
obair bhur lamh.

The Noun governed is sometimes in the Primary, sometimes
in the Aspirated Form.

Proper Names of the Masculine Gender are in the Aspirated
Form; as, bràthair Dhonuill, *Donald's brother;* uaigh Choluim,
*Columba's grave.* Except when a final and an initial Lingual
meet; as, clann Donuill, *Donald's descendants;* beinn Deirg
*Dargo's hill.*

When both Nouns are Appellatives, and no word intervenes between them, the initial Form of the latter Noun
follows, for the most part, that of an Adjective agreeing with
the former Noun. See p. 144.

Thus, d' a ghàradh *f*iona, g' a ghàradh *f*iona, without the
Article, Matt. xx. 1, 2, like do dhuine *m*aith; but do 'n ghàradh
*fh*iona, with the Article *v.* 4, 7, like do 'n duine *mh*aith.
So we should say do 'n ard fhear-*ch*iuil, rather than do 'n
ard fhear-*c*iuil, as in the title of many of the Psalms.

EXCEPT.—If the latter Noun denote an individual of a
species, that is, if it take the Article *a* before it in English,
it is put in the *primary form*, although the former Noun be
feminine; as, sùil caraid, *the eye of a friend*, not sùil *ch*araid,
like sùil *m*hor; duais *f*àidh, *a prophet's reward*, Matt. x. 4,
not duais *fh*àidh, like duais *mh*òr. Chum maitheanais *p*eacaidh,
Acts, ii. 38, signifies *for the remission of a sin;* rather chum
maitheanais *ph*eacaidh *for the remission of sin.*

Acts, ii. 20, *an* la mor agus oirdheirc sin *an* Tighearna. In the Scottish
edition of 1796, the requisite correction is made by omitting the first Article.
It is omitted likewise in the Manks N. T. On the other hand, the Article,
which had been rightly left out in the Edition of 1767, is properly introduced in the Edition of 1796, in 1 Cor. xi. 27, an cupan so an Tighearna.
It is proper to mention that, in the passage last quoted, the first article *an*
had crept, by mistake, into a part of the impression 1796, but was corrected
in the remaining part.

## Section II.

### Of the Government of Adjectives.

Adjectives of fulness govern the Genitive; as, làn uamhainn *full of dread*, Acts, ix. 6, buidheach beidh, *satisfied with meat.*

The first Comparative takes the Particle na *than*, before the following Noun; as, ni 's gile na an sneachdadh, *whiter than the snow;* b' fhaide gach mios na bliadhna, *each month seemed longer than a year.* Smith's "Ant. Poems," p. 9.

The second Comparative is construed thus: is feairrd mi so, *I am the better for this;* bu mhisd e am buille sin, *he was the worse for that blow;* cha truimid a' choluinn a ciall, *the body is not the heavier for its understanding.*

Superlatives are followed by the Preposition de or dhe *of;* as, am fear a 's àirde dhe 'n triuir, *the man who is tallest of the three, the tallest man of the three.*

## Section III.

### Of the Government of Verbs.

A Transitive Verb governs its object in the Nominative or Objective Case; as, mharbh iad an righ, *they killed the king;* na buail mi, *do not strike me.* The object is commonly placed after the Verb, but never between the Verb and its Nominative. [See Part III. Chap. I., Sect. IV.] Sometimes the object is placed, by way of emphasis, before the Verb; as, mise chuir e ris ann am àite, agus esan chroch e, *me he put again in my place, and him he hanged*, Gen. xli. 13. An t-each agus a mharcach thilg e 's an fhairge, *the horse and his rider hath he cast into the sea*, Exod. xv. 1.

Many Transitive Verbs require a Preposition before their object; as, iarr air Donull, *desire Donald*; labhair ri Donull, *speak to Donald;* leig le Donull, *let Donald alone;* beannuich do Dhonull, *salute Donald;* fiosraich de Dhonull, *enquire of Donald.*

Bu *was*, requires the following initial Consonant to be aspirated; as, bu mhaith dhuit, *it was good for you;* bu chruaidh an gnothuch, *it was a hard case;* except initial *d*, and *t* which are not aspirated; as, bu dual duit, *it was natural for you;* bu trom an eallach, *the burden was heavy;* bu ghearr a lo, 's bu dubh a sgeul, *short was her course, and sad was her story.* Smith's "Ant. Poems."

## SECTION IV.

### OF THE GOVERNMENT OF ADVERBS.

The collocation of Adverbs is for the most part arbitrary.

The Adverbs ro, gle, *very*, are placed before the Adjectives they modify, and require the following initial Consonant to be aspirated; as, ro bheag, *very little;* gle gheal, *very white.*

The Negative cha or cho *not*, when followed by a word beginning with a Labial or Palatal, requires the initial Consonant to be aspirated; as, cha mhòr e, *it is not great;* cha bhuail mi, *I will not strike;* cha chuala mi, *I did not hear;* but an initial Lingual remains unaspirated; as, cha dean mi, *I will not do;* cha tog e, *he will not raise;* cha soirbhich iad, *they will not prosper.* *N* is inserted between cha and an initial Vowel or an aspirated *f;* as, cha n-e, *it is not;* cha n-éigin, *it is not necessary;* cha n-fhaca mi, *I saw not.*

The Negative ni requires *h* before an initial Vowel; as, ni h-iad, *they are not;* ni h-eudar, *it may not.*

## SECTION V.

### OF THE GOVERNMENT OF PREPOSITIONS.

The Proper Prepositions aig, air, &c., govern the Dative; as, aig mo chois, *at my foot;* air mo laimh, *on my hand.* They are always placed before the word they govern. The following Prepositions require the Noun governed to be put in the Aspirated Form, viz., de, do, fuidh, fo, fa, gun, mar, mu, o, tre. Air sometimes governs the Noun in the Aspirated Form; as air, bharraibh sgiath na gaoithe, *on the extremities of the*

*wings of the wind*, Psal. xviii. 10.   Gun governs either the
Nominative or Dative ; as, gun chrioch, *without end*, Heb. vii.
16 ; gun chéill, *without understanding*, Psal. xxxii. 9; gun
chloinn, Gen. xv. 2.   Mar, and gus or gu, when prefixed to
a Noun without the Article, usually govern the Dative case ;
as, mar nighin, *as a daughter*, 2 Sam. xii. 13; mar amhainn
mhòir, *like a great river*, Psal. cv. 41; gu crìch mo shaoghail
fein, *to the end of my life-time*, Psal. cxix. 33, xlviii. 10.
But if the Article be joined to the Noun, it is governed in the
Nominative; as, mar a' ghrian, *like the sun*, Psal. lxxxix. 36,
37; gus an sruth, *to the stream*, Deut. iii. 16 ; gus a' chrioch
*to the end*, Heb. iii. 6, 14.   Eadar governs the Nom.; as, eadar
a' chraobh agus a' chlach, *between the tree and the stone.*
Eadar, when signifying *between*, requires the Primary Form ;
as, eadar maighstir agus muinntireach, *between a master and a
servant;* when it signifies *both*, it requires the Aspirated Form ;
as, eadar shean agus òg, *both old and young;* eadar fheara
agus mhnai, *both men and women*, Acts viii. 12.

The Prepositions as, gus, leis, ris, are used before the Monosyllables an, am, a'.   The corresponding Prepositions a, gu,
le, ri, often take an *h* before an initial Vowel; as, a h-Eirin,
*out of Ireland;* gu h-ealamh, *readily;* le h-eagal, *with fear.*

The Improper Prepositions govern the following Noun in
the Genitive; as, air feadh na tire, *throughout the land;* an
aghaidh an t-sluaigh, *against the people;* ré na h-ùine, *during
the time.*   It is manifest that this Genitive is governed by the
Noun feadh, aghaidh, ré, &c., which is always included in the
Preposition.   See Part II. Chap. VII.

Prepositions are often prefixed to a Clause of a sentence;
and then they have no regimen ; as, gus am bord a ghiulan,
*to carry the table*, Exod. xxv. 27 ; luath chum fuil a dhortadh,
*swift to shed blood*, Rom. iii. 15. Edit. 1767; an déigh an obair
a chriochnachadh, *after finishing the work.*

**L**

## SECTION VI.

### OF THE GOVERNMENT OF CONJUNCTIONS.

The Conjunctions agus *and*, no *or*, couple the same Cases of Nouns; as, air feadh chreagan agus choilltean, *through rocks and woods ;* ag reubadh nam bruach 's nan crann, *tearing the banks and the trees.* When two or more Nouns, coupled by a Conjunction, are governed in the Dative by a Preposition, it is usual to repeat the Preposition before each Noun; as, air fad agus air leud, *in length and in breadth ;* 'n an cridhe, 'n an cainnt, agus 'n am beus, *in their heart, in their speech, and in their behaviour.*

Co *as*, prefixed to an Adjective, commonly requires the initial consonant of the Adj. to be aspirated ; as, co mhaith, *as good*, co ghrinn, *as fine.* But sometimes we find co mòr, *as great*, co buan, *as durable*, &c., without the aspirate. Sometimes the aspirate is transferred from the Adj. to the Conjunct. as, cho beag, *as little*, for co bheag. In the North Highlands, an adjective preceded by co is commonly put in the Comparitive form ; as, co miosa, *as bad* ; co treise, *as strong.*

The Conjunctions mur *if not*, gu, gur *that*, are always joined to the Negative Mood ; as, mur 'eil mi, *if I be not ;* gu robh e, *that he was.* M or n is often inserted, *euphoniæ causa*, between gu and an initial Consonant ; viz., *m* before a Labial, *n* before a Palatal or Lingual ; as, gu-m faca tu, *that you saw ;* gu-n dubhairt iad, *that they said* (q).

The Conjunctions ma *if*, o, o'n *because, since*, are joined to the Pres. and Pret. Affirmative, and Fut. Subjunctive; as, ma ta e, *if he be;* o'n tha e, *since he is ;* ma bhuail e, *if he struck ;* o'n bhuail e, *because he struck ;* ma bhuaileas tu, *if you strike ;* o bhitheas sinn, *since we shall be.*

Na'm, na'n *if*, is joined only to the Pret. Subjunctive.

(q) The inserted *m* or *n* is generally written with an apostrophe before it, thus gu'm, gu'n. This would indicate that some vowel is here suppressed in writing. But if no vowel ever stood in the place of this apostrophe, which seems to be the fact, the apostrophe itself has been needlessly and improperly introduced.

The initial Consonant of the Verb loses its aspiration after this Conjunction ; as, na'm bithinn, *if I were;* nan tuiteadh a' chraobh, *if the tree should fall.*

Ged *although,* is used before the Present and Preterite Affirmative, the Fut. Negative, and the Pret. Subjunctive; as, ged tha e, *though he be;* ged bha mi, *though I was;* ge do bhuail thu mi, *though you struck me;* ged bhuail thu mi, *though you strike me;* ged bheireadh e dhomh, *though he should give me* (*r*).

(*r*) I much doubt the propriety of joining the Conjunction ged to the Fut. Affirm.; as, ge do gheibh na h-uile dhaoine oilbheum, *though all men shall be offended,* Matt. xxvi. 33. It should rather have been, ged fhaigh na h-uile dhaoine, &c. The Fut. Subj. seems to be equally improper ; as, ge do ghlaodhas iad rium, *though they shall cry to me,* Jer. xi. 21, Edit. 1786. Rather, ged ghlaodh iad rium, as in Hosea, xi. 7. So also, ged eirich dragh, 's ged bhagair bàs, *though trouble shall arise, and though death shall threaten.* Gael. Paraph. xlvii. 7. Edin. 1787. See page 134. Note (*x*,

# PART IV.

## OF DERIVATION AND COMPOSITION.

# CHAPTER I.

## OF DERIVATION.

THE Parts of Speech which are formed by derivation from other words are Nouns, Adjectives, and Verbs. These are chiefly derived from Nouns and Adjectives, and a few from Verbs.

### I. NOUNS.

Derivative Nouns may be classed as follows, according to the varieties of their termination.

1. Abstract Nouns in *às*, formed from Adjectives or Nouns; as, from ceart *just*, ceartas *justice;* from diomhan *idle, vain*, diomhanas *idleness, vanity;* from caraid *a friend*, cairdeas contracted for caraideas *friendship;* from namhaid *an enemy*, naimhdeas contracted for namhaideas *enmity.*

2. Abstract Nouns in *achd*, formed from Adjectives, and sometimes, though more rarely, from Verbs and Nouns; as, from naomh *holy*, naomhachd *holiness;* from domhain *deep*, doimhneachd contracted for domhaineachd *depth;* from righ *a king*, rioghachd *a kingdom;* coimhid *to keep*, coimheadachd *keeping;* clachair *a mason*, clachaireachd *mason-work;* gobhain *a smith*, goibhneachd contracted for gobhaineachd *iron-work*, or rather *the trade or occupation of a smith.*

3. Abstract Nouns formed from the genitive of Adjectives, by adding *e;* as, from dall gen. doill *blind*, doille *blindness;* from geal gen. gil *white*, gile *whiteness;* from leasg gen. leisg *lazy*, leisge *laziness;* tearc gen. teirc *rare*, teirce *rarity;* trom gen. truim *heavy*, truime *heaviness;* truagh gen. truaigh *unhappy*, truaighe *misery;* uasal gen.

uasail *noble,* uasaile contr. uaisle or by metath. uailse
*nobility.*

4. Abstract Nouns in *ad,* formed from the Comparative of
Adjectives, and used in speaking of the degree of a quality;
as, gilead *whiteness,* boidhchead *beauty,* doimhnead *depth,*
lughad *smallness,* tainead *thinness;* these are construed with
the Prepositions *de, air;* as, cha n-fhaca mi a samhuil air
bhoidhchead, *I have not seen her match for beauty;* air a lughad
or d' a lughad, *however small it be.*

5. Nouns in *air* or *oir, ach, iche,* derived, most of them,
from nouns, and signifying persons or agents; as, piobair *a
player on the pipe,* from piob *a pipe;* clàrsair *a player on the
harp,* from clàrsach *a harp;* cealgair or cealgoir *a deceiver,*
from cealg *deceit;* sealgair or sealgoir *a huntsman,* from sealg
*hunting;* marcach *a rider,* from marc *a horse;* athach *a man
of terror, a gigantic figure,* from atha *fear;* oibriche *a workman,* from obair *work;* sgeulaiche *a reciter of tales,* from
sgeul *a tale;* ceannaiche *a merchant,* from ceannaich *to
buy* (*s*).

6. Diminutives in *an,* and in *ag* or *og,* formed from Nouns
or Adjectives; as, lochan *a small lake,* from loch *a lake;*
from braid *theft,* bradag *a thievish girl;* from ciar *dark-
coloured,* ciarag *a little dark-coloured creature.* These
Diminutives are often formed from the Genitive of their
Primitives; as, from feur gen. feoir *grass,* feoirnean *a pile of
grass;* moll gen. muill *chaff,* muillean *a particle of chaff;* folt
gen. fuilt *hair,* fuiltean *a single hair;* clag gen. cluig *a bell,*
cluigean *a little bell;* gual gen. guail *coal,* guailnean *a cinder;*
smùr gen. smùir *dust,* smùirnean *a particle of dust, a mote;*
clòimh *plumage,* clòimhneag *a small feather, a flake of snow.*

Some Nouns are formed in *an,* which are not Diminutives;
as, from lùb *to bend,* lùban *a bow;* from buail *to beat, thresh,*

(*s*) The terminations *air, oir,* seem from their signification as well as form,
to be nothing else than fear *man,* in its aspirated form fhear. From these
terminations are derived the Latin terminations *or,* orator, doctor, &c., *arius*
sicarius, essedarius, &c.; the French *eur,* vengeur, createur, &c.; *aire,* com-
missaire, notaire, &c., *ter,* chevalier, charretier, &c.; the English *er,* maker,
lover, &c., *ary,* prebendary, antiquary, &c., *eer,* volunteer, &c.

buailtean *a beater,* or *thresher,* applied to that part of the flail which threshes out the grain.

7. Collective Nouns in *ridh* or *ri,* derived from Nouns or Adjectives; as, from òg *young,* òigridh *youth,* in the collective sense of the word; from mac *a son,* macruidh *sons, young men,* Psal. cxlviii. 12; (*t*) from laoch *a hero,* laochruidh *a band of heroes,* Psal. xxix. 1. Macfarlan's Paraph. vi. 15, from ceol *music,* ceolraidh *the muses.* A. Macdonald's Songs, p. 7, from cos the *foot,* coisridh *infantry, a party on foot.* M'Intyre's Songs, Edin. 1768, p. 110, from gas *a lad,* gasradh *a band of domestic attendants.* O'Brien's Ir. Dict. voc. gas; eachradh, eachruith *cavalry.* Fingal. IV. 299, Carthon, 59. —This termination is probably the Noun ruith *a troop.* See Lhuyd et O'Brien, in voc. (*u*)

8. Nouns in *ach,* chiefly Patronymics, formed from Proper Names, thus; from Donull *Donald,* is formed Donullach *a man of the name of Macdonald;* from Griogar *Gregor,* Griogarach *a Macgregor;* so Leodach *a Macleod,* Granntach *a Grant,* &c., from Albainn *Scotland,* Albannach *a Scotsman;* from Eirin *Ireland,* Eirineach *an Irishman.* These Nouns form their Plural regularly, Donullaich, Leodaich, Albannaich, Eirinich. So the following *Gentile* Nouns, which occur in the Gaelic Scriptures, are regularly formed from their respective Primitives, Partuich *Parthians,* Medich *Medes,* Elamuich *Elamites,* Acts ii. 9. Macedonaich *Macedonians,* 2 Cor. ix. 2, 4. See also Gen. xv. 19, 20, 21; Exod. xxiii. 23, 28. (*v*).

(*t*) Timcheal na macraidhe *beside the young men,* Lhuyd, O'Brien. voc. timcheal. This passage proves macraidh to be a singular Noun of the fem. gender, not, as might be thought, the Plural of mac. So laochruidh, madraidh, &c., may rather be considered as collective Nouns of the singular Number than as plurals.

(*u*) The same termination having the same import, is found in the French words cavalerie, infanterie, and in the English cavalry, infantry, yeomanry.

(*v*) In the Gaelic N. Test, the *Gentile* Nouns Κορινθιος, Γαλαται, Εφεσιοι, are rendered Corintianaich, Galatianaich, Ephesianaich. Would it not be agreeable to the analogy of Gaelic derivation to write Corintich, Galataich, Ephesich, subjoining the Gaelic termination alone to the Primitive, rather than by introducing the syllable *an,* to form a Derivative of a mixed and redundant structure, partly vernacular, partly foreign? The word Samari-

9. Collective Nouns in *ach;* as, duille *a leaf,* duilleach *foliage;* giuthas *fir,* giuthasach *a fir wood;* iughar *yew,* iugharach *a yew copse;* fiadh *a deer,* fiadhach *deer, a herd of deer;* crion *diminutive, shrunk,* crionach *decayed wood.*

## II. Adjectives.

1. Adjectives in *ach,* formed generally from Nouns; as, from firinn *truth,* firinneach *true, faithful;* from sunnt *glee,* sunntach *cheerful;* cràdh *pain,* cràiteach *painful;* togradh *desire,* togarrach *willing, desirous.*

2. Adjectives in *mhor* or *or,* derived from Nouns; as, from àdh *felicity,* adhmhor *happy, blessed;* from feoil *flesh,* feolmhor *carnal;* from neart *strength,* neartmhor *strong.*

3. Adjectives in *ail* derived from Nouns; as, from fear *man,* fearail *manful;* from caraid *a friend,* cairdail contr. for caraidail *friendly;* from namhaid *an enemy,* naimhdail contr. for namhaidail *hostile;* from sùrd *alertness,* surdail *alert (w).*

4. A few Adjectives in *ta* or *da,* derived from Nouns; as, Gaelta *belonging to the Gael;* Eireanda *Irish;* Romhanta *Roman;* Kirk. fireanta *righteous,* Matt. xxiii. 35.

## III. Verbs.

Verbs in *ich,* for the most part Transitive, and implying causation, derived from Nouns or Adjectives; as, from geal

tanaich, John iv. 40, is remarkably redundant, having no fewer than three *Gentile* Terminations. From Σαμαρεια is formed, agreeably to the Greek mode of derivation, Σαμαρειται. To this the Latins added their own termination, and wrote *Samaritani;* which the Irish lengthened out still further into Samaritanaich. The proper Gaelic derivation would be Samaraich, like Elamaich, Medich, Persich, &c. The Irish Galiléanach is, in the Scottish Translation 1796, properly changed into Galiléach, Acts v. 37.

(w) The termination *ail* is a contraction for amhuil *like.* In Irish this termination is generally written full, fearamhuil, geanamhuil, &c. From the Gaelic termination *ail,* is derived the Latin termination *alis,* fatalis, hospitalis, &c., whence the English *al,* final, conditional, &c. See page 35. Note (y).

*white*, gealaich *to whiten ;* naomh *holy*, naomhaich *to sanctify ;* cruinn *round*, cruinnich *to gather together ;* lamh *the hand*, laimhsich *to handle ;* cuimhne *memory*, cuimhnich *to remember.* A few are Intransitive ; as, from crith *tremor*, criothnuich *to tremble ;* fann *feeble*, fannuich *to faint.*


## CHAPTER II.

### OF COMPOSITION.

All compound words in Gaelic consist of two component parts, exclusive of the derivative terminations enumerated in the preceding Chapter. Of these component parts, the former may be conveniently named the Prepositive, the latter the Subjunctive term. It sometimes happens, though rarely, that the Subjunctive term also is a compound word, which must itself be decompounded in order to find out the Root.

In compounding words, the usual mode has been, to prefix to the term denoting the principal idea the word denoting the accessory idea or circumstance by which the signification of the principal word is modified. Accordingly we find Nouns, Adjectives, and Verbs modified by prefixing to them a Noun, an Adjective, a Verb, or a Preposition.

In forming compound words, a Rule of very general application is, that when the Subjunctive term begins with a Consonant, it is aspirated. From this Rule, however, are to be excepted, 1. Words beginning with *s* followed by a mute, which never admit the aspirate; 2. Words beginning with a Lingual when the Prepositive term ends in *n;* 3. A few other instances in which there is an euphonic agreement between the Consonants thus brought into apposition, which would be violated if either of them were aspirated.

These observations will be found exemplified in the following Compounds:—

## I. Words Compounded with a Noun prefixed.

### Nouns Compounded with a Noun.

Beart *dress, equipage,* ceann *head*—ceann-bheart *head-dress, armour for the head.*

Fàinn *a ring,* cluas *the ear*—cluas-fhainn *an ear-ring.*

Galar *a distemper,* crith *shaking*—crith-ghalar *distemper attended with shaking, the palsy.*

Oglach *a servant,* bean (in composition, ban) *a woman*—banoglach *a female servant.*

Fàidh *a prophet,* ban-fhaidh *a prophetess.*

Tighearn *a lord,* baintighearn *a lady.*

### Adjectives Compounded with a Noun.

Geal *white,* bian the *skin*—biangheal *white-skinned.*

Lom *bare,* cas the *foot*—caslom *bare-foot ;* ceann the *head*—ceannlom *bare-headed.*

Biorach *pointed, sharp,* cluas the *ear*—cluasbhiorach *having pointed ears.*

### Verbs Compounded with a Noun.

Luaisg *to rock* or *toss,* tonn *a wave*—tonn-luaisg *to toss on the waves.*

Sleamhnuich *to slide,* cùl the *back*—cùl-sleamhnuich *to back-slide.*

Folaich *to hide,* feall *deceit*—feall-fholaich *to lie in wait.*

## II. Words Compounded with an Adjective prefixed.

### Nouns Compounded with an Adjective.

Uisge *water,* fior *true, genuine*—fioruisge *spring-water.*

Airgiod *silver,* beo *alive*—beo-airgiod *quick-silver.*

Sgolt *a crack,* crion *shrunk, decayed*—crionsgolt *a fissure in wood caused by drought or decay.*

Criochan *bounds, regions,* garbh *rough*—garbhchriochan *rude mountainous regions.*

*Adjectives Compounded with an Adjective.*

Donn *brown*, dubh *black*—dubh-dhonn *dark-brown.*

Gorm *blue*, dubh *black*—dubh-ghorm *dark-blue.*

Briathrach (not in use) from briathar *a word*, deas *ready*—deas-bhriathrach *of ready speech, eloquent.*

Seallach (not in use) from sealladh *sight*, geur *sharp*—geur-sheallach *sharp-sighted.*

*Verbs Compounded with an Adjective.*

Ruith *to run*, dian *keen, eager*—dian-ruith *to run eagerly.*

Lean *to follow*, geur *sharp, severe*—geur-lean *to persecute.*

Buail *to strike*, trom *heavy*—trom-buail *to smite sore, discomfit.*

Ceangail *to bind*, dlùth *closer*—dlùth-cheangail *to bind fast.*

### III. Words Compounded with a Verb prefixed.

Art *a stone*, tarruing *to draw*—tarruing-art *load-stone.*

Sùil the *eye*, meall *to beguile*—meall-shuil *a leering eye.*

### IV. Words Compounded with a Preposition.

Radh *a saying*, roimh *before*—roimh-radh *preface, prologue.*

Solus *light*, eadar *between*—eadar-sholus *twilight.*

Mìnich *to explain*, eadar-mhìnich *to interpret.*

Gearr *to cut*, timchioll *about*—timchioll-ghearr *circumcise.*

Lot *to wound*, troimh *through*—troimh-lot *to stab, pierce through.*

Examples of words compounded with an inseparable Preposition are already given in Part II. Chap. VII.

Compound Nouns retain the gender of the principal Nouns in their simple state. Thus crith-ghalar *palsy*, is masculine, because the principal Noun, Galar *distemper*, is masculine, although the accessary Noun crith, by which galar is qualified, be feminine. So cìs-mhaor is masculine though cìs be a feminine Noun, Luke xviii. 11; cìs-mheasadh ought also to be masculine, Acts v. 37. Except Nouns compounded with

Bean *woman*, which are all feminine, though the simple principal Noun be masculine, because the compound word denotes an object of the female sex ; as, oglach *a servant*, masculine, but banoglach *a maid-servant*, feminine, caraid *a friend*, masculine, bancharaid *a female friend*, feminine.

Compound words are declined in the same manner as if they were uncompounded.

In writing compound words, the component parts are sometimes separated by a hyphen, and sometimes not. The use of the hyphen does not seem to be regulated by any uniform practice. In the case of two vowels coming in apposition, the insertion of a hyphen seems indispensable ; because, by the analogy of Gaelic orthography, two Vowels, belonging to different syllables, are scarcely ever placed next to each other without some mark of separation (*x*). Thus so-aomaidh, *easily induced, propense;* so-iomchair, *easily carried;* do-innsidh, *difficult to be told;* and not soamaidh, doinnsidh, &c., without the hyphen.

It was formerly remarked, Part I., that almost all Gaelic Polysyllables are accented on the first syllable. When, in pronouncing compound words, the accent is placed on the first syllable, the two terms appear to be completely incorporated into one word. When, on the other hand, the accent is placed, not on the first syllable of the Compound, but on the first.syllable of the Subjunctive term, the two terms seem to retain their respective powers, and to produce their effect separately, and instead of being incorporated into one word, to be rather collaterally connected. A rule may then be derived from the pronunciation for the use of the hyphen in writing Compounds, viz., to insert the hyphen between the component parts, when the Prepositive term is not accented. Thus it is proposed to write aineolach *ignorant*, antromaich *to exaggerate*, comhradh *conversation*, dobheart *a bad action*,

---

(*x*) Two or three exceptions from this rule occur ; as the Plurals *dée gods*, mnai *women*, lai *days*. But these are so irregular in their form as well as spelling, that they ought rather to be rejected altogether, and their place supplied by the common Plurals diathan, mnathan, lathan or lathachan.

soisgeul *Gospel*, banoglach *a maidservant*, &c., without a
hyphen; but to write an-fhiosrach *unacquainted*, ban-
fhiosaiche *a female fortune-teller*, co-fhreagarach *corresponding*,
so-fhaicsin *easily seen*, &c., with a hyphen (*y*). By this rule,
a correspondence is maintained, not only between the writing
and the pronunciation, but likewise between the written language and the ideas expressed by it. A complex idea, whose
parts are most closely united in the mind, is thus denoted by
one undivided word; whereas an idea composed of parts more
loosely connected, is expressed by a word, whereof the component parts are distinguished, and exhibited separately to
the eye. Thus also the Gaelic scholar would have one uniform
direction to follow in reading, viz., to place the accent always
on the first syllable of an undivided word, or member of a
word. If any exception be allowed, it must be only in the
case already stated of two vowels coming in apposition, as
beo-airgiod *quicksilver.*

Let it be observed that, according to this rule, an Adjective preceding a Noun can never, but in the case just mentioned, be connected with it by a hyphen. For if the accent
be wholly transferred from the Noun to the Adjective, then
they are to be written as one undivided word; as, garbhchriochan *highlands;* but if the accent be not so transferred, the
Adjective and the Noun are to be written as two separate
words; as, seann duine *an old man*, deagh chomhairle *good
advice*, droch sgeul *a bad tale.*

It not unfrequently happens that two Nouns, whereof the
one qualifies the meaning of the other, and connected by the
common grammatical relation of the one governing the other
in the Genitive, come through use to be considered as denoting only one complex object. The two Nouns in this case
are sometimes written together in one word, and thus form
a Compound of a looser structure than those which have been
considered. Such are ceann-cinnidh, *the head of a tribe or*

---

(*y*) As if we should write in English impious impotent, without a
hyphen; but im-penitent, im-probable, with a hyphen.

*clan ;* ceann-tighe, *the head of a family;* ceann-feadhna, *the leader of an army;* fear-turnis, *a traveller;* luchd-faire, *watchmen;* iobairt-pheacaidh, *a sin-offering;* urlar-bualaidh, *a threshing-floor;* fear-bainse, *a bridegroom;* crith-thalmhain, *an earth-quake;* crios-guailne, *a shoulder-belt,* &c. In writ ing Compound Nouns of this description, the two Nouns are never written in one undivided word, but always separated by a hypen. It comes to be a question, however, in many instances of one Noun governing another in the Genitive, whether such an expression is to be considered as a compound term, and the words to be connected by a hyphen in writing, or whether they are to be written separately, without any such mark of composition. An observation that was made in treating of the Government of Nouns may help us to an answer, and furnish an easy rule in the case in question. It was remarked that when one Noun governed another in the Genitive, the Article was never joined to both ; that for the most part, it was joined to the Noun governed, but sometimes to the Noun governing ; that in the latter case, the two Nouns seemed to figure as one compound term, denoting one complex idea. If this last remark hold true, it may be laid down as a rule that in every instance of a Noun governing another in the Genitive, where the Article is or may be pre· fixed to the *governing Noun,* there the two Nouns ought to be connected by a hyphen in writing ; otherwise not. Thus we can say, without impropriety, an ceann-feadhna, *the commander;* an luchd-coimhid, *the keepers;* and the Nouns are accordingly considered as Compounds, and written with a hyphen. But it would be contrary to the usage of the language to say, am mullach craige, *the top of a rock;* an t-uachdar talmhain, *the surface of the ground.* Accordingly it would be improper to write a hyphen between the Nouns in these and similar examples.

The different effects of these two modes of writing, with or without the hyphen, is very observable in such instances as the following:—Ainm dùthcha, *the name of a country,* as Scotland, Argyle, &c.; ainm-dùthcha, *a country name,* or *patronymic,* as Scotsman, Highlander, &c.; clann Donuill, *Donald's children;* clann-Donuill, *the Macdonalds.*

Though few have exerted themselves hitherto in explaining the structure of the Gaelic language, in respect of its inflections, construction, and collocation, this cannot be said to be the case with regard to Etymology. Much has been attempted, and something has been done, toward analysing single vocables, particularly names of places. But this analysis seems to have been too often made rather in a way of random conjecture than by a judicious regard to the analogy of Derivation and Composition. The passion for analysing has even induced some to assert that all true Gaelic Primitives consist of but one syllable, that all Polysyllables are either derived or compounded, and therefore that there is room to search for their etymon. This seems to be carrying theory too far. It appears a fruitless and rather chimerical attempt to propose a system of directions by which all Polysyllables whatever may be resolved into component parts, and traced to a root of one syllable. All I have thought it necessary to do is to methodize and exemplify those general principals of Etymology which are obvious and unquestioned, and which regulate the composition and derivation of those classes of words whereof the analysis may be traced with some probability of success.

# EXERCISES

## READING, EXPLAINING, AND ANALYZING.

---

*From an Address to the Soldiers of a Highland Regiment,* by
D. SMITH, M.D.

THEID an deadh shaighdear gu h-aobhach suilbhear an dàil
gach tuiteamais a thig 'n a chrannchur. Ach 's e a's nòs
do 'n droch shaighdear a bhi gearan 's a' talach air gach
làimh; beadaidh ri linn socair, is diombach ann eiric caoimhneis; lag-chridheach ri h-am cruachais, agus diblidh ri
h-uchd feuma.

### In English.

The good soldier will advance, with spirit and cheerful-
ness, to any service that falls in his way. But it is the
practice of the bad soldier to be complaining and grumbling
on all occasions; saucy in time of ease, and peevish in return
for kindness; faint-hearted under hardships, and feeble in
encountering exigency.

### Analysis.

*Theid.* 3. per. sing. Fut. Affirm, of the irregular Verb *Rach,*
go.

*An.* Nom. sing. of the Article *an,* the.

*Deadh.* An indeclinable Adjective, always placed before its
Noun.

*Shaighdear.* Nom. sing. of the mas. noun *saighdear,* a soldier, in the aspirated form, because preceded by the
Adj. *deadh.* Gram. p. 145.

*Gu.* A proper Preposition, to, for.

*Aobhachh.* An Adject. of the first Declension, joyous, having an *h* before it, because preceded by the Prep. *gu.* Gram. p. 161. *Gu h-aobhach,* joyfully, cheerfully, an adverbial phrase. Gram. p. 109.

*Suilbhear.* An Adject. cheerful. *Gu* is to be supplied from the former phrase; *gu suilbhear,* cheerfully, an adverbial phrase.

*An dàil.* An improper Preposition, to meet, to face, to encounter; made up of the proper Prep. *ann,* in, and the Noun *dàil,* meeting. Gram. p. 121.

*Gach.* An indeclinable Adj. Pronoun, each, every.

*Tuiteamais.* Gen. sing. of the mas. Noun *tuiteamas,* an occurrence, accident, governed in the Gen. case by the improp. Prep. *an dàil* (Gram. p. 161), derived from the Verb *tuit,* Infinitive *tuiteam,* to fall, befal.

*A.* Nom. sing. Relative Pronoun, who, which.

*Thig.* Fut. Affirm. of the irregular Verb *thig,* come.

*'N.* Contracted for *ann,* a proper Prep., in.

*A.* Possessive Pronoun, his.

*Chrannchur.* Mas. Noun, a lot; governed in the Dat. by the Prep. *ann;* in the aspirated form after the adject. Pron. *a,* 'his'—compounded of *crann,* a lot, and *cur,* casting, the Infinitive of the Verb *cuir,* to put, cast.

*Ach.* Conjunction, but. Hebr. אך.

*'S.* for *is,* Pres. Indic. of the Verb *is,* I am.

    *'S e a 's* it is [that] which is.

*Nòs.* Noun mas., custom, habit.

*Do.* Prep. to.

*An.* the article, the.

*Droch.* indeclinable Adject. bad; always placed before its Noun.

*Shaighdear.* mas. Noun, soldier; governed in the Dative by the Prep. *do;* in the aspir. form after the Adject. *droch.*

*A bhi.* for *do bhi* or *do bhith*, Infinit. of the irregular Verb *bi*, to be.

*Gearan.* Infin. of the obsolete Verb *gearain*, to complain, *ag* being understood ; *ag gearan* equivalent to a present Participle, complaining. Gram. p. 86.

*'S.* for *agus*, conjunction, and.

*A' talach.* for *ag talach*, complaining, repining; Infin. of the obsolete Verb *talaich*, to complain of a thing or person.

*Air.* Prep. on.

*Gach.* Adject. Pron. indeclin. each, every.

*Làimh.* dat. sing. of the fem. Noun *làmh*, a hand ; governed in the Dat. by the Prep. *air*, on. *Air gach làimh*, on every hand.

*Beadaidh.* Adject. nice, fond of delicacies, saucy, petulant.

*Ri.* Prep. to, at.

*Linn.* Noun fem. an age, period, season. *Ri linn*, during the time of any event, or currency of any period ; *ri linn Fhearghuis*, in the time, or reign of Fergus; *gu faigheamaid sìth r' ar linn*, that we may have peace in our time.

*Socair.* Noun fem., ease, conveniency ; governed in the Gen. by the Noun *linn*.

*Is.* for *agus*, Conjunct. and.

*Diombach,* or *diùmach.* Adject. displeased, indignant ; derived from the Noun *diom* or *diùm*, indignation.

*Ann.* Prep. governing the Dat. in.

*Eiric.* Noun femin., requital, compensation ; governed in the Dat. by the Prep. *ann.*

*Caoimhneis.* Gen. sing. of the mas. Noun *caoimhneas*, kindness ; governed in the Gen. by the noun *eiric,* derived from the Adject. *caomh*, gentle, kind.

*Lag-chridheach.* Adject. faint-hearted ; compounded of the Adject. *lag*, weak, and *cridhe*, the heart.

*Ri.* Prep. to at.

*Am.* Noun masc., time; governed in the Dat. case by the
Prep. *ri,* and preceded by *h.* Gram. p. 161.

*Cruachais.* Gen. sing. of the mas. Noun *cruachas,* hardship,
strait; governed in the Gen. by the noun *am;*
compounded of the Adject. *cruaidh,* hard, and *càs,*
danger, extremity.

*Agus.* Conjunct., and.

*Diblidh.* Adject., feeble, silly.

*Uchd.* Noun mas. breast, chest; hence it signifies an ascent,
a steep; in the Dat. case, preceded by *h,* after the
Prep. *ri: ri h-uchd,* in ascending, breasting,
encountering, assailing.

*Feuma.* Gen. sing. of the Noun mas. *feum,* necessity, exigency;
governed in the Gen. by the Noun *uchd.*

------

### *Extract from an old Fingalian Tale or Legend.*

Dh' imich Garbh mac Stairn agus Dual a dh' fhaicinn
Fhinn agus a threun fheara colgach, iomraiteach ann an
gniomharaibh arm. Bha Fionn 's an àm sin 'n a thigheadas
samhraidh am Buchanti. 'N an turus d'a ionnsuidh, ghabh
iad beachd air gach gleann agus faoin mhonadh, air gach allt
agus caol choirean. Ghabh iad sgeul de gach coisiche
agus gach fear a thachair 'n an còir. Ann an gleann nan
cuach agus nan lon, chunnaic bùth taobh sruthain; chaidh
a steach, dh' iarr deoch; dh' eirich ribhinn a b' aluinne
snuadh a dh' fhàilteachadh an turuis le sìth. Thug i biadh
dhoibh r'a itheadh, dibhe ri òl; dh' iarr an sgeul le cainnt
thlà. Bhuail gaol o a sùil an Garbh borb, agus dh' innis
cia as doibh. "Thainig sinn o thìr nan crann, far an lionor
sonn—mac righ Lochlainn mise—m' ainm Garbh na'm b'
aill leat—esan Dual, o thìr nam beann, a thuinich ann
Albainn o thuath—a ghabhail cairdeis gun sgàth agus
aoidheachd o 'n àrd righ Fionn, sud fàth ar turuis a Chiabh
na maise—ciod am bealach am buail sinn? seol ar cos gu
teach Fhinn, bi dhuinn mar iùl, is gabh duais." "Duais

cha do ghahh mi riamh, ars an nighean bu bhlàithe sùil 's
bu deirge gruaidh ; cha b' e sud àbhaist Theadhaich nam
beann éilde, 'g am bu lionor dàimheach 'n a thalla, 'g am bu
tric tathaich o thuath—ni mise dhuibh iùl." Gu gleann-sith
tharladh na fir ; gleann an tric guth feidh is loin ; gleann
nan glas charn is nan scor ; gleann nan sruth ri uisg is
gaoith. Thachair orra buaghar bho, is rinn dhoibh iùl ;
thug dhoibh sgeul air duthaich nan creag, air fir agus air
mnaibh, air fàs shliabh agus charn, air neart feachd, air
rian nan arm, air miann sloigh, agus craobhthuinidh nam
Fiann.

### In English.

Garva the son of Starno and Dual, went to visit Fingal
and his brave warriors, renowned for feats of arms. Fingal
was at that time in his summer residence at Buchanti. On
their journey thither, they took a view of every valley and
open hill, every brook and narrow dell. They asked information of every passenger and person that came in their
way. In the glen of cuckoos and ouzles they observed a
cottage by the side of a rivulet. They entered ; asked
drink ; a lady of elegant appearance arose and kindly
bade them welcome. She gave the food to eat, liquor to
drink. In mild speech she inquired their purpose. Love
from her eye smote the rough Garva, and he told whence
they were. "We are come from the land of Pines, where
many a hero dwells—the son of Lochlin's king am I—my
name is Garva, be pleased to know—my comrade is Dual,
from the land of hills, his residence is in the north of
Albion. To accept the hospitality and confidential friendship of the mighty prince Fingal, this is the object of our
journey, O Lady fair (z); say, by what pass shall we
shape our course? Direct our steps to the mansion of Fingal,
be our guide, and accept a reward." "Reward I never took,"
said the damsel of softest eye and rosiest cheek ; "such was
not the manner of [my father] Tedaco of the hill of hinds :

(z) O beautiful ringlet.

many were the guests in his hall, frequent his visitors from the North,—I will be your guide." The chiefs reach Glenshee, where is heard the frequent voice of deer and elk; glen of green mounts and cliffs; glen of many streams in time of rain and wind. A keeper of cattle met them, and directed their course. He gave the information concerning the country of rocks; concerning its inhabitants male and female; the produce of moor and mount; the military force, the fashion of the armour; the favourite pursuits of the people; and the pedigree of the Fingalians.

---

*Extract from Bishop* CARSUEL'S *Gaelic translation of the Confession of Faith, Forms of Prayer, &c., used in the Reformed Church of Scotland;* Printed in the year 1567.

(*From the Epistle Dedicatory.*)

Acht ata ni cheana is mor an leathtrom agas anuireasbhuidh ata riamh orainde gaoidhil alban & eireand, tar an gcuid eile don domhan, gan ar gcanamhna gaoidheilge do chur agcló riamh mar ataid agcanamhna & adteangtha féin agcló ag gach uile chinel dhaoine oile sa domhan, & ata uireasbhuidh is mó ina gach uireasbhuidh oraind, gan an Biobla naomhtha do bheith agcló gaoidheilge againd, marta sè agcló laidne agas bherla agas ingach teaugaidh eile osin amach, agas fós gan seanchus arsean no ar sindsear do bheith mar an gcedna agcló againd riamh, acht ge tá cuid eigin do tseanchus ghaoidheal alban agas eireand sgriobhtha aleabhruibh lámh, agas adtamhlorgaibh fileadh & ollamhan, agas asleachtaibh suadh. Is mortsaothair sin re sgriobhadh do laimh, ag fechain an neithe buailtear sa chló araibrisge agas ar aithghiorra bhios gach én ni dhá mhed da chriochnughadh leis. Agas is mor an doille agas andorchadas peacaidh agas aineolais agas indtleachda do lucht deachtaidh agas sgriobhtha agas chumhdaigb na gaoidheilge, gurab mó is mian leo agas gurab mó ghnathuidheas siad eachtradha dimhaoineacha buaidheartha bregacha saogh-

alta do cumadh ar thuathaibh dédhanond agas ar mhacaibh
mileadh agas arna curadhaibh agas fhind mhac cumhaill gona
fhianaibh agas ar mhóran eile nach airbhim agas nach
indisim andso do chumhdach, agas do choimhleasughagh,
do chiond luadhuidheachta dimhaonigh an tsaoghail dfhaghail
doibhféin, ina briathra disle Dé agas slighthe foirfe na
firinde do sgriobhadh, agas dheachtadh, agas do chumhdach.

---

### English Translation.

[*From the* REPORT *of the Committee of the* HIGHLAND
SOCIETY *of* SCOTLAND, *appointed to inquire into the
nature and authenticity of the Poems of* OSSIAN.]

But there is one great disadvantage which we the Gaeil of
Scotland and Ireland labour under, beyond the rest of the
world, that our Gaelic language has never yet been printed,
as the language of every other race of men has been. And we
labour under a disadvantage which is still greater than every
other disadvantage, that we have not the Holy Bible printed
in Gaelic, as it has been printed in Latin and in English, and
in every other language; and also that we have never yet had
any account printed of the antiquities of our country, or of
our ancestors; for though we have some accounts of the
Gaeil of Scotland and Ireland, contained in manuscripts, and
in the genealogies of bards and historiographers, yet there is
great labour in writing them over with the hand, whereas the
work which is printed, be it ever so great, is speedily finished.
And great is the blindness and sinful darkness, and ignorance
and evil design of such as teach, and write, and cultivate the
Gaelic language, that, with the view of obtaining for themselves the vain rewards of this world, they are more desirous,
and more accustomed, to compose vain, tempting, lying,
worldly histories, concerning the *Tuath de dannan*, and con
cerning warriors and champions, and *Fingal* the son of
*Cumhal*, with his heroes, and concerning many others which

I will not at present enumerate or mention, in order to maintain or reprove, than to write and teach and maintain the faithful words of God, and of the perfect way of truth (a).

---

*From the Preface to a Metrical Version of the Book of Psalms in Gaelic*, by Mr ROBERT KIRK, Minister of the Gospel at Balquhidder; Printed in the year 1684.

Ataid na Psalma taitneamhach, tarbhach: beag nach mion-fhlaitheas lán dainglibh, Cill fhonnmhar le ceol naomhtha. Mur abholghort Eden, lionta do chrannaibh brioghmhoire na beatha, & do luibhennibh iocshlainteamhail, amhluidh an leabhar Psalmso Dhaibhioth, ata na liaghais ar uile anshocair na nanma. Ata an saoghal & gach beó chreatuir da bfuil ann, na chlarsigh; an duine, se is Clairseoir & duanaire, chum moladh an mor-Dhia mirbhuileach do sheinn; & ata Daibhidh do ghná mar fhear don chuideachd bhias marso ag caoin-chaint gu ceolmhar ma nard-Rí. . . . Do ghabhas mar chongnamh don obairsi, dioghlum ughdairidh an uile cháil, ar sheannós, phriomh chreideamh & eachdardha na nGaoidheal, sgriobhta & cló-bhuailte: achd gu ba reula iuil & soluis dhamh, brídh na nSalm fein. Anois maseadh a Chomharbadha ro chaomh, ata mar phlaneidi dhealroidh ag sdiurughadh na ngcorp ioch dardha gan mhonmar, is deaghmhaise dhaoibh an tsaothairse a sgrudadh & a ghnathughadh gu neimhfhiat, gan ghuth ar bheiginmhe & neimhnitheachd an tsaothairigh. Griosam oraibhse a Uaisle, & a Thuatha charthanacha araon, gun

(a) The above is the passage so often referred to in the controversy concerning the antiquity of Ossian's Poems. It was natural enough for the zealous Bishop to speak disparagingly of anything which appeared to him to divert the minds of the people from those important religious truths to which he piously wished to direct their most serious attention. But whatever may be thought of his judgment, his testimony is decisive as to the existence of traditional histories concerning Fingal and his people; and proves that the rehearsal of those compositions was a common and favourite entertainment with the people throughout the Highlands at the time when he lived

bheith mur thacharain ar luaidrean a nunn & a nall go sbailpe
breigi ; achd le gcroidhibh daingne, dosgartha, deagh-fhreumh-
aighte, druididh re Firinn, Ceart, & Ceannsachd, mar
fhuraileas na psalma : Ata clu & tarbha a nsdriocadh don
choir ; call & masladh a ntuitim le heugcoir. .

Imthigh a Dhuilleachain gu dán,
Le Dán glan diagha duisg iad thall;
Cuir failte ar Fonn fial na bFionn,
Ar Gharbh chriocha, 's Indseadh gall.

*In English.*

The Psalms are pleasant and profitable. A church resound-
ing with sacred melody is almost a little Heaven full of
angels. As the Garden of Eden, replenished with trees of life
of potent efficacy, and with medicinal plants, so is this Book
of the Psalms of David, which contains a remedy for all the
diseases of the soul. The world and every living creature it
contains are the Harp ; man is the Harper and Poet, who sings
the praise of the great wonder-working God ; and David is
ever one of the company who are thus employed in sweetly
and tunefully discoursing about the Almighty King. . . .
I was assisted in this work by culling from authors of every
kind, who have treated of the ancient manners, the primitive
religion, and the history of the Gaels, both in manuscript
and in print : but the star and light by which I steered was
the sense of the Psalms themselves. Now, then, my very
dear colleagues, who as shining luminaries guide the inferior
bodies, it becomes you to examine and to use this work can-
didly, without regarding the meanness and insignificancy of
the workman. I beseech you, men of high and of low degree
alike, that you be not, like weak silly creatures, tossed to and
fro by false conceits ; but with firm, resolute, well-established
hearts, adhere to Truth, Justice, and Temperance, as these
Psalms exhort. There is honour and profit in complying
with what is right, loss and disgrace in declining to what is
wrong.

Little Volume, move boldly on ;
In pure godly strains awaken yonder people ;
Salute the hospitable land of the Fingalians,
The highland regions, and the Isles of strangers (*b*).

*(b) i.e.,* the Hebrides.